SAINT ALDHELM'S *RIDDLES*

The first and one of the finest Latin poets of Anglo-Saxon England, the seventh-century bishop Saint Aldhelm, can justly be called "Britain's first man of letters." Among his many influential poetic texts were the hundred riddles that made up his *Aenigmata*. In *Saint Aldhelm's Riddles*, A.M. Juster offers the first verse translation of this text in almost a century, capturing the wit, warmth, and wonder of the first English riddle collection.

One of today's finest formalist poets, A.M. Juster brings the same exquisite care to this volume as to his translations of Horace ("The best edition available of the *Satires* in English" – *Choice*), Tibullus ("An excellent new translation" – *The Guardian*), and Petrarch. Juster's translation is complemented by a newly edited version of the Latin text and by the first scholarly commentary on the *Aenigmata*, the result of exhaustive interdisciplinary research into the text's historical, literary, and philological context. *Saint Aldhelm's Riddles* will be essential for scholars and a treasure for lovers of Tolkien, *Beowulf*, and Harry Potter.

A.M. JUSTER is a poet and translator of classical and post-classical verse. A graduate of Yale University and Harvard University, his work has appeared in *The Paris Review*, *The New Criterion*, and the *North American Review*.

Saint Aldhelm's *Riddles*

TRANSLATED BY A.M. JUSTER

UNIVERSITY OF TORONTO PRESS
Toronto Buffalo London

© University of Toronto Press 2015
Toronto Buffalo London
www.utppublishing.com

ISBN 978-1-4426-3742-9 (cloth)   ISBN 978-1-4426-2892-2 (paper)

Library and Archives Canada Cataloguing in Publication

Aldhelm, Saint, 640?–709
[Aenigmata Aldhelmi. English]
Saint Aldhelm's riddles / translated by A.M. Juster.

Translation of: Aenigmata.
Includes bibliographical references and index.
ISBN 978-1-4426-3742-9 (cloth).   ISBN 978-1-4426-2892-2 (paper)

1. Aldhelm, Saint, 640?–709 – Translations into English   2. Riddles, Latin –
England – Translations into English.   3. Latin poetry, Medieval and modern –
England – Translations into English.   4. Middle Ages – Poetry.   I. Juster,
A. M., 1956–, translator   II. Title.   III. Title: Riddles.   IV. Title: Aenigmata
Aldhelmi. English.

PA8246.A43A2 2015   871'.02   C2015-905131-2

University of Toronto Press acknowledges the financial assistance to its publishing
program of the Canada Council for the Arts and the Ontario Arts Council, an
agency of the Government of Ontario.

Canada Council   Conseil des Arts
for the Arts   du Canada

ONTARIO ARTS COUNCIL
CONSEIL DES ARTS DE L'ONTARIO
an Ontario government agency
un organisme du gouvernement de l'Ontario

Funded by the   Financé par le
Government   gouvernement
of Canada   du Canada

Canadä

Contents

Acknowledgements

I am grateful to *First Things* and *Sewanee Theological Review* for publishing selections from this book.

I want to thank the staff at the libraries of Georgetown University, Harvard University, and the Library of Congress for their assistance. I am grateful to Dumbarton Oaks, where I did most of the research for this book, for allowing an independent scholar to use their magnificent library and consult with their outstanding reference librarians.

In the course of this translation, I imposed on many talented people. Aaron Poochigian, a formidable classicist/poet, was the first reader; he saved me from many a morass. Some of our finest formal poets, including X.J. Kennedy, Rhina Espaillat, Jody Bottum, Deborah Warren, and Melissa Balmain, helped me to bring my translation up several notches. A scholar who has written thoughtfully on Aldhelm, Patrick McBrine, provided extremely helpful early comments. Other scholars, including Scott Gwara, Michael Herren, Anthony Harvey, James Uden, and Jane Stevenson, patiently answered stray questions and provided other assistance. The detailed comments of the two anonymous reviewers and my editor, Suzanne Rancourt, were extremely helpful. I also want to acknowledge the remarkable Stephen Barney, a continuing source of inspiration, who first lured me into the pleasures of medieval literature decades ago.

A.M. Juster

Translator's Note

I decided to translate Saint Aldhelm's *Aenigmata* because I found these riddles fun, fascinating, and deserving of a broader audience. Richard Wilbur, perhaps the best translator into English of all time, translated two of Aldhelm's hundred riddles four decades ago. Aside from these sublime teasers, someone without a solid grasp of Latin who wanted to enjoy these riddles was out of luck. The "literal" translations of Michael Lapidge, Andy Orchard, and Nancy Porter Stork are an indispensable aid to scholars, but they were not intended to be read for pleasure. I wanted to give nonclassicists a faithful literary version of Aldhelm's masterpiece that mimics the many joys of this text.

Aldhelm was a key figure in the early Church who joined the priesthood while Britain was still moving from paganism to Christianity, and I believe that a primary purpose of these riddles was to create a genial platform for introducing and reinforcing the teachings of the Church, a pedagogical ambition suggested in the second line of Riddle 41:

> *Credula sed nostris pande praecordia verbis!*

> But through my words expose your trusting heart!

For Aldhelm, riddles were a form of allegory and religious instruction. The term *enigma* occurs eight times in the *Vulgate Old Testament*, and once in the *New Testament*. As Nancy Porter Stork has noted, Moses sees God *per aenigmata* (*Numbers* 12:8), Solomon solves riddles (3 *Kings* 10:1, 2 *Chronicles* 9:1), Job comforts followers with riddles (*Job* 13:17), and God tells Ezechiel to offer a riddle to the Israelites (*Ezechiel* 17:11). Stork at 60.

While contemporary poets tend to sneer at the riddle as a genre, riddles continue to be a guilty pleasure for the public, particularly for millions of lovers of

Tolkien and Rowlings. In order to meet the expectations of these readers, I tried to produce faithful versions of Aldhelm's riddles with iambic metre, rhythm, and rhyme. I did not use a predictable pattern of rhyme, except in the long final riddle, because I felt that the element of surprise is part of the charm of this text. I have also tried to mimic some of Aldhelm's distinctive alliteration, which echoes the alliteration of Anglo-Saxon poetry that is so clearly heard in Aldhelm's Latin. The only exception is the preface, where I used blank verse and imitated the left-hand side of its double acrostic.

Aldhelm's verse is heavily end-stopped; many scholars believe he was not sufficiently comfortable with quantitative metre to write in the long, flowing sentences of Horace and other classical authors. I tend to think that assertion is at least somewhat overstated, and note that the opening sentence of the *Praefatio* spans eight lines. Reasonably persuasive anecdotal evidence indicates Aldhelm read and wrote Anglo-Saxon poetry, and it may be that the style of the *Aenigmata* was influenced by Anglo-Saxon models. Others have argued that this aspect of Aldhelm's literary style reflects the influence of early Christian poets writing in Latin. Whatever the reason, I have tried to enjamb lines only when Aldhelm did so, though I took small liberties to satisfy various constraints of translation.

I want to stress that this translation is not a "literal" one. I tried to keep as much of the thought as possible in each of the poems, and to avoid injecting thought not reasonably present in the text, but I have been free with syntax, word order, and compounding of concepts in order to produce a fair yet fun version of the text. A student weighing whether to use this book as a trot is thus duly warned.

I expect that this book will be read primarily by people interested in Anglo-Saxon England who do not read Latin. Accordingly, at the risk of upsetting some scholars, I have broken with tradition and separated Aldhelm's titles from his poems. I placed them in the Answer Key after Riddle 100 so that anyone intent on having the excruciating pleasure of puzzling through them can do so without a premature cue. Such readers should be forewarned that only about half of these riddles are readily accessible to a non-medievalist. I aimed the notes primarily at readers with little background in the late seventh century, and have tried to stimulate curiosity about this fascinating era whenever I could.

My secondary audience is the academic community, so I have included notes that exceed a general reader's needs in the hope that my observations will bring more scholarly attention to aspects of the *Aenigmata*. I like to think that this dual approach would have pleased the author, since he wrote his riddles both for the amusement of his people and for their edification about aspects of the religion they had recently embraced.

I hope that scholars and non-scholars will keep my dual mission in mind if certain notes seem either too basic or too obscure. As extensive as the commentary is, by necessity I have not covered some important topics in detail. For instance, I have not tried to track the influence of the *Aenigmata* on the Anglo-Saxon riddle tradition or other medieval poetry; I have raised issues in this area usually only when they have some bearing on the interpretation of the riddle at hand. Similarly, one could write a multivolume treatise on the prosody of the *Aenigmata*, but I have left that task to others.

My efforts to identify parallels between the *Aenigmata* and other texts have been greatly helped by the monumental efforts of Karl Manitius, Rudolf Ehwald, Michael Lapidge, and Andy Orchard. Rather than cluttering the notes with repetitive citations to their work, I have regularly cited Orchard's sections in his *The Poetic Art of Aldhelm* that review his predecessors' comments and his own comments on these parallels; I have cited these and other scholars only when necessary to make a specific point. For those intent on allocating academic credit, I heartily recommend Appendix 4.1 at 225–38 in Orchard (1994), which lays out Orchard's own and previous citations by others of parallels between Aldhelm's poetry and earlier works. I have tried to cite all later published and unpublished observations on parallels with other texts, and have used many databases to identify additional parallels. These databases, for which I am extremely grateful, include Google Scholar, Monumenta.ch., Fontes, Perseus, the Latin Library, Corpus Grammaticorum Latinorum, ProQuest, Thesaurus Linguae Latinae, Monumenta Germaniae Historica, CELT: The Corpus of Electronic Texts, Thesaurus Linguae Hibernicae, Documenta Catholica Omnia, Packard Humanities Institute Latin Texts, and Lacus Curtius. It is wise to remember, however, that the parallels identified with the help of these databases do not necessarily reflect conscious borrowing.

For the text, I followed the Ehwald edition unless I indicated otherwise in the notes, though I have not felt obliged to follow his punctuation. Readers who have Nancy Porter Stork's valuable *Through a Gloss Darkly* should note that she used a manuscript in the British Library, Royal 12.C.xxiii, which differs in some respects from the Ehwald edition, so a numerical reference in this book may refer to her comments on a riddle that her book numbers differently.

Finally, citation style for commentaries varies greatly. My style incorporates certain elements from my legal training that I feel enhance clarity of expression, and I ask readers to be charitable if my citations are unfamiliar in certain respects. I will also welcome suggestions from charitable readers for improvements to future editions; please write to me at the University of Toronto Press if you have such suggestions.

Introduction

The Life of Aldhelm

The facts of Aldhelm's life are sparse and open to debate because his first biographers, Fauricius of Arezzo (ca. 1060–1117) and William of Malmesbury (ca. 1090–1143), wrote centuries after his death and Aldhelm wrote little about himself.[1] The *Historia ecclesiastica* of Bede (672/673–735) includes a brief and somewhat dismissive account of Aldhelm's life.[2]

Aldhelm was born – probably into the royal family of Wessex or one of its noble families – between 635 and 645, the period during which Birinius was converting Wessex to Christianity. William claimed (while later holding that claim at arm's length) that Aldhelm was at least seventy when he died in 709, which has led to the suspect practice of placing the date of Aldhelm's birth at 638 or 639.

Both Fauricius and William assert that Aldhelm was the son of Kenten or Centwine, an unverified brother of King Ine; Ine ruled Wessex from 688 until 726. The unusual breadth and depth of Aldhelm's education, as well as his subsequent role in civic and religious matters, provide strong support for the claim that Aldhelm was at least a member of the nobility. See Thornbury at 149–54.

---

1 Michael Lapidge and Michael Herren, *Aldhelm: The Prose Works* (Cambridge: D.S. Brewer, 1979), 1–10; Michael Lapidge and James Rosier, *Aldhelm: The Prose Works* (Cambridge: D.S. Brewer, 1979), 1–9; Andy Orchard, *The Poetic Art of Aldhelm* (Cambridge: Cambridge University Press, 1994) at 2–5.

2 As venerable as Bede may have been, he seems to have harboured some antipathy toward Aldhelm. Bede's comment that Aldhelm was *sufficienter instructus* ("adequately learned") inescapably seems petty. See Orchard *id.* at 3.

Aldhelm's teachers were probably clergymen, although sometimes men trained in monasteries returned to secular life. The specifics of his early reading are unknown, but one can conjecture that he studied most of Virgil and Lucan's *Bellum civile*. He almost surely studied Old Latin bibles and Jerome's *Vulgate* in addition to such major Christian writers as Augustine of Hippo, Ambrose, and Sedulius. It is likely that he read works of Priscian and other grammarians as well as an assortment of anthologies, reference books, and travel books.

When Aldhelm began his training as a monk, most likely in the late 640s or early 650s, he gained access to a wider range of Christian authors, perhaps including Paulinus of Nola, Prudentius, Fortunatus, and Orientius. One of the hotly disputed aspects of Aldhelm's life is the assertion by his earliest biographers that a shadowy Irishman named Máelduib[3] tutored Aldhelm. Lapidge is dubious about Máelduib; he also embraces the position that "Aldhelm's stylistic connections are with the continent, not with Ireland" and grudgingly concedes only that "(a) case has been made for his knowledge of" the long and quirky Irish poem, the *Hisperica Famina*. Lapidge and Herren at 7.

Orchard takes a more sympathetic view of the Irish influence than Lapidge and observes that "while Irish influence on Aldhelm's prose style is hard to demonstrate, it is clear ... that Aldhelm relied heavily on Hiberno-Latin models in his rhythmical verse." Irish scholars in the seventh century were extremely isolated from the Continent and developed a unique literary sensibility founded more on secondary texts than original texts; their poetry and prose tended to be hyperliterary and often obscure or playful. Regardless of the elusive Irish tutor, my reading of the riddles persuades me that Irish poetry significantly influenced the *Aenigmata*.

Aldhelm became the first abbot of Malmesbury, probably between 670 and 673. As the abbot, he was in an ideal position to buy and borrow manuscripts. He collected texts in an unprecedented way in Britain, including treasures that we have lost, such as Lucan's *Orpheus*, which exists today only in quotations in Aldhelm's prose. It is probable that he first read Ovid's *Metamorphoses* at Malmesbury.

As Aldhelm was becoming a more significant player in British religious and civil issues, Pope Vitalian was growing concerned about the orthodoxy of his unruly island flock of mostly recent converts. In 669 he sent the aging Theodore of Tarsus, a monk and a formidable scholar from what is now Turkey, to become the bishop of Canterbury. Shortly thereafter, he was joined by Hadrian, a younger but similarly formidable North African monk and scholar. Many eager students went to Canterbury to study with these two literary and theological stars.

---

3 There is no consistent spelling of the elusive Irishman's name. Lapidge and Rosier, *Aldhelm: The Prose Works*, 7.

The landmark scholarship of Jane Stevenson recently identified Theodore as the author of the *Laterculus Malalianus*. Influential notes on Theodore's lectures at Canterbury circulated widely among the clergy of Britain, and Theodore experimented with octosyllabic verse. Theodore and Hadrian also brought a wealth of knowledge and many Greek and Latin texts to Britain. Aldhelm studied at Canterbury on at least two occasions, probably between 670 and 675; the influence of Theodore and Hadrian on Aldhelm brought his scholarship up to the level of the top scholars on the Continent.

Aldhelm's life as abbot of Malmesbury kept him so busy that he complained in his letters and in the prose *De Virginitate* that administrative duties interfered with his reading and writing. Along with mundane duties, he became a driving force in building new churches, nunneries, and monasteries, a defender of the orthodox view of "the Easter controversy" about the proper date for observance of Easter, and a busy adviser to King Ine and other powerful figures. He stood as a sponsor for the baptism of King Aldfrith of Northumbria and complained about contentious issues in secular affairs. He made a pilgrimage to Rome and had an interest in travel reflected in the *Aenigmata*.

Upon the death of Bishop Haeddi in 705, the pope split the diocese of Wessex and made Aldhelm the first bishop of Sherborne. According to the *Anglo-Saxon Chronicle*, Aldhelm died in 709. William of Malmesbury reports that he died near today's Doulting in Somerset, and that Ecgwine, the bishop of Worcester, returned the future saint's body to Malmesbury.

Aldhelm's Writings

Unlike most previous Latin poets, Latin was not Aldhelm's native tongue. William of Malmesbury reported that Aldhelm was a great Anglo-Saxon poet who drew audiences for his church services with inspired vernacular recitations, but none of Aldhelm's work in Anglo-Saxon is extant or confirmed by references to specific poems.

Aldhelm's love of Anglo-Saxon verse is palpable, however, in his Latin verse. Some of the poets of Late Antiquity experimented with alliteration and rhyme, but no poet had yet written lines as resonant of Anglo-Saxon poetry as these from the *Aenigmata*:

Ardeo, sed flammae flagranti torre tepescunt	15.4
Fulgida de croceo flavescunt culmina flore	51.2
Prima praecepti complevi iussa parentis	64.3
Carica me currat dum massis pabula praestat	77.6

Scholars debate Aldhelm's fluency with Latin, and some suggest that his heavily end-stopped lines reflect a highly mechanical line-by-line mode of composition, a style that Thornbury has aptly called "stichic."[4] Given Aldhelm's expertise in prosody and the large volume of verse he produced (and we probably do not possess it all), it seems more likely to me that the end-stopped lines at least partially reflect an esthetic preference based on Anglo-Saxon prosody rather than a halting command of classical techniques.

Aldhelm believed his most important literary achievement was his *opus geminatum* ("twinned work") of the verse *Carmen de virginitate* and the prose *Laudibus de virginitate*, but these tributes to early Christian martyrs do not resonate today beyond our expectations of martyrologies. Aldhelm's nineteenth-century editor, Rudolf Ehwald, assigned the title *Carmina Ecclesiastica* to a handful of Aldhelm's dedicatory inscriptions. Although Alcuin and other poets drew on these poems in their own verse, these poems are more interesting from a historical perspective than from a literary perspective. Aldhelm also wrote a number of letters that provide important historical information about himself and his era; many later writers imitated his convolutedly academic prose style. Scholars have rejected Aldhelm's proposed authorship of several other texts and continue to debate whether certain land charters should be attributed to him.

Aldhelm's literary influence relies primarily on two texts: his *Carmen rhythmicum* and his *Epistula ad Acircium*. The *Carmen rhythmicum* is a rhymed octosyllabic poem of two hundred lines that describes a violent storm. It is a pivotal poem in the history of Western poetry that builds on centuries of experimentation in prosody, largely in Late Antique hymns. It breaks fully with classical prosody to adopt both accentual metre and a regular scheme of end-rhyme – in this case, octosyllabic couplets. It is arguably the first ambitious poem of modern European poetry.

The *Epistula ad Acircium* is an eclectic collection of materials addressed to the scholarly King Aldfrith of Northumbria, who reigned from 685 until 705. It includes two essays on prosody, *De metris* and *De pedum regulis*, as well as the *Aenigmata* and remarks about the mystical powers of the number seven. Aldhelm's essays on prosody in this collection were important texts for generations of medieval poets.

Many scholars have assumed that Aldhelm wrote the *Aenigmata* to illustrate the principles expressed in his two essays on prosody. Even if that supposition has some truth to it, the *Aenigmata* became far more than that. With the three-

---

4 Emily Thornbury, *Becoming an Anglo-Saxon Poet* (Cambridge: Cambridge University Press 2014) at 139.

line secular riddles of Symphosius as his primary technical model, Aldhelm accomplished something that had not been done before: he lured readers closer to an unfamiliar God with literature infused with warmth, wit, and wonder.

The *Aenigmata* begins – regrettably in my opinion – with its least impressive piece of poetry, the *Praefatio* ("Preface"). It is a gimmicky piece of work – a double acrostic with the first letters of its lines forming a sentence and the last letters of the lines forming the same sentence in reverse. The technical constraints required by a double acrostic are so extreme that they degrade both the sense and sound of the verse. Having struggled to render the *Praefatio* into a single acrostic in blank verse, I can testify in a way that perhaps no one else can as to how difficult Aldhelm's challenge was.

So why start with such a stunt at all? The *Aenigmata* has become mostly material for philologists, so there has been negligible interest in this and many other questions important to understanding this text. It is possible that Aldhelm was simply interested in acrostics and other figurative poetry, as were some other writers of Late Antiquity. However, I suspect it is important that the addressee of the *Epistula ad Acircium* was Aldfrith, a learned British king and the son of an Irish princess, who would have understood the *Praefatio* as Aldhelm's satirical imitation of Irish literary style.

The *Praefatio* strikes me as Aldhelm's statement of independence from the Irish academic establishment. The double acrostic out-Irishes the Irish at their own linguistic games, and its satirical play upon a classical satire seems to me to be a swipe at an Irish scholarly community that had many secondary texts but precious few original texts. In other words, by satirizing Juvenal Aldhelm is not only showing off his skill as a poet, he is rubbing in the fact that he had actually *read* Juvenal in the faces of his Irish contemporaries.

I believe that Aldhelm wrote the *Praefatio* toward the end of the composition of the *Aenigmata*, and that the riddles are in more or less the order in which they were written. The opening six riddles feel like the original poetic impulse – they are brief, primal, and some of the most beautiful Latin lyrics since Horace. They are also modelled after the secular three-line secular riddles in dactylic hexameter of Symphosius, which probably date to the fourth or fifth century.

These first six riddles lack explicit Christian references and include only one classical reference. I have always found Riddle 6 to be the most stunning of this sequence:

> Nunc ego cum pelagi fatis communibus insto
> Tempora reciprocis convolvens menstrua cyclis.
> Ut mihi lucifluae decrescit gloria formae,
> Sic augmenta latex redundans gurgite perdit.

I share now with the surf one destiny
In rolling cycles when each month repeats.
As beauty in my brilliant form retreats,
So too the surges fade in cresting sea.

Riddle 7 introduces a turn, and Aldhelm incorporates a line from Virgil so he can reject classical religion and substitute Christianity as the ruling force of the universe:

Facundum constat quondam cecinisse poetam:
'Quo Deus et quo dura vocat Fortuna, sequamur!'
Me veteres falso dominam vocitare solebant;
Sceptra regens mundi dum Christi gratia regnet.

A polished poet wrote what's known to all:
"Let us pursue where God and hardship call!"
The ancients dubbed me "mistress," which was wrong;
Christ's grace ruled reigning scepters all along.

Riddle 8 embroiders the point of Riddle 7, then Aldhelm moves on to a string of nine riddles that are less didactic than Riddle 8, although they stress the mysteries of paradox and transformation. Riddle 18, which pokes fun at the mythical ant-lion (who knows whether Aldhelm knew the beast was the product of a translation error?), perhaps is also a poke at Irish wordplay and pedantry; he almost certainly is not referring to Theodore and Hadrian when he takes a crack at "scholars."

Despite intermittent lyrical intensity, the riddles slowly grow more bookish, as in 23 ("Scales") and 24 ("Dragon-stone"), and they slowly grow longer than the riddles of Symphosius. You can also see that Aldhelm sometimes composed related riddles in serial fashion because there is related imagery in adjacent riddles (e.g. 37 "Crab" and 38 "Pond-Strider"). One also hears echoes of the same obscure texts in adjacent riddles. Again in Riddles 37 and 38, for instance, both seem to echo Nonius Marcellus *De compendiosa doctrina*.

Riddle 55 introduces another turn with a long, didactic riddle on the chrismal. Many of the following riddles are similarly didactic and contain more classical imagery and wordplay based on etymology; in short, Aldhelm's initial lyrical impulse appears to have been unsustainable over one hundred riddles (a numerical goal he set for himself because his main model for the riddles, Symphosius, wrote one hundred riddles), and the *Aenigmata* slowly becomes work more of the head than of the heart. It is almost certain that he rummaged through such texts as Basil *Hexaemeron*, Solinus *Mirabilia*, and the anonymous *Physiologus* looking for inspiration for riddles on animals.

Perhaps inspired by Eucheria's *Adynata*, a poem that has fun with the rhetorical device of *adynaton* (a comparison that is impossible), the *Aenigmata* concludes with Riddle 100, an eighty-three line poem that attempts to capture the wonders of the larger canvas of the world. Unchained from the restrictions of the *Praefatio*, it replicates the feel of a classical satire in order to summarize and expand the messages of the preceding riddles.

Aldhelm's Poetic Legacy

Scholars have ably documented Aldhelm's popularization of the riddle as a genre. Some riddles of the Old English *Exeter Book* are virtually translations of riddles of the *Aenigmata*, and the *Aenigmata* stimulated imitative Latin riddle collections by Tatwine, Eusebius, Boniface, and others.

Scholars have not yet documented the full impact of the prosodical innovations of the *Aenigmata* on medieval poetry, particularly its use of alliteration, accentual stress, and end-rhyme, techniques which Aldhelm then used more extensively and systematically in the *Carmen rhythmicum*. Scholars have also tended to overlook the freshness of Aldhelm's insistent vision that close attention to the mysteries of our pedestrian world can lead us closer to an appreciation of the mysteries of God's world and God Himself, so there has been insufficient effort to trace the influence of that mystical strain of Aldhelm's poetry in medieval poetry. Finally, the interest of scholars in philological issues raised by the *Aenigmata* has distracted them from its wit, warmth, and wonder, features which I have tried to resurrect.

SAINT ALDHELM'S *RIDDLES*

Praefatio

Arbiter aethereo iugiter qui regmine sceptrA
Lucifluumque simul caeli regale tribunaL,
Disponis moderans aeternis legibus illuD,
(Horrida nam multans torsisti membra VehemotH,
Ex alta quondam rueret dum luridus arcE),
Limpida dictanti metrorum carmina praesuL
Munera nunc largire, rudis quo pandere reruM
Versibus enigmata queam clandistina fatV!
Sic, Deus, indignis tua gratis dona rependiS!
Castalidas nimphas non clamo cantibus istuC   (10)
Examen neque spargebat mihi nectar in orE.
Cynthi sic numquam perlustro cacumina sed neC
In Parnasso procubui nec somnia vidI.
Nam mihi versificum poterit Deus addere carmeN
Inspirans stolidae pia gratis munera mentI;
Tangit si mentem mox laudem corda rependunT,
Metrica nam Moysen declarant carmina vateM
Iamdudum cecinisse prisci vexilla tropeI
Late per populus illustria qua nitidus soL
Lustrat ab oceani iam tollens gurgite cephaL   (20)
Et psalmista canens metrorum cantica vocE,
Natum divino promit generamine numeN
In caelis prius exortum, quam Lucifer orbI
Splendida formatis fudisset lumina saecliS
Verum si fuerint bene haec enigmata versV,
Explosis penitus naevis et rusticitatE
Ritu dactilico recte decursa nec erroR

Preface

Arbiter, whose eternal reign aloft
Leads sceptres and the star-lit royal court,
Directing it with Your eternal laws,
(Hence You once tortured Behemoth's gross limbs,
Erupting as he fell aghast from Heaven),
Lord of those writing lucid lyrics, help me,
Misguided as I am, to lay out things'
Clandestine mysteries through spoken verse!
O God, freely bestow Your gifts on clods!
My verse won't summon the Castalian nymphs,   (10)
Plus no bees sprinkled nectar on my lips.
Of course, I've never scaled Apollo's peak,
Stretched prostrate on Parnassus, nor seen visions.
Even for me, God will improve verse lyrics,
Dispensing blessings for my sluggish mind;
And if he sways a mind, hearts echo praise,
Thus verses say the prophet Moses once
Had sung of ancient trophies of the soldiers
Of all the tribes, as sun was shining brightly
Upon wild oceans as its head ascended.   (20)
So too the Psalmist, singing hymns in verse,
Announced God came, divinely born, although
No morning star had risen in Earth's sky
Diffusing brilliance in this new-made age.
Long after flaws and crudeness are expunged,
If these verse riddles do, indeed, succeed
(No lines with dactyls overrunning, no

Seduxit vana specie molimina mentiS,
Incipiam potiora, sui Deus arida servI,
Belligero quondam qui vires tradidit IoB,   (30)
Viscera perpetui si roris repleat HaustV.
Siccis nam laticum duxisti cautibus amneS
Olim cum cuneus transgresso marmore rubrO
Desertum penetrat cecinit quod carmine DaviD.
Arce poli genitor servas qui saecula cunctA,
Solvere iam scelerum noxas dignare nefandaS.

INCIPIUNT ENIGMATA ET DIVERSIS RERUM
CREATURIS COMPOSITA

I

Altrix cunctorum quos mundus gestat in orbe
Nuncupor (et merito quia numquam pignora tantum
Improba sic lacerant maternas dente papillas).
Prole virens aestate; tabescens tempore brumae.

II

Cernere me nulli possunt prendere palmis;
Argutum vocis crepitum cito pando per orbem.
Viribus horrisonis valeo confringere quercus;
Nam, superos ego pulso polos et rura peragro.

III

Versicolor fugiens caelum terramque relinquo,
Non tellure locus mihi; non in parte polorum est.
Exilium nullus modo tam crudele veretur,
Sed madidis mundum faciam frondescere guttis.

Efforts at reason tricked with vacant vision),
Someday I'll start on even greater themes
If God, who gave His strength to warlike Job,   (30)
Nourishes servants' thirsty organs with
Vast draughts of dew; throngs crossing the Red Sea
Entered the desert when You made dry rock.
Repulse the streams, as David sang in song;
So, Father who protects our age in Heaven's
Exalted heights, forgive my heinous sins.

RIDDLES ABOUT DIVERSE THINGS MADE BY THE CREATOR BEGIN

1

I'm called the nurse of all that Earth must bear
(and rightly so, since bratty babes don't bite
their mothers' nipples with as much delight),
sprouting in heat then wasting in cold air.

2

No one can hold me in his palms or sight;
I scatter sudden clatter far and wide.
I want to hammer oaks with mournful might;
Yes, I strike sky and scour countryside.

3

Shades shifting as I leave the Earth and sky,
My place is not on land; it's not up high.
No one else dreads his exile with such fears,
But I would make the world be lush with tears.

IV

Crede mihi, res nulla manet sine me moderante
Et frontem faciemque meam lux nulla videbit.
Quis nesciat dicione mea convexa rotari
Alta poli solisque iubar lunaeque meatus?

V

Taumantis proles priscorum famine fingor,
Ast ego prima mei generis rudimenta retexam:
Sole ruber genitus sum partu nubis aquosae.
Lustro polos passim solos; non scando per austros.

VI

Nunc ego cum pelagi fatis communibus insto
Tempora reciprocis convolvens menstrua cyclis.
Ut mihi lucifluae decrescit gloria formae,
Sic augmenta latex redundans gurgite perdit.

VII

Facundum constat quondam cecinisse poetam:
'Quo Deus et quo dura vocat Fortuna, sequamur!'
Me veteres falso dominam vocitare solebant;
Sceptra regens mundi dum Christi gratia regnet.

VIII

Nos Athlante satas stolidi dixere priores.
Nam, septena cohors est, sed vix cernitur una.
Arce poli gradimur nec non sub Tartara terrae.
Furvis conspicimur tenebris et luce latemus;
Nomina de verno ducentes tempore prisca.

4

Trust me, without my guidance nothing stands
And eyes will not perceive my form and face.
Don't brilliant sun, high Heaven's arc though space,
And lunar phases crest at my commands?

5

I'm cast as "child of Thaumas" in quaint speech,
But basics of my birth I'll first reteach:
Born in cloud's water, I am sun's red daughter.
I seek clear skies; in storms I do not rise.

6

I share now with the surf one destiny
In rolling cycles when each month repeats.
As beauty in my brilliant form retreats,
So too the surges fade in cresting sea.

7

A polished poet wrote what's known to all:
"Let us pursue where God and hardship call!"
The ancients dubbed me "mistress," which was wrong;
Christ's grace ruled reigning sceptres all along.

8

"We're born of Atlas," ancient fools would write.
Yes, one's seen faintly, but our group is seven.
We go through Hell beneath the Earth – and Heaven.
We're seen at night and lurk when it is bright;
From spring our former name was brought to light.

IX

En ego non vereor rigidi discrimina ferri,
Flammarum neu torre cremor, sed sanguine capri
Virtus indomiti mollescit dura rigoris,
Sic cruor exsuperat quem ferrea massa pavescit.

X

Sic me iamdudum rerum veneranda potestas
Fecerat ut domini truculentos persequar hostes.
Rictibus arma gerens bellorum praelia patro
Et tamen infantum fugiens mox verbera vito.

XI

Flatibus alternis vescor cum fratre gemello;
Non est vita mihi, cum sint spiracula vitae.
Ars mea gemmatis dedit ornamenta metallis;
Gratia nulla datur mihi, sed capit alter honorem.

XII

Annua dum redeunt texendi tempora telas,
Lurida setigeris redundant viscera filis,
Moxque genestarum frondosa cacumina scando
Ut globulos fabricans tum fati sorte quiescam.

XIII

Quamvis aere cavo salpictae classica clangant,
Et citharae crepitent, strepituque tubae modulentur,
Centenos tamen eructant mea viscera cantus;
Me praesente stupet mox musica chorda fibrarum.

9

Look! I'm not scared by iron's long, hard stress,
Nor in flame's heat do I incinerate,
But goat blood softens my fierce stubbornness,
So gore defeats what scares an iron weight.

10

A holy force once made for me my chore
So I would chase my master's nasty foes.
Armed to the teeth, I brace for bouts of war,
And yet I'm quickly fleeing children's blows.

11

Wheezing with my twin brother, I am fed;
While there are vents for living, I am dead.
My skill gives metals their bejewelled displays;
I'm unthanked, though another steals the praise.

12

When times of year for weaving threads resume,
My hairy threads fill sallow flesh with weight,
And soon I climb the leafy tips of broom
To craft small balls, then rest with twists of fate.

13

Though with their hollow brass the bugles clamour,
Lyres rustle, and resounding trumpets yammer,
Still from my guts a hundred songs are belched;
With me stringed instruments are quickly squelched.

XIV

Sum namque excellens specie, mirandus in orbe;
Ossibus ac nervis ac rubro sanguine cretus.
Cum mihi vita comes fuerit nihil aurea forma
Plus rubet et moriens mea numquam pulpa putrescit.

XV

Ignibus in mediis vivens non sentio flammas,
Sed detrimenta rogi penitus ludibria faxo.
Nec crepitante foco nec scintillante favilla,
Ardeo, sed flammae flagranti torre tepescunt.

XVI

Nunc cernenda placent nostrae spectacula vitae;
Cum grege piscoso scrutor maris aequora squamis.
Cum volucrum turma quoque scando per aethera pennis,
Et tamen aethereo non possum vivere flatu.

XVII

E geminis nascor per ponti caerula concis
Vellera setigero producens corpore fulva.
En clamidem pepli necnon et pabula pulpae
Confero sic duplex fati persolvo tributum.

XVIII

Dudum compositis ego nomen gesto figuris.
Ut leo sic formica vocor sermone Pelasgo,
Tropica nominibus signans praesagia duplis;
Cum rostris avium nequeam resistere rostro.
Scrutetur sapiens gemino cur nomine fungar!

14

Yes, I'm a world-wide wonder, a fine sight;
With bone, red blood, and nerves I was begotten.
While life's my friend, gold does not glow more light,
And during death my flesh is never rotten.

15

I feel no flame while living in the fire,
But mock the pains while deep within the pyre.
As the hearth crackles and the embers glimmer,
I do not burn, though wood's fierce flames grow dimmer.

16

Seeing life's spectacles now entertains;
With fishy, scaly flocks, I search sea plains.
With mobs of birds I also rise through sky,
And yet I can't survive in breeze that's high.

17

I'm born with double shells in deep blue sea
Producing tawny fleece from hairy meat.
Behold! I offer flesh as food – complete
With wool for robes – so twice I pay fate's fee.

18

My name's a hybrid since antiquity.
I'm called a "lion," then an "ant" in Greek,
A blended metaphor, a sign that's bleak;
I can't defend birds' beaks with my own beak.
May scholars probe my name's duplicity!

XIX

Dudum limpha fui squamoso pisce redundans,
Sed natura novo fati discrimine cessit.
Torrida dum calidos patior tormenta per ignes;
Nam, cineri facies nivibusque simillima nitet.

XX

Mirificis formata modis sine semine creta,
Dulcia florigeris onero praecordia praedis;
Arte mea crocea flavescunt fercula regum.
Semper acuta gero crudelis spicula belli,
Atque carens manibus fabrorum vinco metalla.

XXI

Corpore sulcato nec non ferrugine glauca,
Sum formata fricans rimis informe metallum.
Auri materias massasque polire sueta.
Plano superficiem constans asperrima rerum;
Garrio voce carens rauco cum murmure stridens.

XXII

Vox mea diversis variatur pulcra figuris;
Raucisonis numquam modulabor carmina rostris.
Spurca colore tamen sed non sum spreta canendo,
Sic non cesso canens fato terrente futuro.
Nam me bruma fugat sed mox aestate redibo.

19

I was in sea where scaly fish once swarmed,
But with changed fate my nature's frame reformed.
I feel hot pains from fire's torrid glow;
Indeed, my surface gleams like ash and snow.

20

Spawned without seed, produced in ways of wonder,
I load my sweetened breast with floral plunder;
Kings' honeyed fare grows gilded through my flair.
Sharp spears of fearsome war are what I bear,
And I beat – handless! – craftsmen's metalware.

21

With flesh that's furrowed and a bluish glow,
I'm formed to grind crude metal with each row.
Smoothing gold hoards and ore is what I know.
Remaining coarse, I keep a surface sleek;
While lacking speech, I croak a raucous shriek.

22

My sweet voice warbles ways that are unique;
I will not trill songs with a raucous beak.
I'm drab, but still my singing's hard to spurn,
So I keep singing though the future's bleak.
Cold routs me, but in heat I'll soon return.

XXIII

Nos geminas olim genuit natura sorores
Quas iugiter rectae legis censura gubernat;
Temnere personas et ius servare solemus.
Felix in terra fieret mortalibus aevum,
Iustitiae normam si servent more sororum.

XXIV

Me caput horrentis fertur genuisse draconis.
Augeo purpureis gemmarum lumina fucis,
Sed mihi non dabitur rigida virtute potestas
Si prius occumbat squamoso corpore natrix
Quam summo spolier capitis de vertice rubra.

XXV

Vis mihi naturae dedit immo creator Olimpi,
Id quo cuncta carent veteris miracula mundi
Frigida nam chalibis suspendo metalla per auras,
Vi quadam superans sic ferrea fata revinco.
Mox adamante Cypri praesente potentia fraudor.

XXVI

Garrulus in tenebris rutilos cecinisse solebam
Augustae lucis radios et lumina Phoebi;
Penniger experto populorum nomine fungor,
Arma ferens pedibus belli discrimina faxo
Serratas capitis gestans in vertice cristas.

23

Twin sisters, Nature once produced us two
Controlled by laws considered always true;
We hate complainers and to law we hew.
For mortals of our age joy would ensue,
If they could heed the standard sisters do.

24

From a fierce dragon's head I'm born, it's said.
With scarlet hues I help a gemstone's shine,
Though firm control through virtue won't be mine
If scaly serpent flesh has fallen dead
Before I'm plucked, red, from atop its head.

25

Heaven's Maker, not power that's innate,
Provided what all old world wonders lack
For I command cold metals' airy track,
Thus by my power changing iron's fate.
Beside a Cyprus diamond, I'm soon slack.

26

I'm chatty, used to praising late at night
Apollo's glow and rays of great red light.
I'm feathered, named for people of renown;
With foot-borne arms, I'm threatening a fight
While sporting jagged crests upon my crown.

XXVII

Frigidus ex gelido prolatus viscere terrae.
Duritiem ferri quadrata fronte polibo
Atque senectutis vereor discrimina numquam
Mulcifer annorum numerum ni dempserit igne.
Mox rigida species mollescit torribus atris.

XXVIII

Sum mihi dissimilis vultu membrisque biformis.
Cornibus armatus, horrendum cetera fingunt
Membra virum. Fama clarus per Gnossia rura:
Spurius incerto Creta genitore creatus.
Ex hominis pecudisque simul cognomine dicor.

XXIX

Quis non obstupeat nostri spectaculi fata
Dum virtute fero silvarum robora mille?
Ast acus exilis mox tanta gestamina rumpit.
Nam volucres caeli nantesque per aequora pisces
Olim sumpserunt ex me primordia vitae;
Tertia pars mundi mihi constat iure tenenda.

XXX

Nos decem et septem genitae sine voce sorores
Sex alias nothas non dicimus annumerandas;
Nascimur ex ferro rursus ferro moribundae
Necnon et volucris penna volitantis ad aethram.
Terni nos fratres incerta matre crearunt.
Qui cupit instanter sitiens audire docentes,
Tum cito prompta damus rogitanti verba silenter.

27

From frozen bowels of Earth, my birth was frigid.
With my square brow, I'll smooth where iron's rigid
And never face the threat of age with fears
As long as Vulcan's flame won't steal my years.
My stiffness quickly softens as he sears.

28

In limbs and face my look is not the same.
Armed with these horns, my other features frame
A fearsome man. In Gnossian fields my fame
Is clear: Crete's bastard born unclaimed in shame,
A beast and man when I am called my name.

29

Who is not stunned by my amazing fate
When with great strength I prop up countless trees?
Soon, though, a slender spike relieves great weight.
Birds in the sky and fish that swim in seas
Began their life from me in yesteryear;
My hold on one third of the world is clear.

30

Seventeen sisters born without a cry
Declare six other bastards have no worth;
We're born from iron (and by iron die)
Or from birds' feathers darting through the sky.
Three brothers and some mother gave us birth.
For those dead set to hear wise words we speak,
We swiftly give them silent words they seek.

XXXI

Candida forma nitens necnon et furva nigrescens
Est mihi, dum varia componor imagine pennae.
Voce carens tremula nam faxo crepacula rostro,
Quamvis squamigeros discerpam dira colobros.
Non mea letiferis turgescunt membra venenis;
Sic teneros pullos prolemque nutrire suesco
Carne venenata tetroque cruore draconum.

XXXII

Melligeris apibus mea prima processit origo,
Sed pars exterior crescebat cetera silvis;
Calciamenta mihi tradebant tergora dura.
Nunc ferri stimulus faciem proscindit amoenam
Flexibus et sulcos obliquat adinstar aratri,
Sed semen segiti de caelo ducitur almum
Quod largos generat millena fruge maniplos.
Heu tam sancta seges diris extinguitur armis!

XXXIII

Roscida me genuit gelido de viscera tellus;
Non sum setigero lanarum vellere facta.
Licia nulla trahunt, nec garrula fila resultant,
Nec crocea Seres texunt lanugine vermes,
Nec radiis carpor, duro nec pectine pulsor,
Et tamen en vestis vulgi sermone vocabor.
Spicula non vereor longis exempta faretris.

31

My form is gleaming white and growing duller
As I am made with plumes of changing colour.
I do not warble since my beak just shakes,
Although I fiercely slice up scaly snakes.
No deadly toxins cause my limbs to swell,
So I keep feeding chicks – my brood as well –
With filthy serpent's blood and toxic steaks.

32

I got my start from honey-laden bees,
And yet my outside part has grown from trees;
Tough leather made my shoes. An iron spike
Now cuts my gorgeous face and wanders like
A plow that's carving furrows into rows,
But lays down fruitful seed from Heaven's field
Where, from vast harvests, countless bounty grows.
Alas, cruel arms destroy the holy yield!

33

From frozen bowels of dewy Earth I'm bred;
From woolen fleece with bristles I'm *not* made.
They pull no yarn, no humming threads cascade,
No Chinese silkworms weave their yellow thread,
I am not plucked from wheels, no stiff combs beat,
And yet I'm labelled "clothing" on the street.
Long quivers' arrows do not stir my dread.

XXXIV

Quamvis agricolis non sim laudabilis hospes,
Fructus agrorum viridi de cespite ruris
Carpo catervatim rodens de stipite libros.
Iamdudum celebris spolians Nilotica regna
Quando decem plagas spurca cum gente luebant,
Cor mihi sub genibus nam constat carcere saeptum,
Pectora poplitibus subduntur more rubetae.

XXXV

Duplicat ars geminis mihi nomen rite figuris
Nam partem tenebrae retinent partemque volucres.
Raro me quisquam cernet sub luce serena
Quin magis astriferas ego nocte fovebo latebras.
Raucisono medium crepitare per aethera suescens.
Romuleis scribor biblis sed voce Pelasga,
Nomine nocturnas dum semper servo tenebras.

XXXVI

Corpore sum gracilis stimulis armatus acerbis.
Scando catervatim volitans super ardua pennis,
Sanguineas sumens praedas mucrone cruento,
Quadrupedi parcens nulli sed spicula trudo
Setigeras pecudum stimulans per vulnera pulpas.
Olim famosus vexans Memphitica rura
Namque toros terebrans taurorum sanguine vescor.

34

Although for farmers I'm an unloved guest,
I harvest yields from rural, lush terrains
While gnawing bark with swarms on trunks of trees.
Once famed for plundering the Nile's domains
When ten plagues struck their evil dynasties,
My heart is trapped in skin below my chest,
Since, like a toad's, it's tucked beneath my knees.

35

My nature rightly copies my twin name
Since birds and shadows each retain a claim.
I'm rarely seen by people in clear light
For I will hide in star-borne nests at night.
In midflight it is common that I shriek.
I'm in Rome's books, but with a sound that's Greek
As I protect the shadows with my name.

36

My frame is frail, with nasty spurs for arms.
I rise in swarms, ascending high by wing,
Obtaining bloody spoils with bleeding sword,
Sparing no four-hooved beast, yet boldly sting
And torture hides of herds with wounds I gored.
I was once famed for plaguing Memphis farms
And yes, I love bull blood while puncturing.

XXXVII

Nepa mihi nomen veteres dixere Latini,
Humida spumiferi spatior per litora ponti
Passibus oceanum retrograda transeo versis,
Et tamen aethereus per me decoratur Olimpus,
Dum ruber in caelo bisseno sidere scando,
Ostrea quem metuit duris perterrita saxis.

XXXVIII

Pergo super latices plantis suffulta quaternis;
Nec tamen in limphas vereor quod mergar aquosas.
Sed pariter terras et flumina calco pedestris,
Nec natura sinit celerem natare per amnem
Pontibus aut ratibus fluvios transire feroces,
Quin potius pedibus gradior super aequora siccis.

XXXIX

Setiger in silvis armatos dentibus apros
Cornigerosque simul cervos licet ore rudentes;
Contero nec parcens ursorum quasso lacertos.
Ora cruenta ferens morsus rictusque luporum
Horridus haud vereor regali culmine fretus;
Dormio nam patulis non claudens lumina gemmis.

XL

Sum niger exterius rugoso cortice tectus,
Sed tamen interius candentem gesto medullam.
Dilicias epulas regum luxusque ciborum
Ius simul et pulpas battutas condo culinae,
Sed me subnixum nulla virtute videbis
Viscera ni fuerint nitidis quassata medullis.

37

Dubbed "scorpion" by Romans of the past,
I walk wet beaches of the foaming ocean
And cross the seafloor with a backwards motion,
And yet high Heaven's decked out when I rise,
Along with twelve red stars, into the skies,
Which makes the oysters, scared of stones, aghast.

38

I walk on water with four feet that bear me;
In spite of this, submersion doesn't scare me.
Although on land and streams alike I skim,
In rapids Nature will not let me swim
Or cross fierce torrents with a bridge or boat,
Yet on still water, with dry feet, I float.

39

A whiskered beast of woods, I shred each boar,
Though armed with tusks, and antlered stags that roar;
Crushing bears' forearms doesn't give me pause.
Lips bloody, I don't fear wolves' teeth or jaws
And dread no terror by high royal right;
I sleep wide-eyed, with my jewelled beams closed tight.

40

I'm black outside, concealed by wrinkled skin,
And yet I hide a glowing core within.
I season royal feasts and high-class treats
As well as country stews and pounded meats,
But you will never see why I am prized
Until my bright core's guts are pulverized.

XLI

Nolo fidem frangas, licet irrita dicta putentur,
Credula sed nostris pande praecordia verbis!
Celsior ad superas possum turgescere nubes.
Si caput aufertur mihi toto corpore dempto,
At vero capitis si pressus mole gravabor,
Ima petens iugiter minorari parte videbor.

XLII

Grandia membra mihi plumescunt corpore denso.
Par color accipitri, sed dispar causa volandi,
Nam summa exiguis non trano per aethera pennis.
Sed potius pedibus spatior per squalida rura
Ovorum teretes praebens ad pocula testas.
Africa Poenorum me fertur gignere tellus.

XLIII

Lurida per latices cenosas lustro paludes
Nam mihi composuit nomen fortuna cruentum
Rubro dum bibulis vescor de sanguine buccis.
Ossibus et pedibus geminisque carebo lacertis
Corpora vulneribus sed mordeo dira trisulcis,
Atque salutiferis sic curam praesto labellis.

XLIV

Me pater et mater gelido genuere rigore
Fomitibus siccis dum mox rudimenta vigebant,
Quorum vi propria fortunam vincere possum
Cum nil ni latices mea possint vincere fata,
Sed saltus scopulos stagni ferrique metalla
Comminuens penitus naturae iura resolvam.
Cum me vita fovet sum clari sideris instar
Postmodum et fato victus pice nigrior exsto.

41

Don't lose faith, though talk carries little weight,
But through my words expose your trusting heart!
Near lofty higher clouds I can inflate.
If I'm beheaded, all my flesh is shed,
Yet if I'm pressed by weight from someone's head,
I always seem to want to shrink in part.

42

Plumes sprout from giant limbs on my huge hide.
Hawklike in hue, but not in will to fly,
For with frail wings I do not sail high sky.
Instead, I plod through barren countryside
Providing cups from bits of eggs I lay.
Phoenician Africa's my home, they say.

43

Ghostlike, I haunt the filthy pools of mud
For Fortune tagged me with a gory name
While I was gulping mouthfuls of red blood.
I lack bones, arms, both feet, but all the same
I puncture fearful flesh with triforked nips,
And thus I heal with therapeutic lips.

44

Born of my parents' frozen-hard resilience
As tinder quickly added youthful brilliance,
I can surpass their fate with my own force
Since only water knocks me off my course,
But, when I'm freed from Nature's law, I strike
At forests, rocks, tin, iron, and the like.
While I'm alive, I'm like a brilliant star,
Then, crushed by fate, I stay more black than tar.

XLV

In saltu nascor ramosa fronde virescens,
Sed fortuna meum mutaverat ordine fatum.
Dum veho per collum teretem vertigine molam,
Ex quo conficitur regalis stragula pepli;
Tam longa nullus zona praecingitur heros.
Per me fata virum dicunt decernere Parcas.
Frigora dura viros sternant ni forte resistam.

XLVI

Torqueo torquentes sed nullum torqueo sponte
Laedere nec quemquam volo ni prius ipse reatum
Contrahat et viridem studeat decerpere caulem.
Fervida mox hominis turgescunt membra nocentis,
Vindico sic noxam stimulisque ulciscor acutis.

XLVII

Absque cibo plures degebam marcida menses,
Sed sopor et somnus ieiunia longa tulerunt.
Pallida purpureo dum glescunt gramine rura,
Garrula mox crepitat rubicundum carmina guttur.
Post teneros fetus et prolem gentis adultam,
Sponte mea fugiens umbrosas quaero latebras;
Si vero quisquam pullorum lumina laedat,
Affero compertum medicans cataplasma salutis
Quaerens campestrem proprio de nomine florem.

45

I sprang from branches growing greenery,
But, in rank, Fortune altered fate for me.
While on my rounded neck I'm twirling thread,
Which makes the robes that cloak the royal line,
No hero's belt surrounds as much as mine.
The Parcae set men's fates through me, it's said.
If I weren't steadfast, chills would strike men dead.

46

I torture torturers, but freely balk
At harm or torturing – unless a prime
And guilty suspect goes for my green stalk.
His stained limbs swell up, fevered, in no time,
Thus I avenge with barbs and conquer crime.

47

Deprived of food for months, I grew less strong,
Though rest and slumber made long fasting pass.
When purple spreads throughout pale fields of grass,
My ruby throat soon croaks a chatty song.
Once tender young and kindred kids are grown,
I flee for shaded shelter on my own;
Yet if one makes my hatchlings' eyes inflame,
I bring a healing balm of great acclaim
Produced from wildflowers with my own name.

XLVIII

Sic me formavit naturae conditor almus:
Lustro teres tota spatiosis saecula ciclis
Latas in gremio portans cum pondere terras
Sic maris undantes cumulos et caerula cludo.
Nam nihil in rerum natura tam celer esset,
Quod pedibus pergat quod pennis aethera tranet,
Accola neu ponti volitans per caerula squamis,
Nec rota per girum quam trudit machina limphae
Currere sic posset ni septem sidera tricent.

XLIX

Horrida curva capax patulis fabricata metallis,
Pendeo nec caelum tangens terramve profundam.
Ignibus ardescens necnon et gurgite fervens,
Sic geminas vario patior discrimine pugnas
Dum lattices limphae tolero flammasque feroces.

L

Prorsus Achivorum lingua pariterque Latina
Mille vocor viridi folium de cespite natum,
Idcirco decies centenum nomen habebo,
Cauliculis florens quoniam sic nulla frutescit
Herba per innumeros telluris limite sulcos.

LI

Sponte mea nascor fecundo cespite vernans,
Fulgida de croceo flavescunt culmina flore.
Occiduo claudor sic orto sole patesco,
Unde prudentes posuerunt nomina Graeci.

48

Nature's kind Maker formed me as these things:
I'm round and roam all worlds in spacious rings
With my chest lifting Earth's extremities
So I envelop clouds and rough blue seas.
Since nothing real could move with such swift motion –
Nothing that walks or skims the sky with wings,
No fishy friend that zigzags through blue ocean,
No millwheel turning – nothing could surpass me
That runs, except that seven stars harass me.

49

As pounded gaping metal – wide, gross, round –
I hang untouched by boundless sky or ground.
Glowing in flames and fevering with bubbles,
I thus confront two fronts with different troubles
As I survive both being scorched and drowned.

50

In Greek, much like in Latin, I became
The "thousand leaf," which fruitful farmland yields,
So I will have "ten hundreds" as my name,
Since shoots on other plants don't grow the same
In all the countless furrows of the fields.

51

Born in lush farmland, blooming on my own,
Bright blossoms on my crown are glowing gold.
I'm closed at sunset, then at dawn unfold,
So wise Greeks picked the name by which I'm known.

LII

Materia duplici palmis plasmabar apertis.
Interiora mihi candescunt viscera lino
Seu certe gracili iunco spoliata nitescunt,
Sed nunc exterius flavescunt corpora flore.
Quae flammasque focosque laremque vomentia fundunt,
Et crebro lacrimae stillant de frontibus udae,
Sic tamen horrendas noctis repello latebras;
Reliquias cinerum mox viscera tosta relinquunt.

LIII

Sidereis stipor turmis in vertice mundi;
Esseda famoso gesto cognomina vulgo.
In giro volvens iugiter non vergo deorsum,
Cetera ceu properant caelorum lumina ponto.
Hac gaza ditor, quoniam sum proximus axi
Qui Ripheis Scithiae praelatus monibus errat.
Vergilias numeris aequans in arce polorum,
Pars cuius inferior Stigia Letheaque palude
Fertur et inferni manibus succumbere nigris.

LIV

Credere quis poterit tantis spectacula causis
Temperet et fatis rerum contraria fata?
Ecce! Larem laticem quoque gesto in viscere ventris,
Nec tamen undantes vincunt incendia limphae,
Ignibus aut atris siccantur flumina fontis.
Foedera sed pacis sunt flammas inter et undas;
Malleus in primo memet formabat et incus.

52

From two materials, palms molded me.
My insides glow; these guts – for sure a looting
Of flax or some thin reed – shine brilliantly,
Though flesh produced from flowers yellows now.
They're belching fire as flames and sparks are shooting,
And maudlin tears keep dripping down my brow,
So I still clear night's shadows that I feared;
They leave ash smudges where my guts were seared.

53

I'm jammed by mobs of stars on Heaven's peak;
I bear the nickname "wagon" when folks speak.
Revolving endlessly, I never tend
To sink toward sea as other stars descend.
I am more blessed because the North Star nears,
Which over Scythia's Ripheans veers.
I match the Pleiades far overhead,
Whose lower reaches drop to marsh, it's said,
By Styx and Lethe with their dismal dead.

54

Who could believe such reasons for these shows
And that Fate alters clashing fates of things?
Behold! Deep innards hold both flame and juice,
Though eddies do not quell their fiery glows
And deadly fires aren't quenched by streams from springs.
Instead, the waves and flames respect their truce;
A sledge and anvil fashioned my first use.

LV

Alma domus veneror divino munere plena,
Valvas sed nullus reserat nec limina pandit
Culmina ni fuerint aulis sublata quaternis
Et licet exterius rutilent de corpore gemmae
Aurea dum fulvis flavescit bulla metallis.
Sed tamen uberius ditantur viscera crassa
Intus qua species flagrat pulcherrima Christi
Candida sanctarum sic floret gloria rerum.
Nec trabis in templo surgunt nec tecta columnis.

LVI

Hospes praeruptis habitans in margine ripis,
Non sum torpescens, oris sed belliger armis.
Quin potius duro vitam sustento labore
Grossaque prosternens mox ligna securibus uncis.
Humidus in fundo tranat qua piscis aquoso,
Saepe caput proprium tingens in gurgite mergo.
Vulnera fibrarum necnon et lurida tabo,
Membra medens pestemque luemque resolvo necantem.
Libris corrosis et cortice vescor amara.

LVII

"Armiger infausti Iovis et raptor Ganimidis,"
Quamquam pellaces cantarent carmine vates
Non fueram praepes quo fertur Dardana proles.
Sed magis in summis cicnos agitabo fugaces
Arsantesque grues proturbo sub aetheris axe.
Corpora dum senio corrumpit fessa vetustas,
Fontibus in liquidis mergentis membra madescunt;
Post haec restauror praeclaro lumine Phoebi.

55

I'm worshipped, a kind house filled with God's gift,
But no one opens doors or enters in
Unless the roof's four corners rise up higher
Though gems are glowing red upon my skin
As gleaming, gilded baubles are ablaze.
In fact, gross guts are more refined within
Where Christ's most gorgeous splendour is on fire,
So holy matters' glory streams its rays;
With this church roof, no beams or columns lift.

56

I'm living on steep river banks, and yet,
Armed to my teeth for war, I don't relax.
In fact, I make a living through my sweat
And quickly fell big trees with my curved axe.
In murky depths of water where fish swim,
I often dive through currents, my head wet.
I heal both injured bowel and sickened limb,
And ward off plague and other grave disease.
I eat chewed rind and bitter bark of trees.

57

"Ganymede's thief and Jove's unlucky knight,"
Glib poets sang in verse; it wasn't I
Who was the bird who bore Troy's youth in flight.
Instead, I chase escaping swans up high
And drive cranes screeching under Heaven's sky.
When weak from weary flesh that aging brings,
My limbs refresh by dipping in clear springs;
I'm then restored by Phoebus's bright light.

LVIII

Tempore de primo noctis mihi nomen adhaesit;
Occiduas mundi complector cardine partes.
Oceano Titan dum corpus tinxerit almum
Et polus in glaucis relabens volvitur undis,
Tum sequor, in vitreis recondens lumina campis,
Et fortunatus subito ni tollar ab aethra,
Ut furvas lumen noctis depelleret umbras.

LIX

Me dudum genuit candens onocrotalus albam
Gutture qui patulo sorbet de gurgite limphas.
Pergo per albentes directo tramite campos
Candentique viae vestigia caerula linquo
Lucida nigratis fuscans anfractibus arva;
Nec satis est unum per campos pandere callem.
Semita quin potius milleno tramite tendit
Quae non errantes ad caeli culmina vexit.

LX

Collibus in celsis saevi discrimina Martis,
Quamvis venator frustra latrante moloso,
Garriat arcister contorquens spicula ferri,
Nil vereor magnis sed fretus viribus altos,
Belliger impugnans elefantes vulnere sterno.
Heu! Fortuna ferox quae me sic arte fefellit;
Dum trucido grandes et virgine vincor inermi!
Nam gremium pandens mox pulchra puerpera prendit
Et voti compos celsam deducit ad urbem.
Indidit ex cornu nomen mihi lingua Pelasga,   (10)
Sic itidem propria dixerunt voce Latini.

58

The early evening stuck its name on me;
I cloak the western world from my high height.
When Titan dips life-giving flesh in sea
And, lost in gray-blue waves, sky drops from sight,
I follow glassy plains while hiding light –
And I'm not snatched from Heaven, blessedly,
As light keeps clearing gloomy shades of night.

59

The gleaming pelican, who gulps a stream
Of sea in his broad throat, once made me pale.
I'm crossing whitened fields on my straight trail
And leaving deep-blue prints of routes that gleam
While tainting shining land with twists of black;
One pass is not enough for fields to spread.
Indeed, a trail takes countless ways instead
That head to Heaven's heights for those on track.

60

In high terrain a battle's fierce travails –
A foiled hound bays despite the hunter's calling
With iron arrows of the archer falling –
Don't scare me, but bold, trusting my great might,
I wound war elephants before my kill.
Alas, fierce Fortune fooled me with such skill;
I slay beasts – and this unarmed girl prevails!
Breast bare, the beauty wins and brings me right,
As prayed for, to the city on the height.
In Greek my horn has given me my name,　　　　　(10)
So Latinists proclaim I'm just the same.

LXI

De terrae gremiis formabar primitus arte;
Materia trucibus processit cetera tauris
Aut potius putidis constat fabricata capellis!
Per me multorum clauduntur lumina leto
Qui domini nudus nitor defendere vitam.
Nam domus est constructa mihi de tergore secto
Necnon et tabulis quas findunt stipite rasis.

LXII

De madido nascor rorantibus aethere guttis
Turgida concrescens liquido de flumine lapsu,
Sed me nulla valet manus udo gurgite nantem
Tangere ni statim rumpantur viscera tactu
Et fragilis tenues flatus discedat in auras.
Ante catervatim per limphas duco cohortes
Dum plures ortu comites potiuntur eodem.

LXIII

Dum genus humanum truculenta fluenta necarent
Et nova mortales multarent aequora cunctos,
Exceptis raris gignunt qui semina saecli,
Primus viventum perdebam foedera iuris,
Imperio patris contemnens subdere colla,
Unde puto dudum versu dixisse poetam,
'Abluit in terris, quidquid deliquit in undis.'
Nam sobolem numquam dapibus saturabo ciborum,
Ni prius in pulpis plumas nigrescere cernam.
Littera tollatur post haec sine prole manebo.

61

First I was finely crafted from Earth's breast;
From brutal bulls he made up all the rest –
Or, rather, made from goats with their foul smell!
For many of the dead, I close their eyes
As he who guards my lord (though I'm undressed).
Yes, home is made of leather cut to size
And shaved-down wood from lumber that they fell.

62

I'm born from dripping drops in soggy sky
And grow in swelling froth where rivers flow,
But no hand sways me while I'm swimming by
Or else my guts are spilled out everywhere
And fragile breath disperses in thin air.
I lead my team downstream with throngs in tow,
Since many friends have birthdates that we share.

63

When bloody flooding killed the human race
And brand-new seas put mortals in their place
(Except for those who carried mankind's seed),
First among beasts, I snubbed what law decreed,
Deriding yielding to the Lord's command,
For which, I think, a poet would declare,
"The sin revealed on surf was cleansed on land."
Now I won't fill my brood with banquet fare
Until I see plumes blacken on their skin.
Remove a letter, I will lack my kin.

LXIV

Cum Deus infandas iam plecteret aequore noxas
Ablueretque simul scelerum contagia limphis,
Prima praecepti complevi iussa parentis,
Portendens fructu terris venisse salutem,
Mitia quapropter semper praecordia gesto
Et felix praepes nigro sine felle manebo.

LXV

Fida satis custos conservans pervigil aedes,
Noctibus in furvis caecas lustrabo latebras
Atris haud perdens oculorum lumen in antris.
Furibus invisis vastant qui farris acervos,
Insidiis tacite dispono scandala mortis,
Et vaga venatrix rimabor lustra ferarum,
Nec volo cum canibus turmas agitare fugaces,
Qui mihi latrantes crudelia bella ciebunt;
Gens exosa mihi tradebat nomen habendum.

LXVI

Nos sumus aequales communi sorte sorores,
Quae damus ex nostro cunctis alimenta labore.
Par labor ambarum, dispar fortuna duarum
Altera nam cursat, quod numquam altera gessit,
Nec tamen invidiae stimulis agitamur acerbis.
Utraque, quod mandit quod ruminat ore patenti
Comminuens reddit famulans sine fraude maligna.

64

When God's sea punished vile abomination
And water cleansed our sin's contamination,
I, first, fulfilled The Father's proclamation,
Marking with fruit the start of Earth's salvation,
So I will bear a heart that is serene
And stay a joyous bird without dark spleen.

65

Home's watchful, somewhat faithful, guardian,
I'll prowl dark shadows in the pitch-black night
In gloomy caves without my losing sight.
For unseen thieves who raid the barley bin,
I stealthily arrange my fatal snares,
And, a stray huntress, I will search beasts' lairs,
But I don't wish to chase escaping game
With baying dogs who'll pick a savage fight;
A loathsome tribe supplied my given name.

66

We're sisters, partners in this lot we share,
Whose work provides the world its daily fare.
Our labour's paired; both fortunes don't compare
For as one runs the other never stirs,
Yet we're unmoved by envy's bitter spurs.
What each, with our wide maws, has chewed and gnawed
Returns in pieces – served without cruel fraud.

LXVII

Sicca pruinosam crebris effundo fenestris
Candentemque nivem iactans de viscere furvo,
Et tamen omnis amat quamvis sit frigida nimbo;
Densior et nebulis late spargatur in aula.
Qua sine mortales grassantur funere leti
(Sic animae pariter pereunt dum vita fatescit
Et qua ditati contemnunt limina Ditis).
Liquitur in prunis numquam torrentibus haec nix,
Sed, mirum dictu, magis indurescit ad ignem.

LXVIII

Sum cava bellantum crepitu quae corda ciebo
Vocibus horrendis stimulans in bella cohortes.
Idcirco reboans tanto clamore resulto,
Quod nulla interius obtundant viscera vocem,
Spiritus in toto sed regnant corpore flabra.
Garrula me poterit numquam superare cicada,
Aut arguta simul cantans luscinia ruscis;
Quam lingua propria dicunt acalantida Graeci.

LXIX

Semper habens virides frondenti in corpore crines.
Tempore non ullo viduabor tegmine spisso,
Circius et Boreas quamvis et flamina Chauri
Viribus horrendis studeant deglobere frontem,
Sed me pestiferam fecerunt fata reorum.
Cumque venenatus glescit de corpora stipes
Lurcones rabidi quem carpunt rictibus oris,
Occido mandentum mox plura cadavera leto.

67

While dry, through close-set windows I eject
Bright, frosty snow that my dark guts reject,
And though it's cold, it's still adored by all;
Denser than clouds and mist, it sprays the hall.
Without it, mortals march to rites of death
(As when life fades away with failing breath
And those with wealth despise the gates of Hell).
This snow won't melt on embers, but, to tell
Of miracles, near fire it does jell.

68

I'm hollow, I who'll rouse fierce hearts with din
While stirring troops with dreadful calls to war.
It's how I ring with such an echoed roar,
Since my insides don't block a call within,
Though all my body runs on bursts of air.
No chirpy cricket ever could compare,
Nor nightingales in shrubs who join what's sung;
Greeks call them *acalanthus* in their tongue.

69

My leafy body's always crowned in green.
At no time do I lack a woven screen,
Though Circius and Boreas and surges
Of Caurus try to strip my forehead clean,
But still the fates of things have made me mean.
When from my trunk a toxic limb emerges
And frenzied gluttons grab with gaping jaws,
I quickly kill if any body gnaws.

LXX

De terris orior candenti corpore pelta
Et nive fecunda Vulcani torre rigescens,
Carior et multo quam cetera scuta duelli.
Nec tamen in medio clipei stat ferreus umbo.
Me sine quid prodest dirorum parma virorum?
Vix artus animaeque carerent tramite mortis
Ni forsan validis refrager viribus Orco.

LXXI

Me pedibus manibusque simul fraudaverat almus
Arbiter immensum primo dum pangeret orbem.
Fulcior haud volians veloci praepetis ala
Spiritus alterno vegitat nec corpora flatu.
Quamvis in caelis convexa cacumina cernam,
Non tamen undosi contemno marmora ponti.

LXXII

Omnia membra mihi plasmavit corporis auctor,
Nec tamen ex isdem membrorum munia sumpsi.
Pergere nec plantis oculis nec cernere possum,
Quamquam nunc patulae constent sub fronte fenestrae.
Nullus anhelanti procedit viscere flatus;
Spicula nec geminis nitor torquere lacertis.
Heu, frustra factor confinxit corpus inorme,
Totis membrorum dum frauder sensibus intus.

70

I rise from earth, flesh shining like a shield
That's forged in Vulcan's heat and gleams like snow,
And dearer than most plate that takes a blow.
No iron studs constrain my middle, though.
When grim men lack me, what is armour's yield?
Bodies and souls would hardly stop Death's course
Were I not thwarting Orcus with great force.

71

The gentle Judge deprived me right from birth
Of feet and hands as He produced vast Earth.
A swift bird's wing won't cause my elevation
And wheezing stirs no flesh with respiration.
Although I scan sky's vaulted canopy,
I still don't spurn the surging marble sea.

72

My body's maker made my body parts,
Though my limbs' functions I don't utilize.
I cannot walk on feet or see with eyes,
Though now below my brow there's ventilation.
No panting lung provides me respiration;
With my twin arms I can't try throwing darts.
The craftsman botched my giant body size,
Alas, as in all parts I lack sensation.

LXXIII

Per cava telluris clam serpo celerrimus antra
Flexos venarum girans anfractibus orbes.
Cum caream vita sensu quoque funditus expers,
Quis numerus capiat vel quis laterculus aequet
Vita viventum generem quot milia partu?
His neque per caelum rutilantis sidera sperae,
Fluctivagi ponti nec, compensantur harenae.

LXXIV

Glauca seges lini vernans ex aequore campi
Et tergus mihi tradebant primordia fati.
Bina mihi constant torto retinacula filo
Ex quibus immensum trucidabam mole tirannum
Cum cuperunt olim gentis saevire falanges.
Plus amo cum tereti bellum decernere saxo
Quam duris pugnans ferrata cuspide contis.
Tres digiti totum versant super ardua corpus;
Erro caput circa tenues et tendor in auras.

LXXV

Aera per sudum nunc binis remigo pennis;
Horridus et grossae depromo murmura vocis
Inque cavo densis conversor stipite turmis
Dulcia conficiens propriis alimenta catervis,
Et tamen humanis horrent haec pabula buccis.
Sed quicumque cupit disrumpens foedera pacis
Dirus commaculare domum sub culmine querno.
Exemplo socias in bellum clamo cohortes,
Dumque catervatim stridunt et spicula trudunt,
Agmina defugiunt iaculis exterrita diris;   (10)
Insontes hosti sic torquent tela nocenti
Plurima quae constant tetris infecta venenis.

73

Unseen, unheard, I prowl deep cracks of Earth,
Corkscrewing fast through curves in twisted strands.
Devoid of life and any sense of touch,
What number sets or chart equates the worth
Of countless creatures I have brought to birth?
No glowing stars in Heaven's sphere, or sands
Below the choppy seas, provide as much.

74

My start began from flat and blooming fields,
Some leather and the light-blue flaxen yields.
They make me with twin bands of twisted string
With which I slew with stone a brutish king
Back when a crowd of brawlers longed for gore.
I pick a polished stone that ends a war
Instead of hard-tipped iron spears to fight.
Three fingers fling my body to great height;
I loop a head and in thin air I soar.

75

I thrash now through clear air on double wings;
A terror, I exude low grumblings
And in a hollow branch thick swarms increase
While I collect sweet treats to feed our brood,
Though human cheeks are puckered by this food.
If someone wants to break the bonds of peace
So that my oak-roofed house is plagued by woe,
I'll quickly call for war to all my peers,
And while they buzz in swarms and drive home jabs,
The troops escape, afraid of savage stabs;   (10)
Thus, guiltless, they propel their many spears,
Which carry toxins, at a guilty foe.

LXXVI

Fausta fuit primo mundi nascentis origo
Donec prostratus succumberet arte maligni.
Ex me tunc priscae processit causa ruinae;
Dulcia quae rudibus tradebam mala colonis.
En iterum mundo testor remeasse salutem
Stipite de patulo dum penderet arbiter orbis
Et poenas lueret soboles veneranda Tonantis.

LXXVII

Quis prior in mundo deprompsit tegmina vestis
Aut quis elementer miserum protexit egenum?
Irrita non referam verbis nec frivola fingam.
Primitus in terra proprio de corpore peplum,
Ut fama fertur produxi frondibus altis.
Carica me curvat dum massis pabula praestat,
Sedulus agricola brumae quas tempore mandit.

LXXVIII

En! Plures debrians impendo pocula Bacchi
Vinitor expressit quae flavescentibus uvis
Pampinus et viridi genuit de palmite botris
Nectare cauponis complens ex vite tabernam.
Sic mea turgescunt ad plenum viscera musto,
Et tamen inflatum non vexat crapula corpus,
Quamvis hoc nectar centenis hauserit urnis.
Proles sum terrae glescens in saltibus altis,
Materiam cuneis findit sed cultor agrestis,
Pinos evertens altas et robora ferro.

76

Our newborn race was fortunate at first
Until The Devil's cunning made it cursed.
I caused the ancient fall from innocence;
I gave sweet apples to fresh immigrants.
Behold, I witnessed Earth's renewed salvation
When, spread on wood, the Judge of every nation
(And Thunder's Holy Son) paid reparation.

77

Who in the world first covered us with clothes
Or kindly sheltered wretches who were broke?
I'll neither squeal nor make a useless joke.
I was Earth's first, or so reports suppose,
Who wove from lofty leaves a body's cloak.
Figs weigh me down while serving food in clusters,
Which busy farmers eat when winter blusters.

78

Look! I give many drunkards cups of wine
For which the vintner presses golden fruit
He grew on branches from the grape's green shoot
So that a barkeep's tavern reeks of vine.
This way new juice engulfs my bloated trunk,
And yet my swollen frame is never drunk,
Although a hundred nectar jugs may drain.
I'm Earth's child growing in the high terrain,
But peasants' wedges split my wood with whacks,
Destroying pines and oaks by iron axe.

LXXIX

Non nos Saturni genuit spurcissima proles,
Iupiter immensum fingunt quem carmina vatum,
Nec fuit in Delo mater Latona creatrix.
Cynthia non dicor nec frater Apollo vocatur;
Sed potius summi genuit regnator Olimpi
Qui nunc in caelis excelsae praesidet arci.
Dividimus mundum communi lege quadratum;
Nocturnos regimus cursus et frena dierum.
Ni soror et frater vaga saecula iure gubernent,
Heu! Chaos immensum clauderet cuncta latebris
Atraque nunc Erebri regnarent Tartara nigri.

LXXX

De rimis lapidum profluxi flumine lento
Dum frangant flammae saxorum viscera dura
Et laxis ardor fornacis regnat habenis,
Nunc mihi forma capax glacieque simillima lucet.
Nempe volunt plures collum constringere dextra
Et pulchre digitis lubricum comprendere corpus.
Sed mentes muto dum labris oscula trado,
(Dulcia compressis impendens basia buccis)
Atque pedum gressus titubantes sterno ruina.

LXXXI

Semper ego clarum praecedo lumine lumen,
Signifer et Phoebi, lustrat qui limpidus orbem,
Per caelum gradiens obliquo tramite flector.
Eoas partes amo dum iubar inde meabit
Finibus Indorum, cernunt qui lumina primi.
O felix olim servata lege Tonantis!
Heu! Post haec cecidi proterva mente superbus,
Ultio quapropter funestum perculit hostem,
Sex igitur comites mecum super aethera scandunt;
Gnarus quos poterit per biblos pandere lector.

79

We are not spawned by Saturn's blighted son,
Jove, called in bardic verse "The Mighty One,"
And Delian Latona's not our mother.
I'm not called "Cynthia," nor Phoebus "brother";
The Lord who fashioned high Olympus reigns
Instead now from His heavenly domains.
We split the four-part world as we agreed;
Days pass and nights progress as we decreed.
If siblings won't rule passing time by right,
Alas, vast chaos would eclipse the light
And then in Hell dark Erebus would lead.

80

From seams in stone I slowly started streaming
While fire split tough bowels of rock within
And fetters broke as furnace flames were stoked,
And now, like ice, my massive form is gleaming.
Right-handed crowds, for certain, want me choked
And fondle my attractively smooth skin.
I change their minds, though, when I nuzzle lips
(Giving sweet kisses to a mouth pressed thin)
And nudge unsteady feet for nasty trips.

81

I always come before clear light with light,
And, harbinger of sun, which makes Earth bright,
I am deflected angling through air.
I love the East, for brilliance starts out where
India's lands detect an early glow.
O service to God's law was once delightful!
Alas! Proud, I then fell while feeling spiteful,
And so revenge undid a deadly foe,
And thus six friends and I ascend the skies;
Books can reveal them when a reader's wise.

LXXXII

Discolor in curvis conversor quadripes antris,
Pugnas exercens dira cum gente draconum.
Non ego dilecta turgesco prole mariti
Nec fecunda viro sobolem sic edidit alvus
Residuae matres ut sumunt semina partus;
Quin magis ex ore praegnantur viscera fetu.
Si vero proles patitur discrimina mortis,
Dicor habere rudem componens arte medelam.

LXXXIII

Arida spumosis dissolvens faucibus ora
Bis binis bibulus potum de fontibus hausi,
Vivens nam terrae glebas cum stirpibus imis
Nisu virtutis validae disrumpo feraces,
At vero linquit dum spiritus algida membra,
Nexibus horrendis homines constringere possum.

LXXXIV

Nunc mihi sunt oculi bis seni in corpore solo
Bis ternumque caput (sed cetera membra gubernant).
Nam gradior pedibus suffultus bis duodenis.
Sed decies novem sunt et sex corporis ungues
(Sinzigias numero pariter similabo pedestres).
Populus et taxus viridi quoque fronde salicta
Sunt invisa mihi sed fagos glandibus uncas
Fructiferas itidem florenti vertice quercus,
Diligo sic nemorosa simul non spernitur ilex.

82

I live, a multicoloured quadruped,
In burrows fighting snakes, a breed to dread.
My mate's dear children don't increase my size
Nor do I have a womb males fertilize
To reproduce as other mothers do;
My womb's impregnated by mouth instead.
If children, though, remain near death, I brew
A good folk remedy, or so it's said.

83

Relieving my dry mouth with foamy lips,
From twice two fountains I keep taking sips,
For while alive I smash rich clods of soil –
With roots down deep – through my ferocious toil,
But when no life remains in limbs gone cold,
My horrible restraints on men can hold.

84

I've twice six eyes, but flesh that is one whole
And three paired heads (though other parts control).
Two dozen feet suspend me as I stroll.
For nails, though, ninety-six are on my meat
(I look in number like the basic feet).
I hate green willows, poplar trees and yews
But love the nuts of beeches bowing down
And acorn-bearing oaks with flowered crown,
And as for holm-oak shade, I won't refuse.

LXXXV

Iam referam verbis tibi quod vix credere possis
(Cum constet verum fallant nec frivola mentem),
Nam dudum dederam soboli munuscula grata
Tradere quae numquam poterat mihi quislibet alter
Dum Deus ex alto fraudaret munere claro
In quo cunctorum gaudent praecordia dono.

LXXXVI

Sum namque armatus rugosis cornibus horrens.
Herbas arvorum buccis decerpo virentes,
Et tamen astrifero procedens agmine stipor;
Culmina caelorum quae scandunt celsa catervis.
Turritas urbes capitis certamine quasso
Oppida murorum prosternens arcibus altis.
Induo mortales retorto stamine pepli;
Littera quindecima praestat quod pars domus adsto.

LXXXVII

De salicis trunco pecoris quoque tergore raso,
Componor patiens discrimina cruda duelli.
Semper ego proprio gestantis corpore corpus
Conservabo, viri vitam ne dempserit Orcus.
Quis tantos casus aut quis tam plurima leti
Suscipit in bello crudelis vulnera miles?

85

I'll share words now you hardly can believe
(since it's plain truth, not blather to deceive),
For I once gave a blessing to a son
That I could not receive from anyone
As God above denied a gift that's bright
In which the hearts of other men delight.

86

Yes, armed with wrinkled horns, I'm quite a fright.
I chew huge mouthfuls of the meadow grass,
Yet starry swarms escort me as I pass;
They rise in hordes to Heaven's highest height.
Headstrong, I bang the turrets of the town
So its tall fortress walls will tumble down.
With twisted thread I fill man's clothing needs;
I'm right at home if letter fifteen leads.

87

I'm made, a willow-wood shaved-leather blend,
For taking battles to the bitter end.
A body's safety is my body's job
So Orcus will not have a life to rob.
What other soldier bears such hardship or
So many fatal injuries in war?

LXXXVIII

Callidior cunctis aura vescentibus aethrae,
Late per mundum dispersi semina mortis
Unde horrenda seges diris succrevit aristis,
Quam metit ad scelera scortator falce maligna.
Cornigeri multum vereor certamina cervi,
Namque senescenti spoliabor pelle vetustus
Atque nova rursus fretus remanebo iuventa.

LXXXIX

Nunc mea divinis complentur viscera verbis
Totaque sacratos gestant praecordia biblos,
At tamen ex isdem nequeo cognoscere quicquam.
Infelix fato fraudabor munere tali
Dum tollunt dirae librorum lumina Parcae.

XC

Sunt mihi sex oculi, totidem simul auribus hausi;
Sed digitos decies senos in corpore gesto.
Ex quibus ecce quater denis de carne revulsis.
Quinquies at tantum video remanere quaternos.

XCI

Omnipotens auctor, nutu qui cuncta creavit,
Mi dedit in mundo tam victrix nomen habendum
Nomine nempe meo florescit gloria regum,
Martiribus necnon dum vincunt proelia mundi
Edita caelestis prensant et praemia vitae.
Frondigeris tegitur bellantum turma coronis,
Et viridi ramo victor certamine miles.
In summo capitis densescit vertice vellus
Ex quo multiplicis torquentur tegmina pepli;
Sic quoque mellifluis escarum pasco saginis   (10)
Nectare per populos tribuens alimenta.

88

More cunning than all creatures gulping air,
I scatter seeds of death through every field
So toxic crops produce a horrid yield,
Which the Old Goat's grim sickle reaps for sin.
My fights with antlered bucks make me beware,
And, when old, I will shed my ancient skin
And, spurred by newfound youth, again begin.

89

God's holy words now fill my inner part
And bear the sacred books with all my heart,
And yet from them I'm not much edified.
By fate this gift has sadly been denied
As fierce Fates steal the light that books provide.

90

I've six eyes, with as many ears to hear,
But sixty digits on my frame were borne,
Look! From these forty the flesh was torn;
I see that only twenty persevere.

91

Almighty God, who made all with His powers,
Has named me "victor" for world-wide renown,
Since in my name kings' honour surely flowers,
And martyrs too, while thwarting worldly strife
And earning their reward of lofty life.
Soldiers in troops have donned a leafy crown,
And for the battle's victor: a green bough.
The fleece is sprouting thick atop my brow
From which folds tumble down my woven gown;
This way I nourish with a sweetened treat   (10)
So there is nectar everyone can eat.

XCII

Rupibus in celsis qua tundunt caerula cautes
Et salis undantes turgescunt aequore fluctus,
Machina me summis construxit molibus amplam
Navigeros calles ut pandam classibus index.
Non maris aequoreos lustrabam remige campos
Nec ratibus pontum sulcabam tramite flexo,
Et tamen immensis errantes fluctibus actos
Arcibus ex celsis signans ad litora duco
Flammiger imponens torres in turribus altis
Ignea brumales dum condunt sidera nimbi.

XCIII

Quae res in terris armatur robore tanto
Aut paribus fungi nitatur viribus audax?
Parva mihi primo constant exordia vitae.
Sed gracilis grandes soleo prosternere leto,
Quod letum proprii gestant penetralia ventris
Nam saltus nemorum densos pariterque frutecta
Piniferosque simul montes cum molibus altos.
Truxque rapaxque capaxque feroxque sub aethere spargo
Et minor existens gracili quam corpore scnifes.
Frigida dum genetrix dura generaret ab alvo
Primitus ex utero producens pignora gentis.

XCIV

Sambucus in silva putris dum fronde virescit,
Est mihi par foliis nam glesco surculus arvis
Nigros bacarum portans in fronte corimbos.
Quem medici multum ruris per terga virentem,
Cum scabies morbi pulpas irrepserit aegras
Lustrantes orbem crebro quaesisse feruntur.
Cladibus horrendae dum vexat viscera tabo,
Ne virus serpat possum succurrere leprae,
Sic olidas hominum restaurans germine fibras.

92

Where ocean pounds the craggy cliffs in sky
And surging surf is rising with the tide,
A scaffold built my mighty structure high
So I could point out sea-routes like a guide.
I do not roam calm oceans with an oar
Nor plow the deep with rowers as they lurch,
Yet lead lost boats, pushed by huge waves, to shore
While signalling from my exalted perch
In lofty towers, setting inflagrations
As clouds of winter shroud bright constellations.

93

What earthly thing is armed with such great might
Or tries with equal force to terrify?
At first my life's beginnings stayed quite slight.
I tend to slay the great, though I am light,
Since my internal organs carry doom
To both the bushes and the leafy pass,
And lofty piny peeks with rocky mass.
Vile, wild, riled, dry, I spread below the sky
And keep my body smaller than a fly.
When she spawned offspring from her stony womb,
My frigid mother bore me first in class.

94

In woods the elder grows green stinking leaves,
As do I, for I sprout in fields, a shrub
That bears dark berry clusters on its crown.
They've often said that doctors stripping scrub
Have sought me growing far outside of town
When deadly lesions burst through sickened skin.
As dreaded plague attacks your guts within,
I can keep leprosy from creeping in,
Thus, for man's putrid bowels, my bud relieves.

XCV

Ecce molosorum nomen mihi fata dederunt
(Argolicae gentis sic promit lingua loquelis)
Ex quo me dirae fallebant carmina Circae
Quae fontis liquidi maculabat flumina verbis!
Femora cum cruribus suras cum poplite bino
Abstulit immiscens crudelis verba virago,
Pignora nunc pavidi referunt ululantia nautae
Tonsis dum trudunt classes et caerula findunt.
Vastos verrentes fluctus grassante procella
Palmula qua remis succurrit panda per undas,   (10)
Auscultare procul quae latrant inguina circum,
Sic me pellexit dudum Titania proles,
Ut merito vivam salsis in fluctibus exul.

XCVI

Ferratas acies et denso milite turmas
Bellandi miseros stimulat quos vana cupido,
Dum maculare student armis pia foedera regni,
Salpix et sorbet ventosis flatibus auras
Raucaque clangenti resultant classica sistro;
Cernere non pavidus didici trux murmura Martis.
Quamquam me turpem nascendi fecerit auctor,
Editus ex alvo dum sumpsi munera vitae.
Ecce tamen morti successit gloria formae,
Letifer in fibras dum finis serpat apertas.   (10)
Bratea non auri fulvis pretiosa metallis,
Quamvis gemmarum constent ornata lucernis,
Vincere non quibunt falerarum floribus umquam.
Me flecti genibus fessum natura negavit
Poplite seu curvo palpebris tradere somnos.
Quin potius vitam compellor degere stando.

95

Behold my canine name – bestowed by fate
(as Greek vocabularies demonstrate)
When spells of dreaded Circe stained clear flow
Of fountains – she whose words deceived me!
The evil witch's bitter words relieved me
Of shinbones, thighs with calves, along with knees,
The wailing sailors claim now, as they row
Their vessels with their oars and cleave blue seas.
When thrashing through the tempests' driving spray
With broad-blade oars that slice right through the water,   (10)
From near my loins they hear my distant bay,
Thus showing I was tricked by Titan's daughter
As on salt waves I'm justly sent away.

96

As armoured troops and soldiers pack in tight
(Wretches who with vain lust incite a fight
While arms taint sacred civil loyalties),
A trumpet sucks in air with bursts of breeze
And raucous, clanging battle-horns resound;
Fierce, bold, I've come to know their savage sound.
Although God made me ugly at my start,
I picked up gifts of life once I debuted.
Behold! Death sneaks up on my pulchritude
As doom is snaking through each helpless part.   (10)
I can't be beaten by fine sheets of gold,
Although the precious polished metal's decked
With gleaming gems and stylish luxuries.
Nature won't let me kneel when I feel old
Or rest my eyelids while on bended knees.
Indeed, I have to spend my life erect.

XCVII

Florida me genuit nigrantem corpore tellus,
Et nil fecundum stereli de viscere promo,
Quamvis Eumenidum narrantes carmine vates
Tartaream partu testentur gignere prolem.
Nulla mihi constat certi substantia partus
Sed modo quadratum complector caerula mundum.
Est inimica mihi, quae cunctis constat amica
Saecula dum lustrat lampas Titania Phoebi.
Diri latrones me semper amare solebant
Quos gremio tectos nitor defendere fusco.   (10)
Vergilium constat caram cecinisse sororem:
'Ingrediturque solo et caput inter nubila condit
Monstrum horrendum, ingens, cui quot sunt corpore plumae,
Tot vigiles oculi subter mirabile dictu
Tot linguae, totidem ora sonant, tot subrigit auris.
Nocte volat caeli medio terraeque per umbras.'

XCVIII

Ostriger en arvo vernabam frondibus hirtis
Conquilio similis sic cocci murice rubro
Purpureus stillat sanguis de palmite guttis.
Exuvias vitae mandenti tollere nolo
Mitia nec penitus spoliabunt mente venena.
Sed tamen insanum vexat dementia cordis,
Dum rotat in giro vecors vertigine membra.

IC

Consul eram quondam Romanus miles equester
Arbiter imperio dum regni sceptra regebat,
Nunc onus horrendum reportant corpora gippi
Et premit immensum truculentae sarcina molis.
Terreo cornipedum nunc velox agmen equorum
Qui trepidi fugiunt mox quadripedante meatu
Dum trucis aspectant immensos corporis artus.

97

I was born dark, with flesh of Earth in bloom,
And I am sterile with a childless womb,
Though verse describing the Eumenides
Blames me for Tartarus's progeny.
I'm free of stuff with solid pedigrees
But gather the four-cornered world in gloom.
Apollo's torch of Titan, which men see
As friendly light, incurs my enmity.
Grim thieves, for whom I try to give protection
In my dark bosom, always give affection.   (10)
Of my dear sister Virgil has expounded,
"She hides her head in clouds, though she is grounded.
From flesh of this gross monster there appears
A lot of feathers, tongues and watchful eyes
And, strange to say, a lot of mouths and ears;
At night between the earth and sky she flies."

98

Look! Decked with purple in a field, I'll grow
With hairy tendrils like an oyster so
A red-stained branch is dripping crimson flow.
I want no life or loot when men have dined
Nor will my gentle juice destroy a mind.
Although heart flutter makes these people crazed,
Their limbs just whirl around when they are dazed.

99

I once was consul, when a Roman knight
Controlled the royal sceptre as his right,
But flesh now bears my hump's alarming freight
And its large shape is pressed by crushing weight.
Today I scare swift herds of hard-hoofed steeds
Who flee in frightened gallops at high speeds
When my wild frame's huge limbs are in their sight.

C

Conditor aeternis fulcit qui saecla columnis,
Rector regnorum frenans et fulmina lege
Pendula dum patuli vertuntur culmina caeli
Me varium fecit primo dum conderet orbem.
Pervigil excubiis (numquam dormire iuvabit),
Sed tamen extemplo clauduntur lumina somno,
Nam Deus ut propria mundum dicione gubernat,
Sic ego complector sub caeli cardine cuncta.
Segnior est nullus quoniam me larbula terret,
Setigero rursus constans audacior apro.   (10)
Nullus me superat cupiens vexilla triumphi,
Ni Deus, aethrali summus qui regnat in arce.
Prorsus odorato ture flagrantior halans
Olfactum ambrosiae necnon crescentia glebae
Lilia purpureis possum conexa rosetis
Vincere spirantis nardi dulcedine plena,
Nunc olida caeni squalentis sorde putresco.
Omnia quaeque polo sunt subter et axe reguntur
Dum pater arcitenens concessit iure guberno;
Grossas et graciles rerum comprenso figuras.   (20)
Altior en caelo rimor secreta Tonantis,
Et tamen inferior terris tetra Tartara cerno;
Nam senior mundo praecessi tempora prisca.
Ecce tamen matris horno generabar ab alvo,
Pulchrior auratis dum fulget fibula bullis,
Horridior ramnis et spretis vilior algis.
Latior en patulis terrarum finibus exto,
Et tamen in media concludor parte pugilli;
Frigidior brumis necnon candente pruina,
Cum sim Vulcani flammis torrentibus ardens.   (30)
Dulcior in palato quam lenti nectaris haustus,
Dirior et rursus quam glauca absinthia campi.
Mando dapes mordax lurconum more Ciclopum,
Cum possim iugiter sine victu vivere felix.
Plus pernix aquilis Zephiri velocior alis
Necnon accipitre properantior et tamen horrens
Lumbricus et limax et tarda testudo palustris
Atque fimi soboles sordentis cantarus ater.

100

The Maker, whose timeless columns lift the world,
The Lord of lands, with reined-in bolts unhurled
As towers turned in spacious skies, created
My multitudes on lands He generated.
I stay on watch (it never helped to doze),
But still I sleep as eyes abruptly close,
For while God rules the world as He propounds,
I too embrace all things beneath its bounds.
No one's more shy than I, nor fears ghosts more,
Though I stay bolder than a bristly boar.   (10)
No trophy-taker causes my defeat
Save God, who rules from His high airy seat.
More fragrant than ambrosial scents (it's true!)
Emitted by perfume, I can outdo
The scarlet roses, lilies from the yard
As well as, full of sweetness, whiffs of nard,
Though now I rot in filthy, reeking stool.
While God the Archer deigns, by right I rule
The universe beneath the highest star;
I grasp things, gross and graceful as they are.   (20)
Behold! I see God's secrets down through sky,
Yet under land foul Hell attracts my eye;
I lived before time, older than the Earth.
Behold! My mother's womb begets my birth,
More gorgeous than gold amulets that glitter,
More gross than thorns, more vile than low-tide litter.
Behold! I'm wider than the limits of Earth's lands,
Yet can be held within a person's hands;
Colder than gleaming frost and winter, though
In Vulcan's searing blazes I may glow.   (30)
No nectar on the palate is as sweet,
Nor wild gray wormwood quite as foul to eat.
Like hungry Cyclops, I am never sated,
But stripped of food I'd be no less elated.
More swift then eagles, hawks, or Zephyr's wings,
Gross worms, slugs, slow swamp turtles, and those *things* –
Black beetles spawned in putrid dung – outpace
Me faster than my talk about this race.

Me dicto citius vincunt certamine cursus
Sum gravior plumbo scopulorum pondera vergo   (40)
Sum levior pluma cedit cui tippula limphae,
Nam silici densas quae fudit viscera flammas
Durior aut ferro tostis sed mollior extis.
Cincinnos capitis nam gesto cacumine nullos
Ornent qui frontem pompis et tempora setis,
Cum mihi caesaries volitent de vertice crispae
Plus calamistratis se comunt quae calamistro.
Pinguior, en, multo scrofarum axungia glesco
Glandiferis iterum referunt dum corpora fagis
Atque saginata laetantur carne subulci.   (50)
Sed me dira famis macie torquebit egenam
Pallida dum iugiter dapibus spoliabor opimis.
Limpida sum fateor Titanis clarior orbe;
Candidior nivibus dum ningit vellera nimbus,
Carceris et multo tenebris obscurior atris
Atque latebrosis ambit quas Tartarus umbris.
Ut globus astrorum plasmor teres atque rotunda,
Sperula seu pilae necnon et forma cristalli,
Et versa vice protendor ceu Serica pensa
In gracilem porrecta panum seu stamina pepli.   (60)
Senis ecce plagis latus qua panditur orbis
Ulterior multo tendor mirabile fatu.
Infra me suprave nihil per saecula constat
Ni rerum genitor mundum sermone coercens.
Grandior in glaucis ballena fluctibus atra
Et minor exiguo sulcat qui corpora verme
Aut modico phoebi radiis qui vibrat atomo.
Centenis pedibus gradior per gramina ruris
Et penitus numquam per terram pergo pedester;
Sic mea prudentes superat sapientia sofos,   (70)
Nec tamen in biblis docuit me littera dives
Aut umquam quivi quid constet sillaba nosse.
Siccior aestivo torrentis caumate solis,
Rore madens iterum plus uda flumine fontis,
Salsior et multo tumidi quam marmora ponti;
Et gelidis terrae limphis insulsior erro.
Multiplici specie cunctorum compta colorum
Ex quibus ornatur praesentis machina mundi,

I'm heavier than lead – no counterweight
Of stone upon a scale could compensate –   (40)
Lighter than down that makes pond-spiders sprint,
Tougher than flames that spew from bowels of flint
Or iron, softer than a kidney stew.
There are no ringlets on my head to do
Up my high brow with curls or fringe for show,
Though my style lets my forehead's tresses flow
More than a curling iron's crimp allows.
Look, I grow fatter than the greasy sows
With flesh they fill with beechnuts as they eat
While swineherds celebrate their plumper meat.   (50)
I'm drawn and pale; fierce hunger tortures me
While I'm deprived of meals of luxury.
I'm sheer, more clear than Titan's orb, I know;
When clouds shed fleece, I'm brighter than the snow,
Yet darker than a dungeon's blackest glooms
And dismal spirits Tartarus subsumes.
I'm made with round, smooth form or, to be clear,
Like globes, stars' orbits or a crystal sphere,
And, on the other hand, I'm stretched and spread
Like Chinese silk for robes or slender thread.   (60)
Behold with words of wonder: I embrace
Beyond the world's six zones that measure space.
No life persists below or over me
But God, whose Word controls totality.
I'm bigger than black whales in gleaming waves
And smaller than thin worms that bore through graves
Or motes that shimmer in Apollo's glow.
Through lush fields on a hundred feet I go,
Yet never trod ground on a walking trip;
This means my insight outstrips scholarship,   (70)
Though I have never learned books' precious signs
Or anything of syllables' designs.
I'm drier than a scorching summer sun,
Bedewed and drenched more than a river's run,
More salty than an ocean wave that gleams;
I flow more freshly than Earth's crystal streams.
Adorned with countless kinds of coloration
That paint the present world's configuration,

Lurida cum toto nunc sim fraudata colore.
Auscultate mei credentes famina verbi   (80)
(Pandere quae poterit gnarus vix ore magister),
Et tamen infitians non retur frivola lector.
Sciscitor inflatos fungar quo nomine sofos.

EXPLICIUNT ENIGMATA

I'm wan and pale; no colour will remain.
Believers: note my words that *seem* arcane   (80)
(Which skilled speech teachers hardly could explain),
And yet no doubting reader thinks them lame.
I ask the windbag scholars for my name.

THE RIDDLES END

Answer Key

1. Terra/Earth
2. Ventus/Wind
3. Nubes/Cloud
4. Natura/Nature
5. Iris/Rainbow
6. Luna/Moon
7. Fatum/Fate
8. Pliades/Pleiades
9. Adamas/Diamond
10. Molosus/Mastiff
11. Poalum/Bellows
12. Bombix/Silkworm
13. Barbita/Organ
14. Pavo/Peacock
15. Salamandra/Salamander
16. Luligo/Flying Fish
17. Perna/Bivalve Mollusk (*pinna nobilis*)
18. Myrmicoleon/Ant-lion
19. Salis/Salt
20. Apis/Bee
21. Lima/File
22. Acalantida/Nightingale
23. Trutina/Scales
24. Dracontia/Dragon-stone
25. Magnes Ferrifer/Lodestone
26. Gallus/Rooster
27. Coticula/Whetstone

28. Minotaurus/Minotaur
29. Aqua/Water
30. Elementum/Alphabet
31. Ciconia/Stork
32. Pugillares/Writing tablets
33. Lorica/Armour
34. Locusta/Locust
35. Nycticorax/Night-raven
36. Scnifes/Midge
37. Cancer/Crab
38. Tippula/Pond Strider
39. Leo/Lion
40. Piper/Pepper
41. Pulvillus/Pillow
42. Strutio/Ostrich
43. Sanguisuga/Leech
44. Ignis/Fire
45. Fusum/Spindle
46. Urtica/Nettle
47. Hirundo/Swallow
48. Vertico Poli/Sphere of the Heavens
49. Lebes/Cauldron
50. Myrifyllon/Milfoil (Yarrow)
51. Eliotropus/Heliotrope
52. Candela/Candle
53. Arcturus/Arcturus
54. Cocuma Duplex/Double Boiler
55. Crismal/Chrismal
56. Castor/Beaver
57. Aquila/Eagle
58. Vesper Sidus/Evening Star
59. Penna/Pen
60. Monocerus/Unicorn
61. Pugio/Dagger
62. Famfaluca/Bubble
63. Corbus/Raven
64. Columba/Dove
65. Muriceps/Mouser
66. Mola/Mill
67. Cribellus/Sieve

68. Salpix/Trumpet
69. Taxus/Yew
70. Tortella/Loaf of Bread
71. Piscis/Fish
72. Colosus/Colossus
73. Fons/Spring
74. Fundibalum/Sling
75. Crabro/Hornet
76. Melarius/Apple Tree
77. Ficulnea/Fig Tree
78. Cupa Vinaria/Wine Cask
79. Sol et Luna/Sun and Moon
80. Calix Vitreus/Glass Cup
81. Lucifer/Morning Star
82. Mustela/Weasel
83. Iuvencus/Steer
84. Scrofa Praegnans/Pregnant Sow
85. Caecus Natus/Man Born Blind
86. Aries/Ram
87. Clipeus/Shield
88. Basiliscus/Serpent
89. Arca Libraria/Bookcase
90. Puerpera Geminas Enixa/Woman Bearing Twins
91. Palma/Palm
92. Farus Editissima/Tall Lighthouse
93. Scintilla/Spark
94. Ebulus/Dwarf Elder
95. Scilla/Scylla
96. Elefans/Elephant
97. Nox/Night
98. Elleborus/Hellebore
99. Camellus/Camel
100. Creatura/Creation

Commentary

Title & Sources: Janie Steen has noted that "the Christian nature of the *Enigmata* is entirely clear from their title: an *enigma* is both a genre and a trope, a species of allegory, which stems ultimately from biblical *enigmata*, dark sayings that conceal wisdom or truth (*Proverbs* 1:6). Through their allusive language, the *Enigmata* reflect Saint Paul's phrase, *per speculum in enigmate* ('through a glass darkly'; I *Corinthians* 13:12), the assertion that spiritual understanding in this world is obscured." Steen at 90. Aldhelm felt a spiritual need to pierce the world's obscurity and to share the wonders and lessons of his discoveries. See Lapidge and Herren at 59 ("a certain natural curiosity about hidden things … is innate in me … ").

By the time Aldhelm began writing Latin poetry, perhaps during his studies at Canterbury, he had absorbed a stunning amount of literature. Orchard (1994) at 126–238 built on the scholarship of his predecessors to inventory Aldhelm's reading. More than two decades has produced little scholarship that prompts reconsideration of Orchard's painstaking work, and I diverge from his conclusions only in the following ways: 1) I believe that Aldhelm used phrases from Paulinus Petricordia *De vita Martini*, while Orchard is uncertain on that point; 2) I believe that Irish verse, particularly *Hisperica Famina* and *Altus Prosator*, significantly influenced Aldhelm's poetry; 3) I believe that Aldhelm used thoughts and phrases from Theodore of Tarsus *Laterculus Malalianus*; 4) I believe that Aldhelm thought that *Culex* was an authentic Virgilian work and used it as such; 5) I believe that Aldhelm was broadly fluent with many of the works of Corippus, Dracontius, and Claudian, a proposition that Orchard believes is doubtful or unsubstantiated; 6) I believe that Saint Basil's *Hexaemeron* was an important source of subject matter for the *Aenigmata*; and 7) I believe that Aldhelm had largely suppressed *wanderlust* and that his riddles reveal glimmers of his affection for largely forgotten travel books and texts somewhat like almanacs, such as Festus Avienus *Ora maritima*, Priscian *Periegesis*, Justinus *Epitome*, Solinus *Mirabilia*, Valerius Maximus *Facta et dicta memorabilia,* and perhaps Rutilius *De reditu suo.*

The most important source for Aldhelm's allusive *Aenigmata* (which could be translated as either "riddles" or "mysteries"), other than Virgil's *Aeneid*, was the *Aenigmata* of Symphosius, a text that Aldhelm admired despite his concern that it lacked the Christian perspective he wanted in his reading. Similar concerns did not stop Aldhelm from pondering the transformations and paradoxes of Ovid's *Metamorphoses*, although it is not clear whether he read Ovid's racier verse. Isidore of Seville's *Etymologiae* also influenced Aldhelm's science and etymological mindset.

Quotations from Aldhelm's letters as well as his *De metris, De pedum regis, Carmen de virginitate,* and *Laudibus de virginitate* provide reliable information about most of his other reading. In addition to a few lost and misattributed citations, Aldhelm cites Sedulius thirty-five times, Prosper of Aquitaine nineteen times, Lucan twelve times, Juvenal nine times, Juvencus eight times, Arator seven times, and Terence three times, although the references to Terence appear to be derived from secondary sources. See Orchard (1994) at 127–9; see also Lapidge (1996). He quotes from Lucan's sadly lost *Orpheus* twice, which provides us with the only lines we have of that text. *Id.* at 127, 140. Eight of Aldhelm's citations from Juvenal and three from Persius may have been taken from books by Priscian and other grammarians. See generally Ruff, "The Place of Metrics in Anglo-Saxon Latin Education: Aldhelm and Bede," *Journal of English and German Philology* 104, no. 2 (2005) at 149–70. Aldhelm appears to have been familiar with the works of poets such as Statius, Claudian, Prudentius, Paulinus of Nola, Dracontius, and Fortunatus. See Orchard (1994) at 135–224. But see Lapidge and Rosier at 231 (questioning Aldhelm's knowledge of Fortunatus). He seems to have read many of the long Christian poems of the previous three centuries, including the works of Corippus, Orientius, Arator, Juvencus, Cyprianus Gallus, Paulinus Petricordia, and perhaps Claudius Marius Victorius. In addition to a large amount of patristic literature that provided material for his prose and verse works on virginity, Aldhelm read the *Vulgate* and probably read Latin bibles that predated the *Vulgate*. See Marsden at 64–72.

Aldhelm cites Aristotle as a predecessor who used riddles to support serious points. See Ehwald at 75 (*Sed et aristotelis philosophorum acerrimus. Perplexa nihilominus enigmata prosae locutionis facundia fultus argumentatur*). Aristotle used the term *ainigma* three times in his *Rhetoric* and once in his *Poetics*. See Cook at 32. We are fairly sure, however, that Aldhelm spoke no Greek, and no secondary source provides a clear basis for Aldhelm's understanding of Aristotle. More importantly, we do not have actual riddles of Aristotle. Milovanović-

Barham's theory that Aldhelm may have known of pseudepigraphs of Aristotle mentioned by Jerome, as well as other Greek sources through Theodore, deserves more inquiry. See Milovanović-Barham, "Aldhelm's *Enigmata* and Byzantine Riddles," *Anglo-Saxon England* 22 (1993) at 52.

As for other major writers in the rhetorical tradition who discussed riddles, such as Cicero and Quintilian, Aldhelm's silence in his prose and the lack of echoes of those authors in his verse probably reflect his lack of direct knowledge of their work. See Thornbury at 266–7. However, it would be safe to assume from his prose writing that Aldhelm read works of grammarians, such as Donatus, who discussed riddles as a form of metaphor. See e.g. Donatus *Ars minor* 17c (*Aenigma est obscura sententia per occultam similitudinem rerum ut mater me genuit eadem mox gignitur ex me*).

One of the underappreciated inspirations for Aldhelm's *Aenigmata* is the *Hexaemeron* of Saint Basil of Caesarea (330–79), who was also known by the Greek name "*Ouranophantor*" (revealer of heavenly *mysteries*). As with Aldhelm, Basil attempted to explain the wonders and mysteries of God to a lay audience. The subjects of many of Aldhelm's riddles are also subjects in the *Hexaemeron*, a collection of homilies originally written in Greek but then translated into Latin by several authors and widely disseminated in Europe. See e.g. Schaff at 64 (Lucifer); at 68 (stream); at 77–8 (hellebore); at 81 (fig tree); at 85 (ram); at 88 (moon); at 90 (crab); at 90–3 (fish); at 91 (squid); at 96 (swallow); at 97 (rooster, peacock, dove); at 98 (stork); at 99 (owl); and at 105 (elephant). Ambrose's *Hexaemeron*, which relied heavily on Basil's *Hexaemeron*, may also be the source for some riddles. A similar overlooked source appears to be Solinus *Mirabilia*. See 23 (dragon-stone), 27 (whetstone), 39 (lion), 40 (pepper), 42 (ostrich), 60 (unicorn), 77 (fig tree), 96 (elephant), 99 (camel). It is intriguing that there is so little overlap between riddles on subjects in Basil's *Hexaemeron* and subjects in Solinus's *Mirabilia*; one can hardly help imagining Aldhelm rummaging through his *arca libraria* to create a list of possible subjects when he was short on inspiration.

One of Aldhelm's mentors, Theodore of Tarsus (602–90 AD), arrived in Britain in 669 and brought with him knowledge of Greek patristic writers, sometimes in such translations as Eustachius's or Rufinus's translations of Basil's *Hexaemeron*. See Lapidge and Herren at 85. For an indispensable review of the career of Theodore, see Lapidge (1996) at 93–123; see also Corona at 29; Gwara, "His Master's Voice: Late Latin in the Milan Glosses," *Glotta* 73 (1995/1996) at 142–8; Lapidge, "Surviving Booklists from Anglo-Saxon England," in Richards at 108; Lapidge, "The School of Theodore and Hadrian," *Anglo-Saxon England* 15 (1986) at 45–72; Bodden, "Evidence for Knowledge of Greek in Anglo-Saxon England," *Anglo-Saxon England* 17 (1988) at 217–46. Basil's name appears for the first time in Anglo-Latin literature in Theodore's *Penitentials,* a collection of canons compiled, probably as class notes by acolytes of Theodore, late in the seventh century. See Lapidge and Herren at 55; see generally Frantzen (1976 and 1983). Aldhelm praises Basil and his *Hexaemeron* in a paragraph in *Laudibus de virginitate,* Lapidge and Herren at 86–7, and seems to identify closely with Basil's techniques in this passage:

> For in fact it is said to be an ancient practice of skilled orators who, standing high in the pulpits harangue throngs of people, that, in the audience of the diverse assembly with the difference of sexes, they sometimes use a different *persona* just as their own; and, disclosing the secrets of the minds of these persons and unlocking what was hidden in the depths of their hearts, to their astonished audience and their unwitting listeners, they reveal (these things) with the key of their eloquent speech. *Id.* at 86.

It is difficult to be precise about Theodore's influence on Aldhelm because Theodore's paper trail is unclear. While I concur that Theodore inspired but did not write the *Penitentials* often attributed to him, I accept the argument of Stevenson at 8–11 that Theodore is almost surely the author of *Laterculus Malalianus,* a frequently overlooked text that seems to have influenced Aldhelm.

Theodore also knew Roman law and is Aldhelm's most likely instructor on that subject. See Stevenson at 72. He may have even sparked Aldhelm's interest in octosyllabic verse.

Another underappreciated source for the *Aenigmata* is the *Physiologus,* a description of animals combined with a discussion of their Christian import. See Ziolkowski 34–5. The anonymous author of this highly popular volume is believed to have been a Greek speaker who lived in the second, third, or fourth centuries; it is unclear when the text was first translated into Latin. His work spawned many translations and liberal adaptations, and Aldhelm probably had access to both Latin and Old English versions. Most versions of what became a popular educational text discuss about twelve animals, and most of those animals appear, sometimes with parallel themes, in the *Aenigmata.* Examples include dove, elephant, serpent, fig tree, swallow, weasel, heron, lion, and pelican. Cf. Curley; Peebles, "The Anglo-Saxon *Physiologus,*" *Modern Philology* 18, no. 4 (1911) at 571–9; Carmody, "De Bestiis et Aliis Rebus," *Speculum* 13, no. 2 (1938) at 153–9. Aldhelm generally avoided writing riddles about an animal if Symphosius had already written one about that animal. See Bitterli at 22–3.

The extent of Irish influence on Aldhelm remains controversial, but I believe that the seventh-century hyperliterary (or "hermeneutic") *Hisperica Famina* and related texts were significant influences on Aldhelm. Cf. Orchard (1994) at 96–7; Lapidge, "The Hermeneutic Style in Tenth Century Latin Literature," *Anglo-Saxon England* 4 (1975) at 67–111; Grosjean, "Confusa Caligo," *Celtica* 3 (1956) at 64–7; but see Marenbon, "Les Sources du Vocabulaire d'Aldhelm," *Archivum Latintatis Medii Aevi* 41 (1977–8) at 75–90. It is almost certain that Aldhelm knew *Altus Prosator*, an influential Irish hymn of the same era. Cf. Orchard (1994) at 54–60; Stevenson, "Altus prosator," *Celtica* 23 (1999) at 361–4. Nonliterary Irish and arguably Irish Latin sources, such as the *Commentarium in Marcum*, often attributed to Cummian, deserve more scholarly attention than they have received to date. See generally Dempsey, "'Claviger aetherius': Aldhelm of Malmesbury between Ireland and Rome," *Journal of the Royal Society of Antiquaries of Ireland* 131 (2001) at 5–18; see also Herren and Brown at 89–91, 139–40.

Scholars interested in Aldhelm's sources tend to focus on authors they esteem and forget that their preferences do not necessarily match Aldhelm's. For instance, Aldhelm seems to have had a taste for texts that are largely ignored today, many of which were travelogues or had an almanac-like quality. Examples of this type include Solinus *Mirabilia*, Justinus *Epitome*, Valerius Maximus *Facta et dicta memorabilia*, Priscian *Periegesis*, and Festus Avienus *Ora maritima* and *Descriptio orbis terrae*. Katherine O'Brien O'Keeffe makes essentially the same point in "The Geographic List of *Solomon and Saturn II*," *Anglo-Saxon England* 20 (1991) at 127–8. The language of the *Aenigmata* also tends to suggest that Aldhelm was familiar with Ammianus *Res gestae* and Paulinus Petricordia *De vita Martini*; it is unclear from other sources whether those texts had reached Britain by the late seventh century.

There has been little scholarly analysis of the so-called *Bern Riddles*, otherwise known as the *Aenigmata Bernensia*. Since most scholars agree that they were written after Isidore of Seville but before Aldhelm, it is probably a seventh-century text. But see Lapidge and Rosier at 3 (stating that the *Bern Riddles* were "inspired" by the *Aenigmata*). The *Bern Riddles* appear to be modelled after Symphosius in that they have a consistent line length (six lines each instead of Symphosius's three) and a similar secular tone. This text has been attributed to a "Tullius," although curious scholars should probably be looking for a "Paulus" because it has an acrostic with that name in the final riddle. Aldhelm may have borrowed some of the subjects for his riddles from Tullius/Paulus (or vice versa), but there seems to be surprisingly little overlap of language or imagery between these texts.

Preface: The preface is both an acrostic and a telestich communicating the same message twice: "Aldhelm composed a thousand lines in verse." If you are literally minded, this message is incorrect because the lines number less than a thousand, but, to be fair, writers of Latin regularly used words such as *millenis* to mean "a large amount."

An acrostic is a poem that creates a message with the letters in the left-hand margin of a poem. A telestich, which is rarer, does the same thing with the letters on the right-hand margin of a poem (the two in combination are often called a "double acrostic"). In my translation I duplicated the acrostic, but freely admit that duplicating both the acrostic and the telestich was too much for my poetic bag of tricks. Indeed, I reluctantly took some small liberties with the preface that I ordinarily do not take in order to mimic the acrostic. For those who might be unhappy with those liberties, there are very different prose translations of Aldhelm's *Praefatio* at Lapidge and Rosier 70–1, Stark at 98–9, Orchard (forthcoming), and Thornbury, "Aldhelm's Rejection of the Muses and the Mechanics of Poetic Inspiration in Early Anglo-Saxon England," *Anglo-Saxon England* 36 (2007) at 73.

Aldhelm also composed an acrostic and telestich for the preface to his *Carmen de virginitate*, and may have done the same for a loose translation of a Greek devotional poem of debated authorship called *Versus sibyllae de iudicio Dei* that contains an acrostic in the original, although there is no evidence that Aldhelm could translate Greek. See Lapidge and Rosier at 16; Lapidge and Herren at 8–9. Indeed, there is some evidence that his occasional incorrect use of Greek terms suggests he relied upon a glossary, such as the *Hermeneutica*, the *Abolita*, or the *Abstrusa*. See Lapidge and Herren at 183; Stork at 46. Some scholars have argued that the prosody of this translation is too far below Aldhelm's standards to justify an attribution, but (speaking from personal experience) that view may underestimate the difficulty of translating an acrostic from one language into another. See e.g. Orchard (1994) at 196–9.

Aldhelm helped to popularize acrostics, although the tradition of Christian Latin acrostic verse goes at least as far back as Commodianus *Instructiones*, which arguably dates to the middle of the third century. See generally Marshall. Aldhelm was probably unaware that Virgil may have inserted acrostics into his verse. See Grishin, "*Ludis in Undis*: An Acrostic in *Eclogue 9*," *Harvard Studies in Classical Philology* 104 (2008) at 237–40. Some riddles of the *Exeter Book* also contain coded clues of different types. See e.g. Eliason, "Four Old English Cryptographic Riddles," *Studies in Philology* 49, no. 4 (1952) at 553–65.

A likely inspiration for Aldhelm's acrostics is the poetry of Pope Damasus I (304[?]–384), which Aldhelm cited a number of times in his prose works. See Bremmer, Dekker, and Johnson at 154. Although Aldhelm did not cite Damasus's acrostic verse, it is probable that he was familiar with it. See Orchard (1994) at 204–5. A number of anonymous acrostic poems also circulated during this period with the poems of Sedulius. See Orchard (1994) at 164–6. Eugene of Toledo also composed two acrostic poems.

Another likely inspiration for Aldhelm's wordplay was Hisperic Latin, a seventh-century Irish movement of extravagant linguistic playfulness. This playfulness was on display in the anonymous *Hisperica Famina*, the hymn *Altus Prosator* (often attributed, probably wrongly, to Saint Columbanus), and the eccentric writings of the grammarian/satirist Virgilius Maro Grammaticus (whose wordplay intrigued James Joyce).

Unlike most of the riddles, the prologue reflects a fair amount of showing off in the fashionable Irish style of the time with its double acrostic form, rare and elevated vocabulary, and allusions accessible only to fellow scholars. Its self-deprecatory satire is rooted in the classical tradition, and one has to wonder whether Aldhelm felt the need to atone for the sin of pride after such rhetorical displays. By contrast, the riddles that follow are less showy and appear to be intended primarily, although not exclusively, for a broader audience learning Latin and learning more about its Christianity.

Both Aldhelm and Theodore of Tarsus had a strained relationship with their Irish peers. See Aldhelm's *Letter to Heahfrith* in Lapidge and Herren (1997) at 163; Stevenson at 10. Aldhelm's use of the double-acrostic form appears to be a competitive, although gentle, response to Irish writers by one-upping them on their use of acrostics and similar wordplay. He also seems to be one-upping the Irish with his content, since he satirizes a classical satire, a task beyond the reach of Irish writers of the time. The Irish painstakingly read scores of grammars and commentaries on classical texts, but had access to very few, if any, actual classical texts of history or poetry. See generally Herren (1997) at I.1–39.

I scoured the *Aenigmata* looking for other acrostics and found a few candidates. For instance, the first five lines of Riddle 99 begin C-A-N-E-T ("he sings"), a verb that was one of Aldhelm's favourites. The letters of the final lines of the last riddle, Riddle 100, are S-E-M-E-L-A-P-E-S (*semel apes* – "once bees"); the bee was an important symbol for Aldhelm. See n.20 *infra*. As delightful as it would have been to find coded meaning in these riddles, I reluctantly concluded that these discoveries were predictable statistical accidents.

l. 1 The term *Arbiter* ("Arbiter") was a usage of Christian writers of Late Antiquity, particularly Augustine. As strange as this appellation sounds to the modern ear, the sense is closer to "arbitrator" or "mediator" than our more familiar "judge"; I have used both in this translation. Augustine argued that God was a necessary arbitrator between mankind and immortal beings, both good and evil. See e.g. *De civitate Dei* 9.15–17, 20, 11.2; *Confessiones* 7.18.24. Herren and Brown note that the Irish were fond of this image and tended to have a gentler view of Christ's role than continental Christians. See Herren and Brown at 174–8, 260. Aldhelm also used this image in his *Carmen de virginitate*. See Lapidge and Rosier at 102, 109.

The term *aethereo* ("aloft" – literally "in the ether"), a favourite of Lucretius, originally had a scientific sense. By Aldhelm's time the term had a strong religious connotation.

The noun *regmine* ("reign") is an early medieval variant of the classical noun *regimine*. It was not standard even in Aldhelm's time. Cf. Bede *Historia ecclesiastica* 2.15.5, 4.6.6, 4.12.8, 5.19.23, 5.20.2; *Homilae* 1.6.7, 2.8.6. The earliest precedent I have identified for the dropped "i" is Gregory the Great *Moralia in Iob* 19.20.3 (*Quanta disciplina regminis*).

Lapidge and Rosier at 234 are probably correct that Aldhelm was not fussy about theories of government and used varying terms for governing without intending to transmit nuances of meaning that Bede and other later writers intended to transmit. For other uses by Aldhelm of *sceptra* ("sceptres" – in line 2 of translation) as a symbol for civil authority, see Lapidge and Rosier at 48, 155.

l. 2 For *lucifluum* ("-lit" – literally "light-bearing") as a variant of the classical *luciferum*, see O'Sullivan at 294. Cf. *Carmen de virginitate* 2451 (*Florida lucifluae claudent et limina portae*). The earliest use I identified is Juvencus *Evangelia* 3.293 (*lucifluum*); 4.119 (*lucifluo*).

Poets rarely used the noun *tribunal* ("court") in the Augustan era, but Livy, Tacitus, and Cicero regularly used it. *Tribunal* became popular with Christian writers of Late Antiquity, particularly Augustine. They frequently used it in the phrase *tribunal Christi* ("court of Christ"). Aldhelm often used the word at the end of a line even when he was not creating an acrostic. See e.g. *Carmen de virginitate* 2735, 2882, 2901.

l. 3 The phrase *aeternis legibus* ("eternal laws") was surprisingly rare until later in the medieval period. But see Lucan *Bellum civile* 7.1 (*lex aeterna*); Virgil *Georgica* 1.43 (*leges aeternaque*); Boethius *De consolatione philosophiae* 4.P4.1.28 (*aeterna lex*), Seneca *De providentia* 1.1.2 (*aeternae legis*), Arator *De actis apostolorum* 2.57 (*lex aeterna*); cf. Virgil *Aeneid* 1.229–30 (*aeternis regis imperiis*); Augustine *Enarrationes in Psalmos* 110.9 (*aeternis veritatis*); Cicero *De republica* 3.33 (*lex sempiterna*), *De legibus* 2.10 (*lex sempiternam*). The concept was originally a Stoic one, later popularized by Cicero, and then adapted to Christianity by Augustine. See Mousourakis at 123; Dyck at 33; Stone at 41.

ll. 4–5 *Vehemoth* was a monster that God ejected from Heaven. Gregory the Great mentioned it ninety times in *Moralia in Iob*, though he started the name with the more familiar letter "B." Aldhelm's description *Ex alta ... rueret ... arce* ("he fell ... from Heaven") was a somewhat new expression for a familiar scene. Christian writers prior to Aldhelm typically used *cecidit* instead of *rueret*, and preferred *coelo* or other words to *arce*. See e.g. Ambrosiaster *In Epistolas Beati*

Pauli 1.11.20, 2.15.77 (*cecidit de coelo*); Ambrose *In Psalmum David CXVIII Exposito* 12.10 (*cecidit e coelo*), 14.21 (*cecidit ab altitudine*); Augustine *Enarrationes in Psalmos* 93.5, 126.2, *Sermones* 41.297.1 (*cecidit de coelo*); Gregory the Great *Moralia in Iob* 2.14.1, 2.31.1, 2.32.1, 2.47.1 (*cecidit de coelo*); Jerome *Commentarii in Naum* 2.36 (*cedidit de coelo*).

l. 6 The phrase *Limpida … carmina* ("lucid lyrics") appears to be a fresh Aldhelmian expression. The adjective *limpida* typically referred to clear water or a clear voice, not to text, although sometimes writers used it to describe abstractions such as faith and wisdom. Writers over the next century adopted variations of this trope. See e.g. Bede *Historia ecclesiastica* 5.8 (*limpida discipulis dogmata*); Hrabanus Maurus *Martyrologium* 1.13 (*versus cum luce limpida*).

The noun *praesuL* ("Lord") originated in Late Antiquity and was used sparingly, except by Cassiodorus. See e.g. Fortunatus *Vita Sancti Martini* 1.25, 1.202; Prudentius *Cathemerinon* 6.69; Ambrose *De obitu Theodosii oratio* 16, *De fide ad Gratianum Augustum* 3.17.137; Isidore *Etymologiae* 10.205. Cf. *Carmen de virginitate* 1057.

l. 7 Aldhelm's use of the self-descriptive adjective *rudis* ("Misguided") has reinforced the view that the *Aenigmata* is one of Aldhelm's early poetic efforts and, in part, an exercise to develop his prosodical skills. See e.g. Lapidge and Rosier at 61; Ehwald at 76. That view tends to be overstated; there was a long-standing tradition of real and feigned humility in prologues.

l. 8 The term *fatu* ("spoken") hints at legends about Aldhelm's impressive voice. See Frank, "The Search for the Anglo-Saxon Oral Poet," in Scragg at 155–6.

The adjective *clandistina* ("Clandestine") is an unusual variant of the classical *clandestina,* one which might reflect Irish influence. See *Hisperica Famina A Text* at 228, 353 (*clandistinas*); see also Stokes and Strahan at 223 (an Irish gloss using *clandistina*). I am grateful for advice on this point from Anthony Harvey, Director of the Irish Academy *Dictionary of Medieval Latin from Celtic Sources.* Dr. Harvey thoughtfully provided me with an advance copy of his article, "Some Orthographic Features of the Schaffhausen Manuscript," in Bracken and Graf. There he analyses Irish influence on vowels in Anglo-Latin, including substitutions of a short "i" for a short "e" (and *vice versa*) of the type we see here. Other possible examples of Irish-influenced variants are *Aenigmata* 32.6, which has *segiti* instead of the classical *segeti,* and *Aenigmata* 71.4, which has *vegitat* for the classical *vegetat,* although in both cases the Stork text retained the classical version.

l. 9 Particularly given the shared location in their lines, the phrase *dona rependis* ("bestow Your gifts") may echo Prudentius *Apotheosis* 632 (*dona rependam*).

ll. 10–14 These lines are a loose riff on Persius's Prologue to his *Satires*:

I have never dallied to refresh my lips
In the fountain where Apollo's packhorse sips
And have never dreamed (unless I didn't know it)
Of descending from Parnassus as a poet.
I relinquish Helicon's unsullied daughters
And the pleasures of Pirene's depleting waters
To those honored gentlemen whose faces seem
Half-obscured by wreaths of academe.
Since I am among the brashest acolytes,
I use poetry to crash their solemn rites.
But *who* thought these poets should be taught to squawk?
Who determined that these ravens ought to talk?
Probably that maestro – a true prodigy
Called "Will Hunger" spurred these birds to mimicry,
Which suggests that if you found some artifice
That could teach them all the joys of avarice,
Then our flocks of cawing poets might infuse
Their shrill music with the sweetness of a Muse.   (A.M. Juster, trans.)

For a thoughtful analysis of Aldhelm's reinvention of classical tropes used in Persius's prologue, see Thornbury, "Aldhelm's Rejection of the Muses and the Mechanics of Poetic Inspiration in Early Anglo-Saxon England," *Anglo-Saxon England* 36 (2007) at 71–92. This section of the preface tracks lines from the preface of Aldhelm's *Carmen de virginitate*:

I do not seek verses and poetic measures from the rustic Muses, nor do I seek metrical songs from the Castalian nymphs who, they say, guard the lofty summit of Helicon; nor do I ask that Phoebus, whom his mother Latona bore on Delos, grant me a tongue, expressive in utterance. (Lapidge and Rosier at 103)

Lapidge and Rosier at 248 note that these lines may also echo Paulinus of Nola *Carmina* 15.30 (*Non ego castiladas vatum phantasmata Musas*) and that Aldhelm quotes another line from that poem elsewhere in his *Epistola ad Adcircium*. See also Thornbury, "Aldhelm's Rejection of the Muses and the Mechanics of Poetic Inspiration in Early Anglo-Saxon England," *Anglo-Saxon England* 36 (2007) at 74–5; Wright, "Imitation of the Poems of Paulinus of Nola in Early Anglo-Saxon Verse," *Peritia* 4 (1985) at 134–51; Wright, "Imitation of the Poems of Paulinus of Nola in Early Anglo-Saxon Verse: A Postscript," *Peritia* 5 (1986) at 392–6. Cf. Paulinus Petricordia *De vita Martini* 4.251–2 (*fontem Castilias ... lymfas*).

l. 10 Aldhelm seems to be on the cusp of the transition from the classical *nymphas* to the medieval *nimphas* ("nymphs").

l. 11 The bees probably refer to a legend of Saint Ambrose. See Thornbury, "Aldhelm's Rejection of the Muses and the Mechanics of Poetic Inspiration," *Anglo-Saxon England* 36 (2007) at 80; n.20 *infra*. Cf. Lapidge and Rosier at 117; Schaff at 97.

The phrase *nectar in ore* ("nectar on my lips") may echo Horace *Carmina* 3.3.12 (*purpureo bibet ore nectar*), possibly through Paulinus Petricordia *De vita Martini* 4.355 (*oris nectareum*). A similar phrase also appears in the opening lines of Theodore of Tarsus *Laterculus Malalianus* (*labiorum promat nectareis*). See Stevenson at 120. Stevenson at 163–4 notes that the rare *nectareis* also appears in the preface to Sedulius's prose *Opus Paschale*, although it is not clear whether Theodore or Aldhelm had access to that text. Cf. n.4.4 *infra*.

l. 12 The specific phrase *Cynthi ... cacumina* ("Apollo's peak" – *Cynthi* refers here to Mount Cynthus on Delos, home of Apollo) has no clear antecedent, but Claudian or Ovid seem to be the likeliest inspirations. See Claudian *Gigantomachia* 121 (*Cynthi de vertice Nymphae*), *De consulatio Stilichonis* 3.259 (*de vertice Cynthi*); Ovid *Metamorphoses* 6.204 (*summoque in vertice Cynthi*); cf. Statius *Achilleis* (*e vertice Cynthi*). Lapidge and Rosier at 22 cite this line as a rare break from what they see as Aldhelm's monotonous prosody because he ends the line with two monosyllables.

l. 13 The phrase *somnia vidi* ("seen visions") was rare in the classical era. But see Ovid *Metamorphoses* 9.475 (*cur haec ego somnia vidi*). Aldhelm's most likely inspiration may have been *Vulgata Genesis* 41:15 (*vidi somnia*). See also Augustine *De civitate Dei* 18.18.6 (*somnia videbantur*), *Enarrationes in Psalmos* (*somnia sed visum*), *Sermones* 11.13.4 (*somnia ille vidisset*); cf. Jerome *Esdrae II* 14.8 (*somnia quae vidisti*).

l. 15 The phrase *munera menti* ("blessings to my ... mind") was fairly common. See e.g. Ovid *Epistulae ex Ponto* 4.15.37 (*tua munera mente*).

l. 16 The phrase *Tangit si mentem* ("And if He sways a mind") may echo Virgil *Aeneid* 1.462 (*mentem mortalia tangunt*).

l. 17 The *metrica carmina* ("verses") are probably *Exodus* 15:1–18.

l. 18 By using the phrase *vexilla tropei* ("trophies" – literally "flags of victory"), Aldhelm was echoing the Fortunatus hymn *Vexilla Regis Prodeunt*. See Milfull, "Hymns to the Cross: *Vexilla Regis Prodeunt*," in Karkov, Keefer and Jolly at 55; Hunt, "Manuscript Evidence for Knowledge of the Poems of Venantius Fortunatus in Late Anglo-Saxon England," *Anglo-Saxon England* 8 (1979) at 279–95. The noun *vexilla* was rare in classical literature. But see Juvenal 2.101 (*cum iam tolli vexilla iuberet*); Statius *Thebaid* 8.238 (*vexilla triumphi*). By Aldhelm's time the phrase *vexillum crucis* was a common description of a fragment of the Cross. See e.g. Cassiodorus *Variae* 1.5.3; 9.46.1, Jerome *Commentarii in Isaiam* 4.11.33, 13.49.44, *Epistulae* 3.86.1, 1.14.2; Dracontius *De laudibus Dei* 2.496 (*vexilla crucis*); cf. *Carmen de virginitate* at 1104 (*vexilla tropei*).

The adjective *prisci* ("ancient") raises an important point of prosody discussed in detail by Norberg at 2–3 and Orchard (1994) at 75–8. Aldhelm's prosody is exceptionally regular in most respects, but he extended the practice of making vowels under certain circumstances either long or short (a practice known as *communes*) to unconventional consonants and consonant combinations such as *sp*, *sc*, and *st*. See Orchard (1994) at 75–8. This use of *prisci* is the first clear example in the *Aenigmata* of Aldhelmian *communes*.

l. 19 Lapidge and Rosier at 22–3 cite this line as another break from metrical monotony in that it ends with a monosyllable.

l. 20 This use of *cephal* ("its head") appears to be nearly unique and was derived directly or indirectly from the Greek. Aldhelm may have taken the word from the version of *Lorica* in *Hisperica Famina A Text* at 33 (*cephalem*). Cf. Aldhelm *Laudibus de virginitate* 1017; *Miracula Nynie Episcopi* 144 (*cephal*). For more detailed information on *cephal*, see Herren (1987) at 118.

l. 21 For *metrorum cantica* ("hymns in verse"), see *Psalms* 103:3. Cf. *Carmen de virginitate* 24.

l. 22 The term *generamine* ("born") was rare. But see *Appendix Virgiliana Culex* 334 (*hic et Tantaleae Atrides generamen prolis*). Most of Aldhelm's contemporaries wrongly believed that *Culex* was an authentic piece of Virgilian juvenilia. Aldhelm may have had other sources of information on *Culex*, but one was probably Focas's *Vita Vergilii*; Aldhelm cites Focas's grammatical work in *De metris*. Lapidge and Rosier at 193.

l. 23 Aldhelm is using *Lucifer* ("morning star") in its classical sense instead of its later medieval sense of "Satan." See n.81 *infra*. Riddle 81 shows that Aldhelm knew its darker use. See Lapidge and Herren at 67.

l. 24 For *formatis* ("new-made"), cf. Augustine *Confessiones* 13.37.24.1 (*in luminaribus caeli et in affectibus formatis*).

ll. 26–9 These lines are a Christian reinvention of the Roman literary convention (often tongue-in-cheek even in classical times) of apologizing, generally to the emperor, for writing something other than an epic and then promising to deliver something more appropriate in the future. See generally Thornbury, "Aldhelm's Rejection of the Muses and the Mechanics of Poetic Inspiration in Early Anglo-Saxon England," *Anglo-Saxon England* 36 (2007) at 76–9; cf. Ehwald at 75–6.

l. 28 The phrase *molimina mentis* ("Efforts at reason") echoes Juvencus

Evangelia 1.521, 2.308 (*molimina mentis*). Cf. Gregory the Great *Homilae in Ezechielem* 1.2.9 (*molimina in humanis mentibus*).

l. 30 Aldhelm liked adjectives created by combining a noun with the suffixes *-fer* and *–ger*, both of which derive from verbs meaning "to bear" in the sense of carrying. See n.12.2 *infra*. Here the literal sense of *belligero* ("warlike") is "war-bearing." It is possible that Hiberno-Latin, particularly the *Hisperica Famina*, helped to infuse Aldhelm with this affectation. See *Hisperica Famina A Text* at 8 (*florigera*); 52 (*florigerum*); 61 (*propriferum*); 64 (*flamigero*); 65 (*auriferas*); 83 (*florigera*); 84 (*proprifera*); 127 (*clarifero*); 238 (*armigera*); 243 (? *florigera*); 279 (*escifero*); 283 (*esciferas*); 291 (*dulciferos*); 300 (*carniferas*); 347 (*molliferos*); 361 (*umbriferos*); 387 (*Astrifero*); 425 (*mortiferum*); 447 (*Umbrifera*); 533 (*lignifero*); 536 (*florigeros*); 566 (*florigeros*); 576 (*setigerum*); 601 (*armifera*); 605 (*carnifera*); 609 (*mortifera*).

Pitman at 68 notes "the limping metre of this line – an infrequent occurrence with Aldhelm."

ll. 32–4 The references here are *Psalms* 77:16, 106:9; *Exodus* 14:37–15:21. For a thoughtful overview of Anglo-Saxon thinking about *Exodus*, see Howe at 72–107.

l. 33 Previous translators and my advisers have split on *cuneus* ("throngs" in line 32). I concur with Lapidge and Rosier at 71 that in context it has to be translated as a reference to the Israelites, even though philologically it seems it should be "the army" and thus a reference to the Egyptians.

Riddle 1: l. 1 The phrase *Altrix cunctorum* ("the nurse for all") may echo Ambrose *Hexaemeron* 3.15.62 (*altrix omnium*).

The primary meaning of *gestat* would be "to carry in a womb," but that sense does not fit with the tropes of this riddle because the earth is already the metaphorical nurse. But see Pitman at 5.

l. 2 The verb *nuncupor* ("I'm called" – in line 1 of the translation) in the first person was rare. The *Oxford Latin Dictionary* speculates that the word combines *nomen* ("name") and *ceps* ("one who takes or catches").

l. 3 For an unlikely possible source for *lacerant ... dente* ("bite" in line 2 – literally "cut with teeth"), see Augustine *Contra duas epistolas Pelagianorum* 1.3 (*lacerant dente*). Cf. *Carmen de virginitate* 1956 (*Ut lacerare solent latrantes fauce molosi*).

l. 4 Augustine often used the gerund *tabescens* ("it wanes"). See e.g. *Confessiones* 8.1.2, *Enarrationes in Psalmos* 65.14, 118.28.2, *Sermones* 20.219.1.

Riddle 2: For Aldhelm the image of a raging *ventus* ("wind"), an invisible but mighty force, was a reminder of God's unseen might. Images of breath were also a common trope for the soul. *Bern Riddle* 41 (*De vento*) has the same answer.

l. 1 This line may echo Symphosius *Aenigmata* 58.1 (*findere me nulli possunt praecidere multi*). For a discussion of Aldhelm's relation to Symphosius, see Orchard (1994) at 155–61; Lapidge and Rosier at 243–4; Scott, "Rhetorical and Symbolic Ambiguity: The Riddles of Symphosius and Aldhelm," in King and Stevens at 117–44; Ohl, "Symphosius and the Latin Riddle," *Classical Weekly* 25, no. 25 (1932) at 209–12. Aldhelm admired the wit and ingenuity of Symphosius's riddles, but elsewhere in *Epistula ad Acircium* referred to them as *ludibundus apicibus* ("carefree frivolities"). See Ehwald at 75.

l. 2 One could translate *vocis* ("clatter") here in its primary sense of "voices," but I tend to think that Aldhelm intended the secondary sense of noise; it is hard to see how wind can scatter voices. Lapidge and Rosier at 71 translate *vocis* as "voice," but Orchard (forthcoming) translates it similarly as "sound." Cf. OLD 5c.

l. 3 The adjective *horrisonis* ("mournful") combines *horror* ("shudder") and *sonus* ("sound"). Cf. n.Praef.30 *supra*. The term was rare in the classical era, but more common thereafter. It is possible that Aldhelm found the word in Lucan's description of wind in Lucan *Bellum civile* 2.454–5 (*Auster/flatibus horrisonis*). Cf. Virgil *Aeneid* 6.573, 9.55 (*horrisono*).The verb *confringere* ("to hammer") was also rare in classical times, but became popular among Christian writers of Late Antiquity.

l. 4 Aldhelm liked *nam* ("Yes"), which he often used as transitional filler instead of as a causal word, such as "for" or "because." Cf. n.22.5 *infra*.

Riddle 3: Symphosius *Aenigmata* 8 has the same answer.

l. 1 The phrase *caelum terramque* ("the Earth and sky") was formulaic.

l. 4 The literal meaning of the phrase *madidis … guttis* ("tears") is closer to "wet drops." Cf. Cassiodorus *Variae* 9.30.18 (*lacrymarum guttis*).

Riddle 4: l. 1 The phrase *res nulla manet* ("nothing stands") may echo Lucan *Bellum civile* 8.504 (*nulla manet rerum*).

l. 2 The alliterative and internally rhyming phrase *frontem faciemque* ("form and face") appears to be original with Aldhelm. It may have roots in *Vulgata Ezekiel* 3:8 (*Ecce dedi faciem tuam valentiorem faciebus eorum, et frontem tuam duriorem frontibus eorum*).

I have received conflicting advice about *lux* ("eyes"), but followed Lapidge and Rosier at 71. For *lux* as "eyes" see OLD 8. This sense of the term derived from the belief, popular but not universally held since Empedocles in the fifth century BC, that rays emitted by the eyes made vision possible.

l. 3 For the scansion of *nesciat* (collapsed into "Don't" – literally "Is it not known"), see n.Praef.18.

l. 4 The closing words of Lucan, *Bellum civile*, 9.6 are also *lunaeque meatus* ("lunar phases"). For more on Aldhelm's debt to Lucan, see Anlezark, "Poisoned

Places: The Avernian Tradition in Old English Poetry," *Anglo-Saxon England* 36 (2007) at 117–19. Manitius at 17 sees a debatable echo of Virgil *Georgica* 2.478 (*solis varios lunaeque labores*).

The phrase *solisque iubar* ("and brilliant sun") may echo the first paragraph of Theodore of Tarsus *Laterculus Malalianus* (*solis iubar*). See Stevenson at 120, 164. Cf. n.Praef.11 *supra*.

Orchard (forthcoming) would substitute *cumulatus* for *redundans* ("crest"). The meaning would not change; this issue may be a case of a gloss being confused with the word in the text.

Riddle 5: l. 1 Thaumas (from the Greek *thaumatos*: "wonder") was a sea god who married Electra, then fathered Iris, the goddess of rainbows; *iris* is a word for "rainbow" in Latin. The most likely source of this myth is Ovid *Metamorphoses*. See 4.480 (*roratis lustravit aquis Thaumantias Iris*); cf. Virgil *Aeneid* 9.2; Claudian *De raptu Proserpinae* 3.1–2; Cicero *Philosophia de natura deorum* 3.51 (*Thaumante dicitur iris esse nata … arcus enim ipse e nubibus efficitur quodam modo coloratis*). Lapidge and Rosier at 248 place too much weight on the phrase *Taumantis proles* ("child of Thaumas") in suggesting there is a "striking resemblance" to the anonymous poem "Tristicha de arcu caeli" from *Anthologia Latina* 543.1.

It is surprising that this riddle never advances from classical to Christian imagery, such as the rainbow that announced the end of Noah's flood, but there is no explicit Christian content in the riddles until *Aenigmata* 7.4. Herren is particularly surprised by this riddle's absence of a reference to *Genesis* 9:12; he also sees some influence of "Tristicha de arcu caeli." See Herren, "The Transmission and Reception of Graeco-Roman Mythology in Anglo-Saxon England, 670–800," *Anglo-Saxon England* 27 (1998) at 94.

The noun *famine* ("speech") was a rare and fluid word embraced by some Christian writers of Late Antiquity. In the ninth century it was still sufficiently obscure that Remigius glossed the word as "*fabulis, carmina, historia*." See Chance at 297. Its use here may be another hint of the influence of the *Hisperica Famina* on Aldhelm.

l. 2 The verb *retexam* ("I will reteach" – literally "I will reweave" with all the rich associations of weaving in classical literature) was rare in the Augustan era. But see Cicero *Epistulae ad familiares* 11.28.5 (*ac me ipse retexam*). It became more popular in Late Antiquity. See e.g. Paulinus Petricordia *De vita Martini* 2.14 (*retexam*), 2.617 (*retexam*), 3.421 (*retexam*), 5.204 (*retexans*); Paulinus of Nola *Carmina* 12.305 (*retexam*); Sidonius Apollonaris *Panegyricus* 353 (*retexam*); Prudentius *Apotheosis* 1.704 (*retexam*), *Peristephanon* 2.258 (*retexam*).

l. 3 The phrase *nubis aquosae* ("cloud's water") was common in classical literature. See e.g. Virgil *Aeneid* 8.429; Silius *Punica* 2.217; Ovid *Metamorphoses* 4.622.

l. 4 The exact internal rhyme of *solos/polos* is striking and rare in Latin poetry prior to Aldhelm's time.

The verb *lustro* ("I seek") is ambiguous here; it could also mean "illuminate." See OLD 4, 5, 6.

The verb *scando* ("I ... rise") is a significant one for Aldhelm. As in Riddle 12, it reflects a world in which life is a rehearsal for ascending (our English verb "ascend" is derived from *scando*) to Heaven at the Resurrection.

Riddle 6: In the late seventh century the Church was fiercely fighting a centuries-old debate about the proper dating of Easter. See generally Cullen; McCluskey at 77–92. Aldhelm wrote a strong letter to King Geraint defending the view that Rome considered orthodox. Lapidge and Herren at 155–60. In order to participate in this debate, Aldhelm mastered the complexities of the lunar calendar, an area of expertise among the Irish, who held an unorthodox position on the issue. See Cullen at 46–7.

This riddle may embrace Augustine's view that the waxing and waning of the moon is a symbol of Christ's perfection. See Cullen at 134. For the monks of this time period, close attention to the lunar cycle was more than just a lyrical or symbolic exercise, as Bede made clear in his account of the miracles of John of Beverly, a contemporary of Aldhelm's. See Stevenson at 502 quoting Colgrave and Mynors at 460 ("Then he asked when the girl had been bled and, on hearing that it was on the fourth day of the moon, he exclaimed, 'You have acted foolishly and ignorantly to bleed her on the fourth day of the moon; I remember how archbishop Theodore of blessed memory used to say that it was very dangerous to bleed a patient when the moon is waxing and the ocean tide flowing.'"). This view of the moon's powers over the human body was not based on assumptions about magic, which Aldhelm abhorred, but on the Greek medical tradition that assumed direct effects of the environment on a patient. See Stevenson at 51–2.

l. 1 For more information on the sea as a symbol during this period, see Sobiecki; Howe at 83–4; cf. Lapidge and Rosier at 165. The noun *pelagi* ("the surf" – literally "the sea") derives from a Greek term for the sea.

ll. 2–3 The repeating monthly cycle of this line probably cued the reader to the femininity of the answer and foreshadowed the image of feminine beauty in line 3. The phrase *gloria formae* ("beauty ... form") may be taken from *Appendix Virgiliana Culex* 408 (*gloria formae*). See n.Praef.22 *supra*, n.96.9 *infra*.

l. 3 For *lucifluae* ("brilliant"), cf. n.Praef.2 *supra*.

Riddle 7: l. 1 The phrase *cecinisse poetam* ("A ... poet wrote") echoes Virgil *Eclogae* 10.70 (*cecinisse poetam*). Cf. Thornbury at 32–3.

l. 2 The quotation is from Virgil *Aeneid* 12.677. See generally Patterson; see also Murgia, "Aldhelm and Donatus' *Commentary on Vergil*," *Philologus* 131, no. 2 (1987) at 289–99.

Lapidge and Rosier at 248–9 argue that Aldhelm is equating *fatum* ("fate") and *fortuna* ("fortune") in a manner so contrary to the philosophy of the era that they feel this riddle should be retitled *Fortuna*. I disagree, and thus have respected the manuscript tradition, and would suggest that in late seventh-century Britain this metaphysical distinction was less clear to Aldhelm than to earlier authors, such as Boethius. As evidence for this point, *Aenigmata* 44.3–4 seems to use *fata* and *fortunam* interchangeably.

Aldhelm probably knew the Anglo-Saxon concept of *wyrd* ("fate" or "higher law") as well as *fata*. In Aldhelm's time the concept of *wyrd* was transitioning from a pre-Christian concept founded on inexorable outcomes to a more complex one that incorporated the delicate balance between God's plan and man's free will. See Frakes at 82–4; Kasik, "The Use of the Term *Wyrd* in *Beowulf* and the Conversion of the Anglo-Saxons," *Neophilogus* 63, no. 1 (1979) at 128–35; Major, "A Christian *Wyrd*: Syncretism in *Beowulf*," *English Language Notes* 32, no. 3 (1995) at 1–11. For a thoughtful overview of Aldhelm's integration of his Anglo-Saxon heritage into his Christian theology, see generally Dempsey, "Aldhelm of Malmesbury and High Ecclesiasticism in a Barbarian Kingdom," *Traditio* 63 (2008) at 41–88.

l. 3 The word *dominam* ("mistress") suggests here a slaveowner, not a participant in amorous adventures.

l. 4 The sentiment in this line summarizes swaths of Augustine's *De civitate Dei*, although other writers expressed similar sentiments. Aldhelm cited many works of Augustine in his *De metris*. See Lapidge and Rosier at 194.

Riddle 8: In his *Epistola ad Acircium* Aldhelm cites *Job* 38:31 ("Shalt thou be able to join together the shining stars of the Pleiades, or canst thou stop the turning about of Arcturus?") and then adds that the Pleiades "fittingly prefigure the sevenfold distribution of the divine gifts of the universal church by the brightness of just so many stars." Lapidge and Herren at 42–3. Cf. *Altus Prosator* V.1–6; *Job* 9:9. There is a similar and lovely description of the Pleiades in Aldhelm's *Carmen rhythmicum*. Lapidge and Rosier at 178.

ll. 1–2 Nearly a third of Aldhelm's riddles contain a reference to literal or figurative birth or parentage. See Lapidge and Rosier at 64–5. Atlas was a Titan who married the sea nymph Pleione and fathered seven daughters known as the Pleiades. Cf. Lapidge and Rosier at 102, 107, 126, 136, 177. All versions of their story end with Zeus making them seven immortal stars. The one "seen faintly" is Pleione, the only one of the seven stars that is difficult to see with the naked eye.

l. 4 For the striking phrase *luce latemus* ("lurk when it is bright"), see Dracontius *De laudibus Dei* 2.7 (*sub luce latent*); Prudentius *Peristephanon* 11.156 (*luce latente*).

l. 5 In Britain the Pleiades appear in May. Their former name was the *vergiliae*, which Isidore argued derived from *ver* ("spring"), hence the *verno* (literally "springtime" when combined with *tempore*) in this line. See Lapidge and Rosier at 249. Aldhelm discussed the Pleiades in more detail in his *Epistola ad Acircium*. Lapidge and Herren at 42–3; see also Howe, "Aldhelm's *Enigmata* and Isidorian Etymology," *Anglo-Saxon England* 14 (1985) at 51–2. This Roman term for the Pleiades was found in Old Latin bibles, but not the Vulgate.

For *Nomina ... prisca* ("our former name"), cf. Macrobius *Saturnalia* 1.12.37 (*prisca nomina*); Priscian *Periegesis* 837 (*nomine prisco*). For metrical issues, see n.Praef.18.

Riddle 9: l. 1 The phrase *rigidi discrimine ferri* ("by iron's long, hard stress" – capturing both senses of *rigidi* with two adjectives) may echo Claudian *De raptu Proserpinae* 3.94 (*rigidi...ferri*). Cf. *Carmen de virginitate* 1748 (*discrimina ferri*). One has to be wary of this attribution, however, given this statement by Aldhelm: "What, pray, I beseech you eagerly, is the benefit to the sanctity of the orthodox faith to expend energy by reading and studying the foul pollution of base Proserpina, which I shrink from mentioning in plain speech ... ?" Lapidge and Herren at 154. My intuition, however, is that Aldhelm admired Claudian's poetry, particularly Book III of *De raptu Proserpinae*, but was horrified that an educated man writing in the Christian era did not write from a Christian perspective. Cf. Orosius *Historiae adversum paganos* 7.35 (*poeta quidem eximius sed paganos pervicasissimus*) (describing the unnamed Claudian as he quotes him). In other words, Claudian was probably a guilty pleasure. Cf. Orchard (1994) at 152–3.

I have rejected the primary definition of *discrimina*, which would be a "boundary," for a term ("stress") that blends its secondary meanings of "threat" and "test." See OLD 3, 5.

ll. 2–3 There are many possible sources for the idea that goat blood is so hot that it softens diamonds. See e.g. Augustine *De civitate Dei* 21.4; Pliny *Naturalis historia* 20.1, 28.9; Isidore *Etymologiae* 12.1.14–15; Eugene of Toledo *Carmina* 62. Cf. Solinus *Mirabilia* 53. See generally Garrett at 9–10, including citations to *Carmen de virginitate*. For Aldhelm's use of the noun *adamas* and the adjective *adamantinus* in *Laudibus de virginitate*, see Garrett at 8–9.

l. 4 I have translated *cruor* as "gore" instead of "blood" to avoid a duplication of words that Aldhelm avoided and to capture the sense of *sanguine* ("blood") in the second line as "blood in the body" and *cruor* as "blood outside the body." See Bynum at 17–18; Fonrobert, "Blood and Law: Uterine Fluids and Rabbinic Maps of Identity," *Henoch* 30, no. 2 (2008) at 243.

Riddle 10: Riddle 41 of *The Exeter Book* loosely translates this riddle. See Lapidge and Rosier 67. The title/solution *molosus* (the medieval version of the classical *molossus*) refers to an ancient breed of dog similar to a mastiff. The term was also the name for a metrical foot containing three long syllables, which may have amused Aldhelm even though he does not appear to have punned in this riddle. Cf. Quintilian *Institutiones* 9.5; Isidore *Etymologiae* 17.6. Some commentators believe that Aldhelm misunderstood *molosus* and viewed *molosus* as interchangeable with *canis* ("dog") because he used it, not *canus*, in *De laudibus virginitatis* 67.30 in "the homely proverb of Scripture (*Proverbs* 26:11; *2 Peter* 2:22) 'the dog returns to his vomit.'" Lindsay at 100; cf. Bitterli at 108–9.

l. 1 The phrase *veneranda potestas* ("A holy force") probably echoes Lucan *Bellum civile* 5.397 (*veneranda potestas*) or Juvencus *Evangelia* 4.684 (*veneranda potestas*).

l. 3 The phrase *bellorum praelia* ("for bouts of war") introduces a mock-heroic tone by echoing Virgil *Aeneid* 11.541 (*proelia belli*).

For *Rictibus arma gerens* (literally "bearing arms with the jaws") I used the more compact and colloquial "armed to the teeth."

l. 4 The phrase *fugiens mox verbera* ("I'm quickly fleeing … blows") may echo Gregory the Great *Moralia in Iob* 7.22.2 (*verbera fugiens*).

Riddle 11: Lapidge and Rosier at 249 argue, almost certainly correctly, that the previously unknown term *poalum* ("bellows") derives from a misunderstood glossary entry. See also Lindsay, "Columbanus' *Altus* and the Abstrusa Glossary," *Classical Quarterly* 17, no.3/4 (1923) at 198. The answer to Symphosius *Aenigmata* 73 is "bellows," though Symphosius uses the customary term *uter* for "bellows." It is remotely possible that *poalum* is a corruption of the Old English *blawan* ("to blow").

l. 1 The phrase *alternis flatibus* ("wheezing" literally "with alternate breaths") may echo Dracontius. See *De laudibus Dei* 591 (*flatibus alternis*), *Orestis tragoedia* 518 (*flatibus alternis*); cf. Statius *Thebaid*, 6.873 (*flatibus alternis*). For mockery of this phrase, see Bright at 275.

For the phrase *fratre gemello* ("my twin brother"), cf. Ovid *Heroides* 8.77 (*fratresque gemelli*).

l. 2 In order to contrast the superiority of God's craft to mankind's, Aldhelm contrasts a bellows with lungs, much in the same way that Riddle 72 argues that the best of man's craft cannot provide the spirit that only comes from God. Cf. Gregory the Great *Moralia in Iob* 18.50.2, 23.15.2; Gregory of Tours *Historiae* 1.1.1 (*spiraculum vitae*); Jerome *Genesis* 2.7, 7.22 (*spiraculum vitae*); Apuleius *De Platone et eius dogmate* (*per pulmonum spiracula vivacitatem*).

l. 4 The phrase *capit alter honorem* ("another stole the praise") seems to echo (and slightly intensify) a line written in Virgil's voice in an anonymous poem of the *Anthologia Latina* 251.1 (*tulit alter honorem*). Since the *Anthologia Latina* is the probable source of Symphosius for Aldhelm, he was probably familiar with other parts of the anthology. Given Aldhelm's ample appropriation of Virgilian lines, this phrase may be an example of Aldhelmian tongue-in-cheek humility.

Riddle 12: The Romans prized silk, as did their early medieval successors, but did not know how it was made. According to legend, in 552 two Nestorian monks explained the process to the emperor, Justinian, and then at his direction smuggled worms from China to Constantinople. By Aldhelm's time the process for making silk was familiar in Europe. See Evans at 235. In his *Hexaemeron* Basil refers to silkworms as symbols of the resurrection. See Schaff at 100. Aldhelm may have embraced that symbolism, but also saw the products of their efforts as temptations to stray from a godly life. In his *Carmen de virginitate* Aldhelm tells the story of a father who attempts to lead his son away from fervent Christianity with "a silken covering in the form of a purple robe, which a dying silkworm had produced from its fruitful womb." Lapidge and Rosier at 128.

Bern Riddle 43 (*De vermibus bombycibus sericas vestes formantibus*) has the same answer.

l. 1 For *texendi telas* ("for weaving threads"), cf. n.12.4 *infra*.

This line echoes Symphosius *Aenigmata* Praefatio 3 (*annua saturni dum tempora festa redirent*). Aldhelm echoes it again in *Carmen de virginitate* 2221 (*Annua dum redeunt celebrandis tempora festis*). See Orchard (1994) at 159.

l. 2 Twenty of the riddles refer to *viscera* ("flesh"). Lapidge and Rosier at 65. The term can mean either "internal organs" or "flesh" depending on the context. Since the *viscera* here are *lurida* ("sallow"), I chose "flesh" here. Cf. Thornbury at 55.

The text analysed by Stork, Royal 12.C.xxiii (hereinafter "the Stork text"), has *replentur* for *redundant* ("fill").

Aldhelm uses *setigeris filis* ("hairy threads") instead of the classical *saetegeris filis*. It is the earliest example I identified of the dropped "a" with two exceptions, and *setigeris* did not become standard until the Renaissance. But see *Miracula Nynie Episcopi* at 223 (*Setiger*). The adjective *setigerum* also appears at the *Hisperica Famina A Text* 576, another hint that the text might have influenced Aldhelm. See n.Praef.30 *supra*. Steen at 92 (citing a differently numbered text) notes that "the use of *setiger* ... follows Aldhelm's own recommendation in *De metris* to employ compounds with –*fer* and –*ger*. In fact *setiger* is the first such compound mentioned in the list." For more on this term's vowels, see n.Praef.8 *supra*. I have changed the syntax of the line from the literal "sallow flesh expands with bristly strands."

l. 3 Pitman argues that Aldhelm's biology is incorrect, and that local cater-pillars eat broom (a shrub with flowers, usually yellow, that were common in poor soil), whereas choosier silkworms only eat certain types of mulberry. See Pitman at 69. Lapidge and Rosier at 249 go further and support Cameron's ar-gument that Aldhelm was describing the Oak Eggar (*Lasiocampa quercus quercus*). See Cameron, "Aldhelm as Naturalist: A Reexamination of Some of His *Enigmata*," *Peritia* 4 (1985) at 123–4. In my opinion, it is facile to rely on one error to dismiss the possibility that Aldhelm knew many basics of silkworm biology from other sources. See Erhardt-Siebold, "Aldhelm in Possession of the Secrets of Sericulture," *Anglia-Zeitschrift für Englische Philologie* 60 (1936) at 384–9; Cameron at 102; Thomas, "Callimachus, the *Victoria Berenices*, and Ro-man Poetry" in Volk at 222, n.115. If one views Aldhelm as identifying with the silkworm when he uses *scando* ("I climb"), one should sense gentle self-deprecation of the sallow flesh gaining weight, which I can confirm is typical of bookish middle-aged men.

For the phrase *fati sorte* ("twists of fate"), see Statius *Thebaid* 5.534–5; cf. Martial 4.35.2; Maximus of Turin *Contra Paganos* at 251–2 in Spagnolo and Turner, "Maximus of Turin Against the Pagans," republishing the text from *Journal of Theological Studies* 17, no. 68 (1916) at 321–37. This phrase appears to be an idiom with no clear English equivalent. It appears that the point of the idiom is to introduce an allusion to the three Parcae, otherwise known as the three Fates (Nona, Decima, and Morta), who spun, measured, and cut the thread of life. See n.45.6 *infra*.

The phrase *frondosa cacumina* ("leafy tips") echoes Corippus *In laudem Ius-tini Augustis minoris* 2.322 (*frondosa cacumina*).

l. 4 The Stork text has "*Et*" for "*Ut*."

If one accepts Aldhelm's identification with the silkworm's struggle to rise to achieve its destiny, it is tempting to look at *texendi telas* ("for weaving threads") in line 1 and *fabricans globulos* ("to crafting small balls") in line 4 as metaphors for the poet's calling, a calling which promotes the humble resignation to God's will suggested by *quiescam* ("rest"). The image of poetic creation as weaving was a familiar one throughout classical and medieval times, see Schmitt at 300–1, and Aldhelm may have known the Old English phrase *wordcraeft waef* ("wove wordcraft") that appeared a century or so later in Cynewulf. I have including my "crafting" in this line as a tip of my translator's hat to that marvellous phrase. With *globulos* ("small balls"), Aldhelm is referring to cocoons.

Riddle 13: For more information on the medieval organ, see Bowles, "The Or-gan in the Medieval Liturgical Service," *Revue Belge de Musicologie* 16 (1962) at 13–29; Page, "The Earliest English Keyboard," *Early Music* 7, no. 3 (1979) at

309–14. In the Stork manuscript, a glossator explained this rare term (*De barbito id est organo*). See Stork at Riddle 13.

l. 1 The term *salpictae* ("bugles") is an adaptation of the Greek word *salpinx*, a trumpet like the Roman *tuba* only shorter. See n.68 *infra*.

The verb *clangant* ("clamor") was somewhat rare, although a favourite of Jerome. This line probably echoes Prudentius *Cathemerinon* 5.48 (*Ferratasque acies clangere classicum*), which increases the likelihood that Aldhelm's *aere cavo* ("with hollow brass") echoes the same phrase in *Cathemerinon* 1.386, although it also occurred in classical texts familiar to Aldhelm. Cf. Virgil *Aeneid* 3.240, 3.286; Ovid *Metamorphoses* 4.505, 7.317. Aldhelm used this line in *Carmen de virginitate* 1549 (*salpix classica clangit*) and 2459 (*clangit classica salpix*). The phrase *aere cavo* also appears in the anonymous *Versus sibyllae de iudicio Dei* 23, a translation (sometimes attributed to Aldhelm) of a Greek acrostic. See Orchard (1994) at 195–200.

l. 3 For *viscera* ("guts"), see n.12.2 *supra*.

Aldhelm's use of *eructant* ("are belched" – expressed in the active voice in the text with *cantus* ("songs") as its subject) is a common trope of Late Antiquity, perhaps in this case picked up from Ambrose, who favoured *verbum eructat*.

Riddle 14: l.1 The Stork manuscript has *Pulcher et* instead of *Sum namque* ("Yes, I'm"), a version preferred by Orchard (forthcoming). I was reluctant to adopt a line that requires an inferred verb or an extended litany of phrases, so I retained the Ehwald version despite some qualms about *namque*.

For *excellens specie* ("a fine sight"), cf. Velleius *Historiae Romanae* 2.7.2 (*specie excellens*).

l. 2 The Stork manuscript has *ac* for *et* ("and").

The phrase *ossibus ac nervis* ("bones ... and nerves") may echo Jerome *Iob* 10:11 (*ossibus et nervis*).

For *rubro sanguine* ("red blood"), cf. Horace *Carmina* 3.13.7 (*rubro sanguine*).

l. 4 Christian writers of Late Antiquity often associated the peacock with the mythical phoenix, the subject of long poems in Latin before Aldhelm's time and in Old English after Aldhelm's time. See Herren and Brown at 263. An inspiration for this tale is undoubtedly Aldhelm's close reading of the description of a peacock in Augustine's *De civitate Dei* 21.4; this section also includes material on the salamander and the lodestone that parallels *Aenigmata* 15 and *Aenigmata* 25. See Lapidge and Herren at 66, 108; Neville at 26 n.26.

Riddle 15: l. 1 Aldhelm saw the salamander's resistance to fire as analogous to martyrs surviving burning at the stake. Cf. *Carmen de virginitate* 1115 (*Ceu salamandra focus solet insultare pyrarum*). A source of this image may be Augustine *De civitate Dei* 21.4 (*salamandra in ignibus vivet*). See n.14.4 *supra*.

l. 2 The verb *faxo* in the phrase *faxo ludibria* ("mock" – literally "make frivolities") is a variant of *facio*, used frequently by Plautus and Terence, but Aldhelm probably found the shortened version convenient for metrical purposes after seeing the term in Virgil and Ovid. Cf. Ovid *Metamorphoses* 3.271, 12.594; Virgil *Aeneid* 12.313. Aldhelm probably knew of Terence and Plautus only through secondary sources. See Orchard (1994) at 128–9.

l. 3 For *crepitante* ("crackles"), cf. *crepitent* at 13.2.

Riddle 16: Pitman notes Pliny used that the term *loligo* (an earlier form of Aldhelm's *luligo*; most writers, including Pliny, used *lolligo*) in *Naturalis historia* 9.45 to claim that squid and scallops fly over water. Cameron *supra* at 119 notes literature reporting that squid glide above the sea. Other passages in *Naturalis historia* claim that a flying squid is a sign of an impending storm (18.87) and schools of flying squid sink ships (32.6). A recent scientific article, supported by striking photographs, does document that schools of a Pacific squid, *todarodes pacificus*, do indeed fly for distances of at least 100 feet. See Muramatsu, Yamamoto, Abe, Sekiguchi, Hushi, and Sakurai, "Oceanic Squid Do Fly," *Marine Biology* 160 (February 2013). Nonetheless, it appears Aldhelm was using the term *loligo* in a sense that had evolved over the centuries. See Stork at 45 (*luligo* glossed as *pisce volante* – "flying fish"). Aldhelm's use of the adjective *squamis* ("scaly" – literally "with scales") means that we should lean toward this interpretation of "flying fish," notwithstanding Lapidge's adamant statement to the contrary at 249. Squid do not have scales, and I identified no mention of *loligo* with *squamis* except that Pliny notes that squid are *sine squamis* ("without scales"). *Naturalis historia* 32.14.

Monks in Aldhelm's era ate squid. See Bruce at 82.

l. 2 The phrase *aequora maris* ("sea plains") appears to echo Claudian's reworking of a Virgilian line. The phrase *certatim socii feriunt mare et aequora verrunt* appears at *Aeneid* 3.290 and 5.778. Claudian collapses Virgil's *mare* and *aequora* into one image at *De raptu Propserine* 2.1.295 (*quidquid maris aequora verrunt*). One can imagine the appeal for Aldhelm of Claudian's adaptation because the phrase has the ring of an Anglo-Saxon kenning.

I resisted the temptation to translate the term *grege* ("flocks" – singular in the original) as "schools." By Aldhelm's time this word for a group of animals had taken on a decidedly religious sense akin to our "flock." See e.g. Ambrose *In Psalmum David CXVIII Exposito* 14.2 (*grex Domini*), Augustine *Sermones* 10.4.18 (*grex Domini*), 10.46.34 (*grex Christi*), 10.56.15 (*grex Christi*), 11.10.1 (*grex Domini*), 20.265.6 (*grex Christi*); Jerome *Commentarii in Ezechhielem* 11.34.17 (*grex Domini*), *Commentarii in Ieremiam* 3.13.17, 3.13.18 (*grex Domini*).

l. 3 For *scando* ("I ... rise"), see n.5.4 *supra*. The phrase *aethera pennis* ("on wings through sky") echoes Virgil *Georgica* 1.409 (*aethera pennis*).

Riddle 17: The title *perna* ("ham") puns on the ham-shaped *pinna nobilis*, a common bivalve mollusk of the Mediterranean which grows silky threads with which many ancient cultures wove highly prized cloth. See Cameron *supra* at 120; cf. Laufer, "The Story of the Pinna and the Syrian Lamb," Volume 28 No. 128 *Journal of American Folklore* (1915) at 103-22.

The answer to Symphosius *Aenigmata* 85 is also *perna*, but without the pun.

l. 1 The Stork manuscript has the more common *conchis* instead of the Ehwald *concis*, but I have retained *concis* because at least one text read carefully by Aldhelm used the rarer version of the term. See Isidore *Etymologiae* 20.4.11 (*conca*); cf. Gregory the Great *Homilae in Ezechielem* 1.8.7 (*conco*).

The phrase *caerula ponti* ("in deep blue sea") was rare in classical Latin. But see Lucretius *De rerum natura* 1.1091 (*ponti...caerula*); Virgil *Aeneid* 12.18 (*caeruleo ponto*). It was formulaic for Christian writers. See e.g. Augustine *De civitate Dei* 18.23.3 (*caerula ponti*); Dracontius *De laudibus Dei* 1.675 (*caerula ponti*); Sedulius *Carmen Paschale* 1.120, 2.222, 3.219 (*caerula ponti*).

l. 2 For *setigero* see n.12.2 *supra*.

For *vellera ... fulva* ("tawny fleece"), cf. Ovid *Heroides* 6.16 (*vellera fulva*).

l. 3 The exact nature of a *clamidem pepli* ("for robes" – in line 4 of the translation) is unclear; both *clamidem* and *pepli* were rare words that together probably meant "a ceremonial robe." See Owen-Crocker at 110. Aldhelm may have been punning bilingually here. The Old English noun *clam* had primary meanings of a "prison" and "clay-like substance," but it also meant "a shellfish with claws" – not quite the contemporary "clam" perhaps, but close.

l. 4 I have not been able to identify an earlier use of the striking phrase *fati tributum* ("fate's fee"). The *tributum* was originally a complex tax similar to a broad property tax; its burden fluctuated frequently, which may hint at the genesis of the trope. As typically happens with taxes, over time officials applied *tributum* to an increasing variety of other activities. This line may echo Juvencus *Evangelia* 3.395 (*duplex dissolve tributum*).

Riddle 18: Poor Aldhelm was confused about his *myrmicoleon* ("ant-lion"), but he had distinguished company. This nonexistent being (whose name was spelled many ways) was also called a *formicaleon*.

The mysterious ant-lion sprang to life based on a mistranslation of the Hebrew term *lajisch* in the Septuagint version of the Old Testament, a translation project which commenced in the third century BC. For the Septuagint, see generally Rajak; Rajak, "The Septuagint Translation of the Bible: Between Jews and Christians," a 26 November 2007 lecture at Boston College, at frontrow.bc.edu/

program/rajak. *Lajisch* was a rare term for "lion," but according to legend the project's seventy or seventy-two experts all independently mistranslated *lajisch* into Greek as *myrmicoleon* ("ant-lion") – yet another lesson about the dangers of an overly large committee. Aldhelm's most likely sources were Gregory the Great *Moralia in Iob* 5.20.40 and Isidore *Etymologiae* 12.3.10. Lapidge and Rosier at 247 note that one of the glossators cited *Moralia in Iob*. See also Stork at Riddle 18.

The myrmicoleon myth endured at least into the thirteenth century, and the creature appeared in medieval bestiaries such as Vincent Beauvais's *Speculum Naturale* and Guillaume de Clerc's *Bestaire*. Sometimes the ant-lion was viewed as a super-ant that preyed on lesser ants, and sometimes as the hybrid spawn of a lion and an ant (the mechanics of such unions are, thankfully, unclear). The latter version of the myrmicoleon invariably starved to death because its ant part could not digest meat and its lion part could not digest grain. Today "ant lion" is another name for the larval form of the lacewing fly, an insect that preys on ants.

Translators are duly warned about the enduring consequences of their mistakes.

l. 3 For *tropica ... duplis* as "blended metaphor," see Howe, "Aldhelm's *Enigmata* and Isidorian Etymology," *Anglo-Saxon England* 14 (1985) at 47–8. But see Stork at *Aenigmata* 18 (rendering *tropica* as "mystical" on the basis of a gloss).

I have rendered *praesagia* (literally "prognostication") as a phrase ("a sign that's bleak").

l. 4 I rejected the emendation by Orchard (forthcoming) of *rescindere* for *resistere* ("defend") because a verb of defensive action makes more sense here.

l. 5 Orchard (1994) at 207–8 notes that this line strongly parallels a line from an anonymous collection of epigrams in Paris Bibliothèque Nationale, lat. 8071, fl. 60–1 (P). See 21.4.9 (*Scrutetur sapiens lector quo nomine fungit*).

Riddle 19: This riddle is one of two translated by Richard Wilbur in a 1975 limited-edition broadside. Both translations are also available in Wilbur, *Collected Poems 1943–2004* (New York: Harcourt, 2004), a book which should be enjoyed on a regular basis.

Romans prized salt, and Anglo-Saxons produced enough for it to be a staple of their diet. Although there is some disagreement, the Old English term *wich* seems to have referred to a place where salt was manufactured or traded (a bit akin to the American English term "lick"). This suffix or the more generic suffix derived from the Anglo-Saxon *wic* ("dwelling place") survives in the names of municipalities such as Sandwich, Greenwich, and Eastwick.

The answer of Riddle 3 (*De sale*) of the *Bern Riddles* is also "salt."

l. 1 For *squamoso pisce* ("scaly fish"), cf. Cicero *De natura deorum* 2.114 (*squamoso corpora pisces*).

l. 2 For *discrimine* as "frame," see OLD 1a.

l. 3 Both this line with *per ignes* ("from fire's ... glow") and *Bern Riddle* 3.1 (*me pater ignitus*) share the image of salt emerging through heat.

l. 4 For *cineri* ("ash") see n.52.8.

Riddle 20: In *Laudibus de virginitate*, Aldhelm effuses about bees and states that bees "signify a type of virginity and the likeness of the Church." Lapidge and Herren at 62. See Casiday, "St. Aldhelm's Bees (*De virginitate prosa*, cc. iv–vi): Some Observations on a Literary Tradition," *Anglo-Saxon England* 33 (2004) at 1–22; Randle argues that Aldhelm sees bees as a symbol of virginity and service to authority. Randle, "The Homiletics of the *Vercelli Book* Poems," in Orchard and Zacher 202–9. In *Carmen de virginitate* Aldhelm's metaphor and wordplay connect Saint Ambrose with "the sweet words of nectared honeycombs, from which the hearts of people become abundantly sweetened." Lapidge and Rosier at 117; cf. Lapidge and Herren at 84–5, 161, 169. Randle at 205–9 *supra* connects this riddle with *Homilectic Fragment I*. Another commentator relies on this riddle to argue that the much-debated solution to *Exeter Book* Riddle 17 is *leo* and *beo* (Old English for "lion" and "bee"). See Murphy, "Leo and Beo: *Exeter Book* Riddle 17 as Samson's Lion," *English Studies* 88, no. 4 (August 2007) at 371–87.

Bern Riddle 21 (*De ape*) has the same answer in the singular.

l. 1 Randle *supra* at 208 argues (probably overargues) that *creta* ("spawned") is deliberately ambiguous in that it can be the past tense of either *cresco* ("spawn") or *cerno* ("understand"). The phrase *sine semine creta* ("spawned without seed") alludes to the birth of Christ. Cf. Juvencus *Evangelia* 4.242 (*semine cretas*).

l. 2 The term *florigeris* ("floral" – literally "flower-bearing") appears to have been a rare term of Christian writers of Late Antiquity. See e.g. Sedulius *Carmen Paschale* 2.2 (*florigera*); Cassiodorus *Institutiones* 32.4 (*florigeri*). A likely source is the *Hisperica Famina*. See *A Text* at 52 (*florigerum*), 83 (*florigera*), 243 (*? florigera*) 536 (*florigeros*); see also n.Praef.30 *supra*.

l. 3 The phrase *crocea ... fercula regum* ("Kings' honeyed fare") may echo Prudentius *Apotheosis* 1.609 (*auratis regalia fercula*); cf. Gregory of Tours *Historiae* 3.15.4 (*fercula regalia*).

l. 4 Randle at 208 *supra* argues that *acuta* ("sharp") carries two senses of the term: "pointed" and "intelligent."

Riddle 21: Aldhelm introduces significant end-rhyme in this riddle, then adds more in the following riddle.

l. 3 The Stork manuscript has *suesco* for the Ehwald *sueta* ("is what I know" – literally "familiar"). Emendation is tempting, but I retained the Ehwald text.

l. 3 The verb *polire* ("smoothing") may refer to the practice of clipping coins (filing the edges to retain a small amount of metal) that plagued governments long before and long after Aldhelm. See Stenton and Dolley at 5.

l. 4 The Stork manuscript has *constant* for the Ehwald *constans* ("staying").

l. 5 This line appears to echo Ovid *Metamorphoses* 13.567 (*coepit et haec missum rauco cum murmure*), which describes Hecuba's transformation into a barking dog. Cf. Paulinus Petricordia *De vita Martini* 2.412 (*rauco ... murmure*).While Ovid's poetry undoubtedly posed a challenge to Aldhelm's views on sexual matters, Aldhelm, with his fascination about physical transformations, nonetheless made room in his reading for *Metamorphoses*. Orchard (1994) at 147–50 provides evidence for this conclusion and notes that much of Aldhelm's knowledge of mythology could have come from *Metamorphoses*.

I have tried to mimic the onomatopoeia of the original line by incorporating the clustered sounds of the letter "c" that mimic the clicking of a file on a hard surface.

Riddle 22: Bitterli at 47–53 thoughtfully places this riddle in the context of writings on the nightingale in Pliny, Ambrose, Isidore, Eugene of Toledo, and Old English poetry, and then discusses Aldhelm's influence on Alcuin's nightingale poem. The great classical scholar H.W. Garrod made the mistake of publishing a dreadful translation of this riddle, but his chapter on "The Nightingale in Poetry" is worthwhile reading. See Garrod at 139–60. See also Williams, particularly at 34–74, for the "Christianization" of this classical image.

Whether intentional or not, Aldhelm's AABBB rhyme scheme would have horrified classical poets. End-rhyme was probably a recent Irish import.

l. 4 The phrase *fato ... futuro* (combined as "the future's") has no obvious precedent, and *futuro* feels like metrical filler.

l. 5 In a dense line I sacrificed one word to retain the metre; the word *nam* would have been best rendered at the beginning of the line as "Yes" or "Indeed" instead of the more common "for" or "because." Cf. n.2.4 *supra*.

Riddle 23: For more information on the subject of this riddle, see Shull, "Scales and Weights in Early Anglo-Saxon England," *Archaeological Journal* 147 (1990) at 183–215. Shull argues that scales were used primarily for weighing coin or bullion used as currency. *Id.* at 209. It is possible that one of the patristic writings Theodore introduced to Britain was the Syriac text, Epiphanius *On Weights and Measures*, which was a source for Bede. See P. Kitson, "Lapidary Traditions in Anglo-Saxon England: Part II, Bede's *Explanatio Apocalypsis* and Related Works," *Anglo-Saxon England* 12 (1983) at 73–123; cf. Priscian *De ponderibus et mensuris*. Stevenson at 66, 182–84 notes that the only Greek author cited in Theodore *Laterculus Malalianus* is Epiphanius. For Aldhelm the image of weights in balance almost surely reminded him of monastic life. See n.23.5 *infra*. To see photographs of Anglo-Saxon scales in the Ashmolean Museum, link to anglosaxondiscovery.ashmolean.org/Life/dailylife/scales.html.

l. 1 The phrase *geminas ... sorores* ("twin sisters") probably echoes Ovid *Metamorphoses* 4.773 (*geminas ... sorores*). Cf. Symphosius *Aenigmata* 68.1 (*aequales sorores*).

l. 2–3 Aldhelm indicates in his letter to Lothere that he had studied *legem Romanorum* ("Roman law"). Cook argues that few source materials were available in the Anglo-Saxon world at this time, and that the most likely text for his studies was the *Breviary of Alaric*. Cook, "Aldhelm's Legal Studies," *Journal of English and German Philology* 23, no.1 (1924) at 105–113. Cook's conclusion merits reconsideration.

l. 3 For *personas* ("complainers") in its litigious sense, see OLD 5.

l. 4 The phrase *mortalibus aevum* ("mortals of our age") is classical. See Virgil *Georgica* 3.66 (*mortalibus aevi*); Lucan *Bellum civile* 9.981(*mortalibus aevum*); Silius *Punica* 15.57 (*mortalibus aevi*), 15.63 (*mortalibus aevum*).

l. 5 The image of the scales in balance and the *Iustitiae normam* ("standard" – literally "measure of justice") may allude to "Basil's Rule" for monks as explained in Basil's *Hexaemeron*. See *Carmen de virginitate* in Lapidge and Herren at 119 ("BASIL, at one time the greatest author of learned works, in his divine doctrine founded an excellent law from which proceeds the norm of a balanced life, which releases nothing to bend under perverse weight but balances the elect by the scale of just weight, returning in alternating turns messages to holy men, in such a way that the true harmony of brothers may be adorned ... "). Cf. Ambrose *De officiis ministrorum* 5.31 (*iustitiae ... normam*); Augustine *Enarrationes in Psalmos* 140.18 (*normam iustitiae*); Gregory the Great *Moralia in Iob* 25.8.4 (*normam iustitiae*).

Riddle 24: The term *dracontia* ("dragon-stone") appears to have originated with Aldhelm; it fuses *draconitis* ("precious stone") and *draconteus* ("snake-like"). See Garrett at 16. Several glosses equate it with the Old English *gimrodor* ("very bright gem"). See Meritt at 72. Retsch at 157–8 argues, wrongly in my opinion, that these glosses indicate that Aldhelm used *dracontia* to refer to a generic stone rather than a specific one. His argument relies on a logical fallacy; the glossator's use of *gimrodor* almost certainly simply reflects the lack of an equivalent term for *dracontia* in Old English. Cf. Ehwald at 244.

The ultimate source of this riddle is Pliny *Naturalis historia* 37.158, but likely direct sources include Solinus *Mirabilia* 31.16 and Isidore *Etymologiae* 16.14.7. See Howe, "Aldhelm's *Enigmata* and Isidorian Etymology," *Anglo-Saxon England* 14 (1985). Based on his exposure to Theodore of Tarsus, Aldhelm might have been influenced by a Syriac text, Epiphanius, *On Twelve Stones*.

l. 2 This line may echo Claudian *De III Consolatu Honorii Augusti* 1.4 (*augescat purpura gemmis*). See Orchard (1994) at 154. Cf. Horace *Carmina* 16.7 (*gemmis ... purpura*).

l. 4 The noun *natrix* ("serpent") was rare, but did appear in texts of writers familiar to Aldhelm. See e.g. Isidore *Etymologiae* 12.4.25; Lucan *Bellum civile* 9.720; Pliny *Naturalis historia* 1.27.83.

For the phrase *squamoso corpore* ("scaly ... flesh"), see Juvencus *Evangelia* 2.519 (*squamoso corpore*); Dracontius *De laudibus Dei* 1.459 (*squamoso corpore*).

Riddle 25: This riddle probably derives from Isidore *Etymologiae* 16.4.1–2. Cf. Pliny *Naturalis historia* 37.58; see Howe, "Aldhelm's *Enigmata* and Isidorian Etymology," *Anglo-Saxon England* 14 (1985) at 46. There Isidore tries to persuade us that the *Magnes* in the answer/title is a proper name based on a dubious legend, not an adjective. Lodestones, which are natural magnets mined from the earth, were probably discovered independently in Europe, Asia, and perhaps Central America, by around 400 BC. Another possible source is Eugene of Toledo *Carmina* 60 (*De Magnete*).

l. 1 The term *creator* ("Maker") was rare in the Augustan era, then became popular with Christian writers of Late Antiquity.

l. 2 The phrase *miracula mundi* ("world wonders") was not yet a familiar one in Aldhelm's time. Cf. Isidore *Etymologiae* 7.5.17 (*miracula in mundo*).

l. 4 For a thoughtful discussion of Aldhelm's dropping of a hint about the answer in this line with *ferrea* ("iron's"), see Howe, "Aldhelm's *Enigmata* and Isidorian Etymology," *Anglo-Saxon England* 14 (1985) at 46. The unusual phrase *ferrea fata* ("iron's fate") may be a playful use of Prudentius *Contra Symmachum* 2.1.462 (*ferrea fata*).

l. 5 The phrase *potentia fraudor* ("I'm ... slack" – literally closer to "I am deprived of power") has no clear antecedent.

Scholars disagree as to whether *adamante* in this line means the special hard steel of Cyprus or its diamonds.

Riddle 26: This riddle may be the first example in British literature of a joke at the expense of the French. The joke relies in part on the pun between *gallus* ("rooster") and *Gallus* ("a resident of Gaul"). Some translators have pushed the point by translating the title of this riddle as "cock" instead of "rooster," but I think the raunchiness of that choice pushes the joke past Aldhelm's intentions. Cf. Bitterli at 123–4. Aldhelm may have had the rooster of Prudentius *Cathemerinon* 65–8 in mind while composing this riddle.

It is undoubtedly a coincidence, but there is an intriguing, if not amazing, telestich in this riddle (M-I-R-O-S "amazing").

l. 1 Howe *supra* at 47 notes wordplay linking the opening word, *garrulus* ("chatty") and the title/answer *gallus* ("rooster").

The verb *cecinisse* ("praising") could be construed in several ways, but I think it has some sense of "celebrate," which provides a kind of preemptive defence for the speaker's annoying routine. One anonymous reviewer astutely suggested that *cecinisse* might be onomatopoeic.

ll. 1–2 For *rutilos ... radios* ("rays ... of red"), cf. Cassiodorus, *Variae*, 7.35.1 (*rutliantes radios*).

l. 2 The phrase *lumina Phoebi* ("Apollo's glow" – Phoebus/Apollo was a symbol of the sun) may echo Claudian *De raptu Proserpinae* 2.1.28 (*lumina Phoebi*); see also *Carmen de virginitate* 775 (*lumina Phoebi*); cf. *Appendix Virgiliana Culex* 373 (*lumine Phoebi*).

Augustae ("great") could have either a secular or religious sense.

l. 3 Aldhelm may have learned the adjective *penniger* ("feathered" – literally "feather-bearing") from Fortunatus. See *Vita Sancti Martini* 2.326, 3.289 (*pennigero*), 4.510 (*penniger*); see also Silius *Punica* 8.375 (*pennigeris*); Dracontius *De laudibus Dei* 1.260 (*pennigerum*); cf. 1474 *Carmen de virginitate* (*Pinniger*); Dracontius *Hylas* 2.5 (*pinniger*). See n.Praef.30 *supra*. Gildas is another possible source. See Schlutter, "Gildas, Libellus Querulus de Excidio Britannorum as a Source of Glosses in the Cottoniensis (Cleopatra A III=WW. 338–473) and in the Corpus Glossary," *American Journal of Philology* 29, no.4 (1908) at 437. Cf. Pliny *Naturalis historia* 11.48 (*pinniger*). The phrase *Penniger ... fungor* ("I'm feathered") is literally closer to "I function feather-bearing." Cf. Symphosius *Aenigmata* 1.2.

l. 4 For *faxo* see n.15.2 *supra*. The best literal translation of *belli discrimina faxo* ("I'm threatening a fight") is "I make threats of war." It probably echoes either Lucan *Bellum civile* 8.389 (*discrimina belli*) or Corippus *Iohannid* 1.103 (*discrimina belli*), 1.407 (*discrimine belli*), 1.565 (*belli in discrimine*), 2.334 (*in discrimine belli*). Cf. *Miracula Nynie Episcopi* 60 (*discrimine belli*). For a helpful discussion of Lucan's use of *discrimina*, see Masters at 64.

l. 5 The phrase *serratas cristas* ("jagged crests") appears in Solinus *Mirabilia* 33.26 (*dorsa serratas habent cristas*) in a description of the rooster's distant relative, the crocodile. Cf. Ammianus *Res gestae* 22.15.18 (*serratis ... cristis*); Isidore *Etymologiae* 12.6.16, 12.6.20 (*serratam ... cristam*).

Aldhelm may be adding a mock-heroic tone to the line by echoing Virgil with *in vertice cristas* ("crests upon my crown"). See *Aeneid* 10.701 (*vertice figere cristas*), 12.493 (*vertice cristas*); cf. Claudian *In Rufinum* 2.355 (*cristato vertice*); Dracontius *De laudibus Dei* 10.598 (*cristato ... vertice*).

Riddle 27: Solinus discusses the whetstone at *Mirabilia* 16.10, 28.11, 28.40,

34.14, 35.3. Aldhelm saw it as a symbol of resistance to opponents of the Church. See Lapidge and Herren at 94.

l. 1 For the phrase *viscere terrae* ("bowels of Earth"), see n.33.1 *infra*.

l. 3 For *discrimina* ("threat"), cf. n.26.4 *supra*.

l. 4 *Mulcifer* is a rare variant of *Mulciber*, an alternative name for Vulcan, the blacksmith of the gods. For a discussion of its etymology, see Postgate, "Etymological Studies," *American Journal of Philology* , no. 11 (1882) at 329–39. Milton named one of his fallen angels "Mulciber," and J.K. Rowling gave the name to one of the wizards in her *Harry Potter* series.

The Stork manuscript has *ignis* instead of *igne*.

l. 5 I have taken liberties in translating *torribus atris* (literally "with dark torches") as "as he sears."

Riddle 28: For a discussion of possible wordplay in the title, see Howe, "Aldhelm's *Enigmata* and Isidorian Etymology," *Anglo-Saxon England* 14 (1985) at 42.

ll. 1–2 Counterintuitively, the phrase *cornibus armatus* ("Armed with these horns") is rooted in science, not poetry. See Pliny *Naturalis historia* 8.72 (*cornibus armatos*); Isidore *Etymologiae* 12.1.8 (*cornibus armata*). There may be a Senecan echo; the words *cornigero*, *membra*, and *biformis* appear in *Phaedra* 8.14–18.

ll. 2–3 Aldhelm's wrote almost exclusively in end-stopped lines; these lines are a rare example of his use of enjambment.

l. 3 The term *Gnossian* is a synonym for "Cretan." Knossos is a town in north-central Crete believed to be the site of the Minotaur's labyrinth.

l. 5 For *dicor* ("I am called"), cf. Symphosius *Aenigmata* 38.1 (*a fluvio dicor*).

Herren sees this line as influenced by Isidore *Etymologiae* 11.3.38. See Herren, "The Transmission and Reception of Graeco-Roman Mythology in Anglo-Saxon England," *Anglo-Saxon England* 27 (1998) at 94.

Riddle 29: l. 2 For *mille* as "countless," see the note on the Preface *supra*.

l. 3 The term *acus* ("a … spike") has a primary meaning of a needle, spike, or other sharp object. It can also refer to types of fish, such as pipefish, which are too thin and small to puncture the shell of a boat. I searched for evidence that *acus* could refer to a swordfish or a narwhal, but found no support for that intriguing thought. I suspect that *acus* alludes to the menacing battering ram called a *rostrum* ("beak") that Romans placed on the bows of their warships. In Aldhelm's time the *rostrum* had been abandoned for several centuries and would have been the subject of history and legend. See Charles, "Transporting the Troops in Late Antiquity: *Naves Onerariae*, Claudian and the Gildonic War," *Classical Journal* 100, no. 3 (2005) at 288. Henig and Ross, "A Roman Intaglio

Depicting a Warship from the Foreshore at King's Reach, Wichester Wharf, Southwark," *Britannia* 29 (1998) at 325–7. But see Lapidge and Rosier at 250.

For *gestamina* as "weight," see OLD 2. For its prosody, see n.Praef.18 *supra*.

l. 5 The phrase *primordia vitae* ("yesteryear") echoes Symphosius *Aenigmata* 14.1 (*primordia vitae*). Cf. Juvencus *Evangelia* 2.203 (*primordia vitae*); *Carmen de virginitate* 176 (*primordia vitae*).

l. 6 This line's *tertia pars mundi* ("on one third of the world") may echo Corippus *Iohannis* 1.47 (*tertia pars mundi fumans perit africi flammis*). Orchard (1994) at 215–16 rejects Manitius's argument that this line echoes Sidonius Apollonaris *Carmina* 5.56 (*venio pars tertia mundi*).

Riddle 30: Aldhelm follows Isidore *Etymologiae* 1.4.10 and assumes that h, k, q, x, y, and z are not native letters, and that u/v and i/j are duplicates of one letter. See O'Keeffe at 52; Bitterli at 114–15. Bitterli at 115 notes the possible influence of *Bern Riddle* 25 (*De litteris*).

l. 1 The Stork manuscript has *denae* for *decem* ("seventeen" – literally the "ten" of "ten and seven").

l. 2 The term *annumerandas* ("have no worth") is an adjective of Late Antiquity more literally translated as "not in our number." Cf. Isidore *Sententiae* 3.13.

For *nothas* as "bastards," see Lees and Overing at 192–3; Lambert, "Varia VI," *Ériu* 36 (1985) at 187–8.

l. 3 The term *ferrum* ("iron") alludes primarily to a stylus here, but has other associations. See O'Keeffe at 53.

l. 4 For *penna* ("feathers" – an allusion to a writing quill), see Bitterli at 144 suggesting this image may derive from *Bern Riddle* 25 (*De litteris*).

l. 5 The "three brothers" are the thumb, forefinger, and middle finger that hold a stylus or quill.

Riddle 31: Storks are not native to Britain. A gloss on an eleventh-century manuscript of the *Aenigmata* notes that storks are from Africa. Stork (no pun intended) at 136. Storks are mentioned in a number of places in the Old Testament, such as *Leviticus* 11:19, *Deuteronomy* 14:18; *Jeremiah* 8:7 and *Zecharaiah* 5:9.

l. 1 The phrase *candida forma nitens* ("My form is gleaming white") may echo Sedulius *Carmen Paschale* 3.282 (*candida forma*).

l. 2 The Stork manuscript has *conponor* not *componor* ("I'm made").

l. 3 For *faxo crepacula rostro* ("my beak just shakes" – literally "I make a rattle in my beak"), see n.15.2 *supra*.

l. 4 The Stork manuscript has the standard *colubros* over the variant *colobros* in the Ehwald text.

The adjective *squamigeros* ("scaly" – literally "scale-bearing") was rare, but a favourite of Lucretius. See *De rerum natura* 1.162 (*squamigerum*), 1.373 (*squamigeris*), 1.378 (*squamigeri*), 2.344 (*squamigerum*), 2.1087 (*squamigerum*); cf. *Carmen de virginitate* 2399 (*squamigerum*); cf. n.Praef.30 *supra*. Aldhelm probably had not read Lucretius, but may have read a refutation of his cosmology in Lactantius *De opificio Dei*, particularly chapter 6. See Lockett at 223.

l. 5 The words *membra* ("limbs") and *venenis* ("toxins") appear in the same locations in Ovid *Metamorphoses* 15.359.

ll. 5–7 Basil's *Hexaemeron* also discussed certain animals able to eat substances toxic to most other animals. Schaff at 77–8. Aldhelm undoubtedly viewed nourishment from poison as another paradox.

Riddle 32: Writing tablets, a common teaching tool, were typically made of wax and framed in wood and leather. See Bischoff at 14. Incredibly, less than a century ago a writing tablet from around 600 AD containing lines from *Psalms* 30–2 was discovered in Ireland. It probably was lost by a travelling priest in training. See Armstrong and Macalister, "Wooden Book with Leaves Indented and Waxed Found Near Springmount Bog, Co. Antrim," *Journal of the Royal Society of Antiquaries of Ireland* 10 (1920) at 160–6; see also Wright, "The Tablets from Springmount Bog, a Key to Early Irish Palaeography," *American Journal of Archaeology* 67 (1963) at 219. Tablets were sometimes made of expensive materials and used in church services. See Rock at 147–8. The term *pugillares* spawned the Old Welsh *puolloraur* and the Middle Welsh *peullawr*. Bitterli at 140 suggests a possible influence of the writing tablets in *Bern Riddle* 19 (*De cera*).

l. 1 The adjective *melligeris* ("honey-laden") is an Aldhelmian modification of the rare *melliferis*. See Ovid *Metamorphoses* 15.383 (*melliferarum*); Claudian *De raptu Proserpinae* 2.1.127 (*mellifer*); see also n.Praef.30 *supra*.

l. 3 Most translators render this line in a way that assumes that the tablet has "shoes" – leather feet on its base. But see Milovanović-Barham, "Aldhelm's *Enigmata* and Byzantine Riddles," *Anglo-Saxon England* 22 (1993) at 58–60.

l. 4 For *ferri stimulus* ("iron spike"), cf. *Aenigmata* 30.3. See Milovanović-Barham *supra* at 58.

ll. 5–7 The plowing metaphor was a popular classical trope, perhaps originally drawn from Plato's *Phaedrus*. The seed metaphor was a popular early Christian trope; in Aldhelm's *Carmina Ecclesiastica* he associated it with Saint Paul. See Lapidge and Rosier at 51. Aldhelm returned to the metaphor in his *Letter to Heahfrith*. See Lapidge and Herren at 162 (" … open your throat and moisten the thirsting fields of the mind, so that the seed of heavenly ecstasy, sown by the sweat of the Creator, may swell and blossom in the living and fertile furrows of the orthodox without hindrance of parching drought, and that the thickly sown crop at length come richly to fruition by the will of God."). Cf. Thornbury at 54.

l. 6 The Stork text has the classical *segeti* for the Ehwald/Pitman *segiti* ("field"). For a discussion of possible Irish influence here, see n.Praef.8 *supra*.

l. 8 Aldhelm was punning on *arma* (hands/weapons).

Riddle 33: This riddle is another example of Aldhelm connecting a concrete item and a spiritual concept. The term *lorica* referred to a broad range of body armour, but it also referred to a prayer recited by monks for protection from evil. The most famous of these prayers was *The Lorica of Saint Patrick*, which would be a fourth-century composition if Patrick is the author, although some scholars suggest it was composed as late as Aldhelm's era. Regardless of its exact dating, this type of prayer was popular in Ireland during Aldhelm's time and crossed the water to Britain. At least one linguistic echo suggests that Aldhelm was familiar with the version of *The Lorica* contained in the *Hisperica Famina*. See Herren (1974) at xxii. Herren and Brown at 255 note that the image of the sacerdotal Christ as the *lorica* of the faithful was common in the art of Ireland during Aldhelm's era. Steen at 93 notes the elevated connotations of *lorica* and argues that the title alludes to the Pauline imagery of spiritual armour by citing Jerome *Ad Thessalonicenses* I 5:8 (*lorica fidei*) and *Ad Ephesios* 6:11 (*lorica iustitiae*).

The "Leiden riddle" appears to be a translation of Riddle 33, as is Riddle 36 of *The Exeter Book*. Lapidge and Rosier 67. See also Klein, "The Old English Translation of Aldhelm's Riddle *Lorica*," *Review of English Studies, New Series* 48, no. 191 (1997) at 345–9; Steen at 91–8.

l. 1 The precise phrase *roscida ... viscera tellus* ("frozen bowels of ... Earth") may have been novel with Aldhelm, but the concepts were familiar. Aldhelm would have known "frozen earth" from Dracontius *De laudibus Dei* 1.65 (*roscida tellus*), which may in turn have been influenced by Seneca *Phaedra* 0.42 (*roscida tellus*). Pairing the noun *corpus* with *tellus* was also common. See e.g. Lucretius *De rerum natura* 6.633 (*corpore tellus*); Cicero *De divinatione* 1.8 (*corpore tellus*); Silius *Punica* 4.294 (*corpora tellus*); Augustine *De civitate Dei* (*corpora tellus*). To complete the phrase, Aldhelm had many possible sources. See Ovid *Metamorphoses* 1.138 (*viscera terrae*); Solinus *Mirabilia* 5.9 (*terrae viscera*); Statius *Thebaid* 8.109, 9.451 (*viscera terrae*); Silius *Punica* 12.141, 14.15 (*viscera terrae*); Damasus *Epigrammata* 4.7 (*viscera terrae*); Dracontius *De laudibus Dei* 2.450 (*viscera terrae*); *Romulea* 3.12 (*viscera terrae*); Claudius Marius Victor *Alethia* 1.215, 1.487 (*viscera terrae*); Paulinus Petricordia *De vita Martini* 1.269 (*viscera terrae*).

l. 2 See n.12.2 *supra*.

l. 3 The adjective *garrula* ("humming") describes the sound of the loom, not the *fila* ("threads") themselves. Typically, *garrula* would mean something closer to "chatty," but I wanted a word that sounded more like the sound of a loom. See n.26.1–2 *supra*.

The verb *resultant* ("cascade") could mean either "leap rhythmically" or "echo"; translators have made both choices.

l. 4 See n.12 *supra*. Steen at 92 notes that *texunt* ("weave") has the central position in what prosodists call a "golden line."

l. 5 The *radiis* ("wheels") and *duro ... pectine* ("stiff combs" – singular in the text) were parts of a spinning wheel.

l. 6 The phrase *vulgi sermone* ("on the street" – literally "in common parlance") was uncommon, but dated back to the Augustan era. See e.g. Cicero *Epistulae Ad Atticum* 2, *Epistula* 21.1 (*vulgi sermonibus*). The most likely source is Jerome. See *Epistulae* 3.57.12 (*vulgi sermone*), 4.117.1 (*vulgi sermone*), 4.128.4 (*vulgi sermonibus*).

Riddle 34: I followed Ehwald and Lapidge in the ordering of the lines of this riddle rather than the ordering of Orchard (forthcoming).

l. 2 This line echoes Ovid *Metamorphoses* 13.395 (*purpureum viridi genuit de caespite florem*).

l. 4 For more on "the Nile's domains," see *Exodus* 10:5–14.

Riddle 35: *Nycticorax* (or *nicticorax*) is a Greek compound word for "night-raven." Lapidge and Rosier argue that the term was another name for a screech owl. See 250 ("Aldhelm plays on the Greek etymology of the name (which, for once, is not derived from Isidore"). Isidore, *Etymologia* at 12.7.39–42 appears to distinguish a *nycticorax* from a *strix* ("screech owl") and a *noctua* ("night-owl"). While some later glossators and writers identify the *nycticorax* (cf. OE *nihthrae-fn*) as an owl, others identify it as a heron. The term *nycticorax* survives as a scientific name for herons, and, in fact, a "night heron" exists that makes precisely the sound described by line five's *raucisono* ("I shriek") and looks more like a raven than an owl. While it is unclear, I believe that Aldhelm's *nycticorax* is a heron. Cf. Whitman, "The Birds of Old English Literature," *Journal of German Philology* 2 (1898) at 149–98; Kitson, "Old English Bird-names," *English Studies* 78 (1997) 481–505. The *nycticorax* appears in the works of authors familiar to Aldhelm, including Ambrose, Paulinus of Nola, Augustine, Prosper of Aquitaine, and Jerome, and in versions of the *Physiologus*.

l. 1 The challenge of this line is choosing the word for the open-ended *ars*.

Orchard (1994) at 235 sees *rite* ("rightly") *figuris* (combined with *duplicat* as "copies") as possibly echoing Arator *De actis apostolis* 1.795 (*rite figuram*).

l. 3 For the phrase *sub luce serena* ("in clear light"), see Prudentius *Cathemerinon* 6.51 (*lux serena*); Silius *Punica* 13.17 (*luce serena*).

l. 4 The striking phrase *astriferas … latebras* ("star-borne nests") has eluded scholarly comment. Aldhelm may have picked up the adjective *astriferas* from Sedulius *Carmen Paschale* 3.221 (*astriferas*) or Lucan *Bellum civile* 9.5 (*astriferis*). Cf. Martial 8.28.8, 9.20.6 (*astrifero*); Boethius *De consolatione philosophiae* 4.1.2.5 (*astriferas*); Valerius Flaccus *Argonautica* 6.751 (*astriferas*); Isidore *Differentiae* 1.C.82 (*astriferus*); Statius *Thebaid* 2.400 (*astriferum*), 8.83 (*astriferos*); Augustine *Sermones* 21.179.2 (*astriferi*). Another possibility is the *Hisperica Famina*. See *A Text* 387 (*Astrifero*); cf. n.Praef.30 *supra*.

l. 6 The phrase *Romulei biblis* ("Rome's books") is literally "the books of Romulus." Romulus – a cofounder of Rome – was also a pseudonym of one or more writers from around the fifth century AD and one of the many popular translators of Aesop's *Fables*. See aesopus.pbworks.com/romulus; Ziolkowski at 19–20.

l. 7 I have used the identical rhyme "name" to mimic the repetition of *nomen* in line 1 and *nomine* in line 7.

Riddle 36: Scholars disagree about the exact nature of Aldhelm's *scnifes* ("midge"). Pitman discusses flies, lice, and fleas as possibilities. Pitman at 72. Since Cameron's "Aldhelm as Naturalist" *supra* at n.12.3, scholars tend to agree on "midge," an explanation given in one gloss. An Egyptian midge is not the equivalent of the harmless North American gnat; it has a stinger and transmits diseases. Aldhelm may have found the term in *Exodus* 8:16–18 and *Psalms* 104:31 or in Isidore *Etymologiae* 12.8.14. See Forbes, "Book Worm or Entomologist? Aldhelm's *Enigma XXXVI*," *Peritia* 19 (2005) at 21–2.

l. 1 With *armatus* ("for arms" – literally "armed") Aldhelm again puns on arms as limbs and weapons.

l. 2 For *scando* ("I rise"), see n.5.4 *supra*. As Orchard (1994) at 159 has noted, this line may echo Symphosius *Aenigmata* 35.2 (*culmina de facile peragrans super ardua gressu*), but it also seems to combine Dracontius *Romulea* 7.154 (*et volucer veneris volitans super aequora pennis*) and Virgil *Aeneid* 12.892 (*ardua pennis*). For Aldhelm's debt to Dracontius, see *id*. at 185–8.

Aldhelm placed *catervatim* ("in swarms") in the same location in *Aenigmata* 34.3, 75.9 and *Carmen de virginitate* 2454, 2878. See Forbes, "Book Worm or Entomologist? Aldhelm's *Enigma XXXVI*," *Peritia* 19 (2005) at 23.

l. 3 The phrase *mucrone cruento* ("bleeding sword") appears in the same location in the line in Dracontius *De laudibus Dei* 2.295 and *Carmen de virginitate* 1749.

l. 7 The verb *vescor* ("I love") can mean either "feed on" or "enjoy." Either meaning works in this line.

Riddle 37: The title may be another example of Aldhelm's intermittently dicey science; the term *nepa* means "scorpion," but he is clearly talking about a crab, particularly in line 4, which is referring to the constellation Cancer. In fairness to Aldhelm, Isidore wrote that crabs transformed into scorpions, and Aldhelm probably believed him. See Isidore *Etymologiae* 11.4.3; Lapidge and Rosier at 250–1; Howe, "Aldhelm's *Enigmata* and Isidorian Etymology," *Anglo-Saxon England* 14 (1985) at 54–5. Ehwald at 113 points to a possible source for both Isidore and Aldhelm, Nonius Marcellus's *De compendiosa doctrina* (*Nepam quidam cancrum putant … nam vere nepa scorpius dicitur*). See Lindsay at 211. Thornbury at 55 makes the helpful argument that this riddle is not so much about the crab "but the Latin word *cancer*." She also makes a case that the source might have been a quotation from Plautus *Casina* 443 in Pomponius Festus *De verborum significatu epitome*. Thornbury at 257–8.

l. 2 Both *spumifer* ("foaming" – literally "foam-bearing") and its synonym *spumiger* were rare. This line's *spumiferi … ponti* ("foaming ocean") echoes Ovid's *Metamorphoses* 11.140 (*spumigeroque … fonti*); another likely source is Statius. See *Thebaid* 5.56, 9.438 (*spumifer*); *Achilleis* 1.59 (*spumiferos*).

l. 3 The adjective *retrograda* ("backwards"), from which we derive our word "retrograde," is an overlooked example of Aldhelm's love of exotic language and quiet wit. It was a term used in astronomy that Aldhelm almost certainly learned from Isidore. See *De natura rerum* 22.3 (*retrograda*), 23.3 (*retrograda*), *Etymologiae* 3.66.3 (*retrograda*), 3.67.1 (*retrograda*) (twice); cf. Avianus *Fabulae* 1.2 (on the crab) (*retro cedens*). Isidore probably learned the term from Pliny. See *Naturalis historia* 2.77 (*retrogradum*). But see Meccariello, "An Echo from Nonius Marcellus in Aldhelm's *Aenigmata*," *Classica et Mediaevalia* 61 (2010) at 264. In this line Aldhelm takes a technical term used to describe stars and applies it not just to a collection of stars, but to the humble symbol of those stars as well. For a thoughtful overview of Aldhelm's astronomical knowledge, see Stevens, "Sidereal Time in Anglo-Saxon England," in Kendall and Wells at 125–55.

l. 6 The likely sources for this line are Isidore *Etymologiae* 12.6.51–2 and Ambrose *Hexaemeron* 5.8.22. Although the story may be opaque for modern readers, the oyster fears that the crab will toss a stone to break its shell and eat its meat. The same myth appears in the *Exeter Book* riddles. See Salvador, "The Oyster and the Crab: A Riddle Duo (nos. 77 and 78) in the *Exeter Book*," *Modern Philology* 101, no.3 (2004) at 400–19. One can easily imagine Aldhelm wryly bridging from this riddle to *John* 8:7 (" … he that is without sin among you, let him first cast the stone at her").

I have not translated the largely redundant *duris* ("hard").

Riddle 38: It is tempting to look at this riddle as a platform for a homily on *Matthew* 14:22–33. In addition to the obvious comparison between the water-strider and Christ, line 2 echoes lines verse 27 ("Take courage! It is I. Don't be afraid.") and the reference to *ratibus* ("with ... a boat") in line 5 is an opportunity to address verse 29 in which Peter leaves his boat and walks on water until he takes his eyes off of Jesus and loses faith.

The exact nature of the *tippula* ("pond strider") was unclear even to Aldhelm's early readers. See O'Keeffe, "The Text of Aldhelm's *Enigma* no.C in Oxford Bodleian Library, Rawlinson C.697 and Exeter Riddle 40," *Anglo-Saxon England* 14 (1985) at 61–73. The best source we may have is Nonius Marcellus's *De compendiosa doctrina*. See Orchard (1994) at 130. I am also grateful to Scott Gwara for bringing to my attention Meccariello, "An Echo from Nonius Marcellus in Aldhelm's *Enigmata*," *Classica et Mediaevalia* 61 (2010) at 257–65. This article argues that Aldhelm may have found *tippula* in Nonius, *De compendiosa doctrina* or possibly Paulus's compendium of Festus *De verborum significatu*. See Lindsay (1903) at 264. Meccariello's case is strengthened by his comments on Aldhelm's use of the *tippula* as an example of lightness, which closely parallels a similar observation by Nonius. Meccariello also makes a clever, but strained, argument that the description of the *tippula* "assures [*sic*]" that the insect is a *gerris gerridae*, or pond-skater. *Id.* at 262–3.

l. 2 Perhaps the insect's bravery about submersion reminded Aldhelm of the fears less brave members of his flock displayed prior to baptism.

l. 3 The phrase *calco pedestris* ("I skim" – literally "I tread on feet") raises an interesting issue of translation. The verb *calco* originally had the sense of a heavy step – perhaps not a stomp, but certainly not a tiptoe. It may be that the choice of this verb was a bit of Aldhelmian humour, a little like describing the noise of a kitten as a roar. However, I think the more likely explanation is that the sense of the verb changed. At least by the time of Isidore the noun *calcus* ("a light weight" or "pebble") came into fashion, and that usage seems to have pushed the sense of the verb *calcare* at least to "walk," if not all the way to "skim." See e.g. Isidore *Etymologiae* 16.25.8; Augustine *Confessiones* 12.2.2.1 (*terramque quam calco*); Prudentius *Hamartigenia* 1.772 (*calcare viam*). I will leave it to *sapientes* to decide whether my hypothesis is fair or not, but I have selected "skim" in the belief that by Aldhelm's time *calcare* no longer necessarily connoted a heavy foot.

l. 5 Meccariello argues, unpersuasively in my opinion, that *fluvios transire feroces* ("cross fierce torrents") echoes Varro *Menippeae* 50.1, a line that refers to the pond skater (*levis tippula lymphon frigidos transit lacus*). See "An Echo of Nonius Marcellus in Aldhelm's *Aenigmata*," *Classica et Mediaevalia* 61 (2010) at 263–4.

l. 6 This line echoes Ovid *Metamorphoses* 14.50 (*summaque decurrit pedibus super aequora siccis*).

Riddle 39: A primary source for this riddle is probably Isidore *Etymologiae* 12.2.3–5. In early Christian exegeses the lion was a symbol of Christ – and was often represented in medieval bestiaries as sleeping with its eyes open. See Cramp at 48. See e.g. bestiary.ca/beasts/beast78.htm. See also Solinus *Mirabilia* 28, 53.

l. 1 For *setiger* ("whiskered"), see n.12.2 *supra*.

The closing words *dentibus* ("with tusks") *apros* ("each boar") may echo the closing words of Juvenal 15.162 (*dentibus apri*). See also Ovid *Metamorphoses* 10.550 (*dentibus apri*); cf. Silius *Punica* 4.559 (*dentibus apri*); Lucretius *De rerum natura* (*dentibus apri*); Pliny *Historiae naturalis* 8.95 (*dentibus aprorum*).

l. 2 The phrase *cornigerosque … cervos* ("and antlered stags") may echo Claudian *De Consulatu Stilichonis* 2.353 (*cornua cervos*) or Ovid *Ars Amatoria* 3.78 (*cervos cornua*). See also n.Praef.30 *supra*.

l. 4 The *ora cruenta* ("Lips bloody") at the beginning of this line may echo the *ora cruentatum* in the same location as Sedulius *Carmen Paschale* 4.296. Cf. Statius *Thebaid* 6.247 (*ore cruenta*); Fortunatus *Vita Sancti Martini* 1.181 (*Ore cruentatis*).

l. 6 Orchard (1994) at 231 noted that this line echoes Pseudo-Claudian *Epithalamium Laurentii* 36 (*non tibi nam gemmae sed tu das lumina gemmis*). A reference to this poem in the *Carmen de virginitate* shows that Aldhelm was familiar with this poem. See Lapidge and Herren at 97. For Aldhelm's relation to Claudian, see Orchard (1994) at 152–5.

The phrase *lumina gemmis* ("my jeweled beams") may echo *Appendix Virgiliana Culex* 185 (*lumina gemmis*). It is an ornate description of eyes, which for centuries people believed emitted beams to allow vision.

Riddle 40: Although pepper was a staple in the later medieval era, it was a luxury in Aldhelm's day. Cuthbert reports that pepper was among the *preciosa* distributed by Bede before his death. See *Cuthbert's Letter on the Death of Bede* in Colgrave and Mynors at 584–5. This riddle has some parallels with Solinus *Mirabilia* 64 and the same answer as *Bern Riddle* 37 (*De pipere*).

l. 1 The phrase *rugoso cortice* ("by wrinkled skin") may echo Ovid *Heroides* 5.30 (*rugoso cortice*). Cf. Ovid *Metamorphoses* 7.626 (*rugosoque suum servantes cortice callem*); Persius 5.56 (*rugosum piper*); Isidore *Etymologiae* 17.8.8 (*piper album quod vero cute rugosa*). It appears that Aldhelm viewed pepper as a metaphor for man with the dark husk being the body and the white core the soul. However, it is difficult to extend that metaphor to the closing line. Perhaps sometimes pepper is just pepper.

l. 2 For the phrase *candentam … medullam* ("glowing core"), cf. Pliny *Naturalis historia* 18.17 (*candidiorem medullam*).

Riddle 41: As suggested in my translator's note, Aldhelm may be identifying with the pillow in this riddle. In lines 1 and 2 he meditates on his Christian mission. Line 3 hints at the transcendence possible by embrace of that mission, and line 4 hints at the possible price of such transcendence. It might be possible to stretch this analysis into lines 5 and 6, but as in the previous riddle it seems that Aldhelm is returning to the visible world.

For a comparison of this riddle with Alcuin's Riddle 101, see Bayless, "Alcuin and the Early Medieval Riddle Tradition," in Halsall at 170–1.

l. 1 The direct address and language of *licet irrita dicta putentur* ("though talk carries little weight") may echo Virgil *Aeneid* 10.244 (*mea si non inrita dicta putaris*).

l. 2 Aldhelm later echoed this line in *Carmen de virginitate* 1806 (*Credula virgineis pandentem pectora verbis*). Cf. Paulinus of Nola *Carmina* 18.62 (*pandite corda*).

l. 4 For *caput aufertur* ("I'm beheaded"), cf. Gregory the Great *Moralia in Iob* 14.35.2, 14.35.3 (*de capite aufertur*). Aldhelm refers to the pillow case as a "head," a comparison that does not resonate with modern readers.

l. 6 The phrase *ima petens* (collapsed into *minorari* as "to want to shrink") echoes Virgil *Aeneid* 8.67 (*ima petens*). See also Sedulius *Carmen Paschale* 3.206 (*ima petunt*).

Riddle 42: Since no ostriches lived in Britain, Aldhelm's information came from sources such as Pliny *Naturalis historia* 10.1, Isidore *Etymologiae* 12.7.20, or Gregory the Great *Moralia in Iob* 31.8–23. Aaron Poochigian also pointed me toward *Job* 39:13–18 ("The wing of the ostrich is like the wings of the heron, and of the hawk. When she leaveth her eggs on the earth, thou perhaps wilt warm them in the dust. She forgetteth that the foot may tread upon them, or that the beasts of the field may break them. She is hardened against her young ones, as though they were not hers, she hath labored in vain, no fear constraining her. For God hath deprived her of wisdom, neither hath he given her understanding. When time shall be, she setteth up her wings on high: she scorneth the horse and his rider"). Old English had the term *stryta* derived from the Latin *struthio*, which in turn was derived from the Greek *struthion*.

l. 2 This line may echo Sedulius *Carmen Paschale* 5.206 (*par est poena trium sed dispar causa duorum*).

l. 3 The phrase *aethera* ("sky") *pennis* ("wings") is Virgilian. See *Aeneid* 11.272 (*aethera pennis*), 11.867 (*aetherium pennis*), *Georgica* 1.406, 1.409 (*aethera pinnis*).

I adopted *Nam summa* ("For ... high") of Orchard (forthcoming) over the Ehwald *Summa dum*.

l. 5 Many cultures have prized cups made from ostrich eggs since at least 3000 BC. See generally Laufer, "Ostrich Egg-shell Cups of Mesopotamia and the Ostrich in Ancient and Modern Times," Chicago: Field Museum of Natural History, Anthropology Leaflet No. 23 (1926).

Riddle 43: l. 2 The phrase *nomen … cruentem* ("a gory name") plays on *sanguine* ("blood") in line 3 and the word for a leech, *sanguisuga*. See Howe, "Aldhelm's *Enigmata* and Isidorian Etymology," *Anglo-Saxon England* 14 (1985) at 45–6. If I had chosen the more colloquial, but less precise, "bloodsucker" to translate the answer, it would have better captured this wordplay. The exact medicinal uses of leeches by Anglo-Saxons are unknown. See Cameron at 25.

l. 3–6 The four end-rhymes and substantial internal rhymes in these lines give this riddle a music that would have been highly novel at the time Aldhelm wrote it.

l. 6 Doctors use leeches today for removing pockets of blood after certain kinds of surgery, and the successful blood thinner Angiomax is a synthetic molecule derived from the saliva of the leech. Leech saliva contains substances that keep a wound open as the insect sucks.

Riddle 44: l. 1 The phrase *gelido … rigore* ("frozen-hard resilience") is a reference to a flint. See n.93 *infra*. Cf. Fortunatus *Vita Sancti Martini* 1.51 (*frigore sub gelido*); Valerius Maximus *Facta et dicta memorabilia* 3.3.106 (*gelido rigore*).

ll. 3–4 For *fortunam* ("fate") and *fata* ("course"), see n.7.2 *supra*.

l. 6 The phrase *naturae iura* ("Nature's law") is classical. See e.g. Ovid *Ars amatoria* 2.42. Aldhelm's understanding of this phrase came primarily from Augustine and other Christian writers. See e.g. Augustine *Sermones* 21.128.1, 41.245.3; Dracontius *De laudibus Dei* 3.338; Ambrose *De Noe et Arca* 1.26.94.

l. 7 The phrase *Cum me vita fovet* ("While I'm alive") is literally closer to "While my life warms me."

The last two words of Symphosius 67.2 are also *sideris instar* ("like a … star").

l. 8 The phrase *pice nigrior* ("more black than tar") echoes Ovid *Metamorphoses* 12.402 (*pice nigrior*).

I retained Ehwald's *Postmodum* ("Then") over the *Post haec* of Orchard (forthcoming).

Riddle 45: For a thorough overview of Anglo-Saxon weaving and textile production, see Owen-Crocker at 272–316. The Ehwald text places the lines of this riddle in a different order from previous editors. See Pitman at 73. I have rejected the Ehwald rearrangement for literary, not textual, reasons, and similarly rejected the order proposed by Orchard (forthcoming).

l. 2 The Stork manuscript has *natura* for *fortuna* ("Fortune").

l. 3 Pitman at 73 notes that Aldhelm probably learned *molam* ("thread" – literally "a clump of flax held on the distaff, from which the thread is spun") from Isidore *Etymologiae* 20.8.6. Pitman notes that this line is virtually repeated in *Carmen de virginitate* 1464.

l. 5 The *zona* ("belt") is the coiled strap that spins the spindle's wheel. Cf. Lapidge and Herren at 104.

l. 6 The Parcae were three female personifications of "the Fates." Nona, one of the three, chose a person's date of death on his or her birthday by spinning the thread of life from her distaff to her spindle. The Parcae were discussed in many texts familiar to Aldhelm, particularly Virgil's *Aeneid* and Ovid's *Metamorphoses*. See also Isidore *Etymologiae* 1.37.24 (arguing their name is derived from the verb *parcere*, which means "to spare"). Aldhelm echoes this etymological explanation in *Carmen de virginitate* 1462–3. See Lapidge and Rosier at 135, 259.

A gloss on the Stork text notes that *virum* ("men's") is a shortened *virorum*. Stork at 35.

l. 7 Aldhelm echoes himself almost as much as he does any other writer. Here the *frigora* ("chills") *dura* ("steadfast") reminds one of *gelido rigore* from the first line of the previous riddle.

Riddle 46: Pitman notes at 73 that this riddle is an adaptation of Symphosius *Aenigmata* 44 on the onion. The title/answer *urtica* and the use of the verb *adurat* may be wordplay influenced by Isidore *Etymologiae* 18.9.44. See Rusche, "Isidore's *Etymologiae* and the Canterbury Aldhelm *Scholia*," *Journal of English and German Philology* 104, no. 4 (2005) at 439. I have taken some poetic liberties in the first three lines in the name of fun; Lapidge and Rosier at 79 render these lines more literally as "I torment my tormentors, but I willingly would torment no one, nor do I wish to harm anyone, unless he were first to incur the guilt and seek to pluck my green stalk."

According to folklore which is almost certainly untrue, Caesar introduced nettles to Britain. See Nearing, "Local Caesar Traditions in Britain," *Speculum* 24, no. 2 (1945) at 218–19.

l. 1 Orchard (1994) at 159 notes an echo of Symphosius *Aenigmata* 44.1 because *Torqueo*, *torquentes*, and *torqueo* are in the same locations as *Mordeo*, *mordentes*, and *mordeo*.

l. 4 The phrase *membra nocentis* ("stained limbs") at the end of this line may echo the *membra nocentes* in the same location of Cyprianus Gallus *Heptateuchus Exodus* 20. The phrase *turgescunt membra* ("limbs … swell up") recalls the same phrase in *Aenigmata* 31.5.

Riddle 47: l. 2 The phrase *ieiunia longa* ("long fasting") may echo Augustine *Confessiones* 21.175.2 (*ieiunia longa*) or Solinus *Mirabilia* 2.37 (*longa ieiunia*).

Cf. Cassiodorus *Variae* 11.40.4 (*ieiunia longa*). The noun *ieiunia* was uncommon, although it became a term for Lent; the phrase *caput ieiunia* became a term for Ash Wednesday.

l. 3 The verb *glescunt* ("spreads") is the medieval version of *gliscunt*.

l. 4 The description of the *hirundo* ("swallow") as *garrula* ("chatty") probably echoes Virgil *Georgica* 4.307 (*garrula quam tignis nidum suspendat hirundo*).

l. 5 The phrase *prolem gentis adultam* ("kindred kids are grown") may echo Virgil *Aeneid* 1.431 (*gentis adultos*).

ll. 7–9 The plant is the *chelidonium*, which comes from the Greek word *chelidon* ("swallow"). Likely sources are Pliny *Naturalis historia* 8.41 and Isidore *Etymologiae* 17.9.36. To make this balm, medieval physicians mixed the toxic orange juice of the plant with honey in a brass or copper pot. See Cameron at 121.

l. 9 For this sense of *quaerens* ("Produced"), see OLD 7.

Riddle 48: l. 1 The adjective *almus* was rare in Aldhelm's time, which increases the possibility that Aldhelm took the phrase *conditor almus* ("kind Maker") from a lovely anonymous late sixth- or early seventh-century hymn sung for Vespers during Advent called *Conditor alme siderum*. The hymn was butchered about a thousand years later by Vatican priests who viewed its Latin as insufficiently classical. The suggestion that Aldhelm was thinking of this hymn during composition is more compelling when one recalls that the title of the hymn is "Kind Maker *of the Stars*" and this is a riddle about the movement of the heavens. There are also slight parallels in vocabulary. The words *saeculum* appears in line 6 of the hymn and *saeculi* in line 18; *saecula* ("worlds") appears in line 2 of this riddle. The noun *siderum* ("stars") appears in the title and first line of the hymn; *sidera* appears in line 9 of this riddle.

l. 2 For *saecula* as "worlds," see OLD 10. Cf. Lapidge and Rosier at 79 ("the universe").

l. 6 The phrase *pennis aethera tranet* ("skims the sky with wings") may echo Virgil *Aeneid* 10.265 (*aethera tranant*).

l. 9 The *septem sidera* ("seven stars") were the Earth, Sun, and five planets visible to the eye.

Riddle 49: This riddle is the second of two translated by Richard Wilbur in a 1975 broadside. See n.19 *supra*. For Aldhelm it is likely that the cauldron was an image associated with the mouth of Hell. See Hofmann at 79 (" … devils cooking or at least tormenting the damned in a cauldron is also the imagery used in the second most common sanction with infernal imagery among extant Anglo-Saxon charters"); see generally Schmidt. Bubbling water also had connotations of psychological distress. See n.54 *infra*.

l. 1 This line clearly echoes Symphosius *Aenigmata* 89.1 (*horrida curva capax patulis fabricata metallis*).

l. 3 The phrase *ignibus ardescens* ("Glowing in flames") echoes Isidore *Etymologiae* 16.1.10.

My use of "bubbles" for *gurgite* is a slight poetic liberty – literally it means "a whirlpool" or "a swirling mass of water." It seemed fair, though, that boiling, swirling water in a cauldron would have bubbles, and the term did evolve into Italian and Portuguese verbs for "bubble up."

Riddle 50: The source here appears to be Isidore *Etymologiae* 20.8.4. Milfoil, also known as yarrow, is a common weed (a pejorative opinion, perhaps, but one also expressed in line five) similar to Queen Anne's lace.

l. 1 The adjective *Achivorum* ("Greek") is classical and perhaps best rendered as "Achaean."

l. 2 The phrase *mille … folium* ("thousand-leaf") describes the plant, but also puns on the answer. This line echoes Ovid *Metamorphoses* 13.395 (*purpureum viridi genuit de caespite florem*).

l. 3 The closing phrase *nomen habebo* ("I will have … as my name") also closes Symphosius *Aenigmata* 74.3.

l. 4 The noun *cauliculis* ("shoots") appears regularly in Pliny and rarely elsewhere.

Riddle 51: The primary sources here appear to be Pliny *Naturalis historia* 2.41, 22.29 and Isidore *Etymologiae* 17.8.37, although this plant fascinated classical writers. See generally von Erhardt-Siebold, "The Heliotrope Tradition," *Osiris* 3 (1937) at 22–46; cf. Priscian *Periegesis* 254. Priscian's grammatical texts were a major influence on Aldhelm. See Manitius at 59–62.

The answer "sunflower" doesn't work because sunflowers are native to the Americas. Cameron *supra* at 129 argues that the heliotrope is the dandelion, but his argument seems unlikely. The Stork text, which varies significantly from the Ehwald text, perhaps offers the best clue. Scribes, undoubtedly worried that readers would be baffled by an obscure Greek reference, expanded and explained Aldhelm's title to "DE ELIOTROPO GRECE QUOD EST SOLESQUIUM LATINE." Unfortunately, the word *solesquium* is as obscure to us as *eiliotropo* was to the scribes. Above the word *solesquium*, however, a glossator has added the Old English term *goldwyrt*, a term generally, but not definitively, associated with *calendula officinalis*, the pot marigold, which is somewhat heliotropic.

l. 3 This line may slightly echo Ovid *Metamorphoses* 1.63 (*vesper et occiduo quae litora sole tepescunt*).

The phrase *orto sole* ("at dawn" – literally "at risen sun") was a particular favourite of Jerome, who used it at least a dozen times.

Riddle 52: l. 3 The term *spoliata* ("a looting" in line 2 of the translation) had strong martial connotations and is striking as a trope for picking. A possible inspiration is the fig tree in Gregory the Great *Moralia in Iob* 8.48.3 (*spoliata ficus*).

I identified only one unlikely possible source for *iunco gracilis* ("some thin reed"). Cf. Petronius *Satiricon* 135 (*iunco gracilis*).

l. 6 The adjective *udae* ("maudlin") literally means "wet," but I have interpreted it here as "excessively wet" to avoid redundancy, and thus jumped to "maudlin" without a philological rationale.

l. 8 The noun *cinerum* ("ash") may have reminded Aldhelm of *Genesis* 3:19 ("Remember, man, thou art dust and unto dust thou shalt return"), even though the *Vulgate* used *pulvis* for "dust." At the time of Aldhelm, both burial and cremation were common. See Dunn at 86–8. In his *Letter to Geraint*, Aldhelm referred to the purifying qualities of gravel and ash. See Lapidge and Herren at 158. Whether *cinerum* would have thus reminded Aldhelm of *dies cinerum* ("Ash Wednesday") is less clear. One of the earliest descriptions of Ash Wednesday in Britain is in the homilies of Aelfric (955–1020 A.D.); most scholars believe that their observance of Ash Wednesday began somewhere in the eighth century. The phrase *reliquias cinerum*, though, was common in epitaphs before Aldhelm's time. See e.g. Colafrancesco and Bücheler at 92, 126, 322, 739.

Riddle 53: Arcturus is the brightest star of the constellation Boötes. There is a tradition that associates Arcturus with the legendary King Arthur. See Anderson at 29. It is likely that Aldhelm relied on Gregory the Great *Moralia in Iob* 29.31.7–8 for the material of this riddle. For a thoughtful overview of this riddle, see Bitterli at 61–6; see also Lapidge and Rosier at 251.

l. 1 For the phrase *in vertice mundi* ("on Heaven's peak"), see Statius *Thebaid* 3.218 (*e vertice mundi*); cf. Rutilius *De reditu suo itinerarium* 1.17 (*mundani verticis*); Boethius *De consolatione philosophiae* 4.6.2.5 (*vertice mundi*); Columella *Rei rusticae* 10.1.1.53 (*vertice mundi*); Manilius *Astronomica* 1.564 (*de vertice mundi*), 2.906 (*de vertice mundi*).

l. 2 The term *Esseda* refers to a light two-wheeled military wagon used as a platform for battle that over time civilians made heavier and more lavish; people eventually regarded it as an affectation, much like the Hummer in the United States after Operation Desert Storm. See Straus at 29–30. Aldhelm is engaging in wordplay; Arcturus was often known as the "Wain" or "Wagon."

For a vitriolic, and yet wrong, analysis of *gesto* ("I bear"), see Brae, "Arthur's Slow Wain," *Notes and Queries* (July 29, 1871) at 91–2. Brae continued his tirade in Brae, "Arthur's Oven at the Carron: Ritson and Dr. Maginn," *Notes and Queries* (February 27, 1875) at 171–2, never noticing the irony of his comment that " … an unjust and malevolent attack, always unpleasing, becomes especially so when it exposes the critic's own ignorance." *Id.* at 172.

For a helpful discussion of Aldhelm's use of *vulgo* ("when folks speak"), see Howe, "Aldhelm's *Enigmata* and Isidorian Etymology," *Anglo-Saxon England* 14 (1985) at 51n.38. Cf. Suetonius *De vita Caesarum* 8.3.3 (*famoso vulgoque*).

l. 6 Though many authors mentioned the Riphean mountains, they knew little about them except that they were distant and cold. Perhaps the most likely source is Justinus *Epitome* 2.2, which sets the Riphean mountains as one of Scythia's boundaries. See Crick, "An Anglo-Saxon Fragment of Justinus' *Epitome*," *Anglo-Saxon England* 16 (1987) at 181–96; cf. Priscian *Periegesis* 307; Solinus *Mirabilia* 21.1; Isidore *Etymologiae* 13.21.24; Claudian *In Eutropium* 2.1.151. For Aldhelm, Scythia would have been a large but vague tract of land north of Parthia (Persia) and Greece. Justinus *Epitome* 2.2 also provides a detailed, and exceptionally bleak, description of Scythia. See also Virgil *Georgica* 1.240; Isidore *Etymologiae* 14.3–4; Ovid *Epistulae ex Ponto* 3.2.45, 3.2.96, 4.6.5; Priscian *Periegesis* 23; Solinus *Mirabilia* 16.22–9; Claudian *De raptu Proserpinae* 3.21.

This line's last two words, *monibus errat* ("Ripheans [*monibus* combined with *Ripheis*] … veers"), may echo the end of Sedulius *Carmen Paschale* 1.211 (*monibus errans*). Aldhelm's knowledge of the non-fixed location of the North Pole reflects astronomical sophistication that might surprise readers, but he probably learned this fact through research on the Easter controversy. Bede was also keenly interested in Arcturus. In *De temporibus* 34.5–6, probably written about five years before Aldhelm's death, Bede discusses Arcturus in some detail.

l. 7 The words *stigiaque palude* ("to marsh … By Styx") may echo Virgil *Aeneid* 6.323 (*stygiamque paludem*) and 6.369 (*stygiamque … paludem*).

l. 8 I have retained the *Pars cuius* ("Whose ... reaches") of Ehwald over the *Cui pars* of Orchard (forthcoming).

Riddle 54: There has been debate about the details of this cooking vessel, most of which tries to read too much into the riddle. See generally von Erhardt-Siebold, "An Archaeological Find in a Latin Riddle of the Anglo-Saxons," *Speculum* 7, no. 2 (1932) at 252–6. For Anglo-Saxons, images of seething water often stirred unease. Cf. n.49; Lockett at 59.

ll. 1–2 These lines are probably corrupt. The Stork manuscript has *tantarum foedera rerum* for *tantis spectacula causa* at the end of line 1 and *morum* for *rerum* in line 2, a version also supported by Orchard (forthcoming). I have identified no precedent for *spectacula causis* ("reasons for these shows"), but have for the alternative. See Lucan *Bellum civile* 2.2 (*foedera rerum*). Nonetheless, I have followed Ehwald because I think the observation about the "shows" better reflects Aldhelm's fascination with this image. Cf. *Aenigmata* 49. Moreover, it is unlikely that Aldhelm would have used *foedera* twice in one riddle.

l. 2 The phrase *contraria fata* ("clashing fates") echoes Virgil *Aeneid* 1.239 (*contraria fata*). Cf. *Carmen de virginitate* 1171 (*contraria fata*).

l. 3 The term *larem* ("flame") refers to one of the Lares, the minor household gods who ruled the hearth. Here it is a metonym for fire.

I collapsed *viscere ventris* (literally "organs of the stomach") into the more concise but less alliterative "innards."

l .4 The phrase *vincunt incendia* ("quell their fiery glows") echoes Sedulius *Carmen Paschale* 1.187 (*vincunt incendia*).

l. 5 The phrase *ignibus … atris* ("deadly fires") echoes Sedulius *Carmen Paschale* 3.300 (*ignibus atris*).

The phrase *flumina fontis* ("streams from springs") echoes Ovid *Metamorphoses* 14.788 (*flumina fontis*).

l. 6 The phrase *foedera pacis* ("truce" – literally "bonds of peace") was common. Cf. *Carmen de virginitate* 2628 (*foedera pacis*).

Riddle 55: A chrismal (or *ciborium*) is a container for holding the Eucharist. Many seventh-century chrismals were portable and worn with a chain around the neck. See von Erhardt-Siebold, "Aldhelm's Chrismal," *Speculum* 10, no. 3 (1935) at 276–80.

l. 1 The phrase *divino munere* ("with God's gift") was rare among classical authors. But see Cicero *Orationes de Haruspicium Responso* 6. Likely sources are Augustine or Gregory the Great. See e.g. Augustine *De civitate Dei* 13.18.3, *Sermones* 10.10.1, 21.130.2, 41.258.2; Gregory the Great *Moralia in Iob* 11.10.3,16.41.2, 23.24.4 (twice), 23.25.10, 23.27.2, 24.7.3, 29.23.2.

l. 3 Glosses suggest that "corners" is the best translation of *aulis*, which makes more sense than standard definitions given *quaternis* ("four"). See von Erhardt-Siebold *supra* at 278.

l. 4 Several commentators have suggested that *fulvis … metallis* ("gilded") might echo Corippus *In laudem Iustini* 3.100 (*fulvo metallo*). Another possibility is Fortunatus *Vita Sancti Martini* 4.315 (*fulva metallis*).

l. 5 Orchard (1994) was the first to note parallels between this riddle and Eucheria's delightful sixth-century *Carmen Eucheriae*, also known as her *Adynata* ("Impossibilities"), which is the earliest extant humorous poem in Latin by a woman. Her poem in elegiac couplets has many aspects that undoubtedly appealed to Aldhelm: its dry self-deprecatory humour, its delight in paradoxical fusions, its poke at class distinctions, and even its use of the classical "golden line." Eucheria was probably the wife of one of Fortunatus's literary friends, Dinamius of Marseille.

This line may echo the poem's opening line (*Aurea concordi quae fulgent fila metallo*). Cf. Corippus *In laudem Iustini*, 3.100 (*fulvo chrysatica vina metallo*). For your amusement and comparisons with Riddle 100, I offer my loose translation of the *Carmen Eucheriae*:

Eucheria's Impossibilities

I'm longing for my golden metal threads that shine
  and bristly knotted hair to intertwine.

I chat about a gemstone-studded Chinese coat
  as if it were a garment made of goat.

A prince's purple and a homely rag are wed;
  a brilliant gem is fused with heavy lead.

Now let the pearl be robbed of glittering appeal
  and may it glow inside some gloomy steel.

Let emeralds be guarded with the Gallic brass;
  may sapphires now equal stones in class.

The jaspers, cliffs, and boulders are the same, it's said.
  The moon now chooses darkness of the dead.

Let us tend lilies now where mingled bramble grows;
  may dreaded hemlock clutch the crimson rose.

So, piling on, let us now wish for garbage fish
  while passing up a tasty seafood dish.

Let a toad love a bream, a bass his serpent too;
  may trout and snail pursue their rendezvous.

Let noble lioness and lowly fox romance;
  may a chimp give a pretty lynx a chance.

Let buck and donkey, tigress, and wild ass now date;
  may nimble deer and sluggish cattle mate.

Now let a bitter herb befoul the sweet rose wine;
    may honey and repulsive gall combine.

Let's blend a canyon's crystal water with the mud;
    may our refreshing fountain stir up crud.

Let ghastly buzzard and swift swallow have their fling;
    may gloomy owl and nightingale now sing.

Let somber screech-owl and his flashy partridge nest;
    may raven and sweet dove embrace at rest.

Let creatures trade their turf for unknown area
    as hick and slave pursue Eucheria.   (A.M Juster, trans.)

For the original Latin text and an uneven "literal" translation, see Marcovich and Georgiadou, "Eucheria's *Adynata*," *Illinois Classical Review* 13, no. 1 (1988) 165–74; see also Santelia, "Per amare Eucheria Anth.Lat. 386 Shackleton Bailey Saggio introduttivo, traduzione e note," *Collection Margini* no. 68, Palomar di Alternative, Bari (2005). A comparison of this poem with the *Aenigmata* reveals some parallels in vocabulary. Line 25 contains the word *hirundo* ("swallow"), the answer to Riddle 47. Line 30 has *corvo* ("crow") and *columba* ("dove"), the answers to Riddles 63 and 64 respectively. Line 12 also has the rare *Sericeum* ("Chinese"). Cf. n.12 *supra*.

l. 7 This line's *species flagrat pulcherrima* ("most gorgeous splendour") may echo line 28 of the *Versus sibyllae de iudicio Dei*, a Latin translation of a poem from an obscure Greek collection of acrostics. See Bischoff and Lapidge at 185–6; Orchard (1994) at 195–200.

l. 8 The phrase *gloria rerum* ("matters' glory") may echo Juvencus *Evangelia* 1.436 (*gloria rerum*).

l. 9 The last two words of this riddle, *tecta columnis* ("roof … columns"), may echo the last two words of Statius *Thebaid* 7.44 (*tecta columnis*). The word *columnis* probably resonated for Aldhelm with important figurative connotations. In the *Laterculus Malalianus*, see Stevenson at 146–7, Theodore of Tarsus used the phrase *duodecim ecclesiae columnae* ("twelve pillars of the Church") to describe the Apostles. See also Stevenson at 212–13; cf. *Altus prosator* M.4 (*columnis sustentatibus*).

Riddle 56: Beavers were not yet extinct in Britain during Aldhelm's time. Their fur, meat, teeth, and most of all, their inguinal glands (which produce a musky material they called *castoreum*) were highly prized. Medicine for many ills had been treated with *castoreum* for hundreds of years before Aldhelm. Authors who confused the inguinal glands with testicles, such as Claudius Aelianus (ca. 175–ca. 235 A.D.) in *De natura animalium*, claimed that beavers chewed off their own testicles and left them behind to placate hunters. Scholfield at 51 (" … it understands the reason why hunters come after it with such eagerness and impetuosity, and it puts down its head and with its teeth cuts off its testicles and throws them in its path, as a prudent man who, falling into the hands of robbers, sacrifices all that he is carrying, to save his life, and forfeits his possessions by way of ransom. If however it has already saved its life by self-castration and is again pursued, then it stands up and reveals that it offers no ground for their eager pursuit, and releases the hunters from all further exertions, for they esteem its flesh less"). For less entertaining, but similar, accounts, see Pliny *Naturalis historia* 8.47; Isidore *Etymologiae* 12.2.21. One Old English gloss even suggests, wrongly, that the Latin word *castor* ("beaver") is derived from the gerund *castrando* ("castrating"). See Stork at 170. Cf. Katz, "Hittite taskŭ- and the Indo-European Word for Badger," *Historiche Sprachforschung* 11, no.1 (1998) at 77–9.

l. 1 The phrase *in margine ripae* ("on … river banks") is Ovidian. See *Metamorphoses* 1.730 (*in margine ripae*), 5.559 (*margine ripae*), *Heroides* 5.29 (*margine ripae*); cf. Silius *Punica* 6.165 (*margine ripae*); Statius *Thebaid* (*margine ripae*).

l. 2 The phrase *belliger armis* ("armed … for war") echoes Fortunatus *Vita Sancti Martini* 1.112, 1.458 (*belliger armis*). See n.Praef.30 *supra*.

l. 3 The phrase *duro … labore* ("through my sweat" – literally "through hard work") probably echoes Virgil *Georgica* 4.114 (*ipse labore manum duro terat*); cf. Corippus *Iohannid* 1.2 (*durosque labores*).

ll. 5–9 This poem concludes with a succession of powerful Christian images: fish, immersion in water, healing, and the taking of fragments of wood, but the poem remains playful in an offhand way instead of didactic.

l. 9 The phrase *cortice … amara* ("bitter bark") may echo *Appendix Virgiliana Culex* 281 (*cortice amara*) or Virgil *Eclogae* 6.62 (*amarae cortices*).

Riddle 57: l. 1 Jove, in the form of an eagle, kidnapped Ganymede, a Trojan of royal birth, on Mount Ida because he lusted after the gorgeous young man. The phrase "Troy's heir" in line 3 refers back to Ganymede. This line is not an exact quotation, but the phrase *Iovus armiger* ("Jove's … knight") appears to be taken from Virgil *Aeneid* 5.255 (*Armiger … Iovus*). Cf. Apuleius *Metamorphoses* 3.23 (*supremi Iovis nuntius vel laetus armiger*). Michael Herren has discussed this anomaly, which he attributes to Aldhelm's anxieties about the tensions between the Christian and classical traditions. See Herren, "The Transmission and Reception of Graeco-Roman Mythology in Anglo-Saxon England, 670–800," *Anglo-Saxon England* 27 (1998) at 95. One might extend Herren's argument to even more intense anxieties arising from an analogue for God engaging in homosexual adultery.

l. 5 *Arsantesque* ("screeching") may be a literary joke. Stork at 30 notes that the term appears eight times in Aldhelm's *De pedum regulis* and that in prosody it means "the raising of the voice on an emphatic syllable." Scott, in his article "Rhetorical and Symbolic Ambiguity: The Riddles of Symphosius and Aldhelm," notes that one of Aldhelm's sources, Isidore, also used the verb *arsare*, but to describe the sound of cranes. King and Stevens at 140. One can easily imagine Aldhelm chuckling at the image of pedants screeching like cranes.

The phrase *sub aethera axe* ("under Heaven's sky") is Virgilian. See *Aeneid* 2.512, 8.28. See also Ovid *Tristia* 1.174 (*ab aetherio personat axe*).

l. 6 The phrase *corpora fessa* ("from weary flesh") is another Virgilian echo. See *Aeneid* 4.522–3 (*placidum carpebant fessa soporem/corpora*).

l. 8 The phrase *praeclaro lumine* ("bright light") echoes *Anth.Lat.Ries*.678 (*praeclaro lumine*). Apollo ends both this riddle (*Phoebi*) and *Anth.Lat.Ries*.678 (*Phoebe*). See generally Housman, "*Anth.Lat.Ries*.678," *Classical Quarterly* 12, no. 1 (1918) at 29–37. Cf. Priscian *Periegesis*, 1072 (*praeclaro lumine*).

The verb *restauror* ("I'm ... restored") was rare in classical times. But see Tacitus *Annales* 3.72 (*restaurando*), 4.43 (*restaurari*). With its connotation of resurrection, it became more popular with Christian writers of Late Antiquity. Aldhelm's use of the Christian verb *restaurare* reinforces the identification of Apollo with the Christian God during this period.

Riddle 58: This riddle echoes vocabulary of the *Hisperica Famina A Text* at 133–6 (*Titaneus, polum, almi*) as Aldhelm is looking in the direction of Ireland. Those interested in this parallel should also gingerly consider corrupt line 288 as well as line 303 (*Titaneus occiduum*).

l. 1 The phrase *nomen adhaesit* ("stuck its name") may echo Horace *Sermones* 2.2.56 (*cognomen adhaeret*). See Orchard (1994) at 145. Cf. Symphosius *Aenigmata* 28.1 (*Nox mihi dat nomen primo de tempore noctis*).

The phrase *prima noctis* ("early evening") would have been powerful for Aldhelm. He would have joined observances, including the singing of hymns, for Vespers early each evening. See generally Lapidge (1996) at 321–31. The sight of Lucifer (literally "light-bearer") would have been a familiar part of Vespers. For "Lucifer" as a Biblical label for Heaven's rebel angel, see Lapidge and Rosier at 253.

l. 2 For the phrase *occiduas mundi ... partes* ("the western world" – literally "western parts of the world"), see Isidore *Etymologiae* 14.6.25 (*parte occidua*); Ammianus *Res gestae* 22.3.7 (*occiduas partes*). Cf. Jordanes *Getica* 1.4, 14.3, 58.9 (*parte occidua*); Bede *Historia ecclesiastica* 2.4.5 (*occiduis partibus*).

l. 3 In *Carmen de virginitate* Aldhelm equates Titan with Christ. See Lapidge and Rosier at 102. Cf. *id.* at 107, 126, 137, 177. Dipping *corpus ... almum* ("life-giving flesh") into dark liquid suggests the rite of Holy Communion. Line 16 of the epitaph at Bobbio for Aldhelm's approximate contemporary from Ireland, Saint Cummian, refers to the saint's remains as *almum ... corpus*. Stokes at 173.

For the phrase *oceano ... tinxerit* ("dips ... in sea"), cf. Jerome *Commentarii in Ecclesiasten* 1.5 (*oceano tinxerit*); Isidore *Etymologiae* 3.2.1 (*oceano se tinxerit*), *De rerum natura* 17.2 (*oceano se tinxerit*).

l. 4 Lucretius is an unlikely direct source for *glaucis ... undis* ("gray-blue waves"). *De rerum natura* 1.71 (*Ionium glaucis aspargit virus ab undis*). A more likely source is *Hisperica Famina A Text* 416 (*glaucis sub fluctibus ludicat seminarium*). Cf. Aldhelm *Carmen de virginitate* 813 (*aequora per vitreos bullirent turgida campos*).

I have rejected the *descendens* of Orchard (forthcoming) and retained the Ehwald *relabens* ("lost").

l. 5 This line probably echoes Sedulius *Carmen Paschale* 3.235 (*libera per vitreos movit vestigia campos*). Sedulius's line also drew the attention of Bede. Cf. *De orthographia* D 40.

I have rejected the *abscondens* of Orchard (forthcoming) and retained the Ehwald *recondens* ("hiding").

Riddle 59: The pelican was largely overlooked by classical authors. But see Martial 11.21.10 (*onocrotali*); Pliny *Naturalis historia* 1.10.66 (*onocrotali*), 10.131 (*onocrotali*).

During Late Antiquity the pelican was a symbol of Christ based on ancient tales that pelicans killed their chicks and then brought them back to life by wounding themselves and pouring the blood from their wounds on their victims. Without this background information, this verse of the Saint Thomas Aquinas hymn *Adoro Te* would be inexplicable:

> Pie Pelicane, Jesu Domine
> Me immundum munda tuo sanguine:
> Cujus una stilla salvum facere
> Totum mundum quit ab omni scelere.

> Faithful Pelican, Lord Jesus,
> Cleanse loathsome me in your blood,
> One drop of which can save
> The whole world from all its sins.   (A.M. Juster, trans.)

Jerome is the most likely source for much of Aldhelm's knowledge of pelicans. See *Isaias* 34.11, *Sophonias* 2.14, *Commentarii in Isaiam* 10.34.14, 10.34.15, 10.35.2, *Commentarii in Sophoniam* 2.41, 2.44, 2.45, *Leviticus* 11.18, *Deuteronium* 14.18, *Commentarii in Isaiam* 10.34.19. At least one scholar has questioned, incorrectly in my opinion, whether Aldhelm thought the term applied to a swan. See Bitterli at 143.

ll. 1–2 The phrase *de gurgite limphas* ("a stream/Of sea") echoes Virgil *Aeneid* 9.23 (*de gurgite lymphas*).

l. 3 The phrase *directo tramite* ("on my straight trail") may echo Ambrose *Hexaemeron* 5.7.18 (*directo tramite*).

l. 5–8 These lines may have multiple distant echoes of Prudentius *Contra Symmachum* 2.1.895 (*Cernis ut una via est multis anfractibus errans*).

l. 6 I believe the pun on "fields" is present in the original because *campos* can refer to the subject matter of a writer or orator. See OLD 5b.

l. 8 For a thoughtful analysis of how the phrase *caeli culmina* ("Heaven's heights") exemplifies Aldhelm's compositional techniques, see Lapidge (1996) at 261–70. This phrase predates the Christian era, see e.g. Silius *Punica* 3.624 (*culmina caelo*), but became more popular during early Late Antiquity. See e.g. Boethius *De consolatione philosophiae* 4.6.2.1 (*culmina caeli*); Augustine *Sermones* 41.297.1 (*coeli culmina*); Martianus Capella *De nuptiis Philologiae et Mercurii* 6.601 (*caeli culmina*), 9.919 (*culmina caeli*).

The phrase *Quae non errantes* ("for those on track" – literally "for those not straying") was rare. But see Cassiodorus *Exposito in Psalterium* 2.52.8 (*non errantes*).

Riddle 60: Aldhelm's sources appear to be Isidore and perhaps Pliny or Solinus. See Pliny *Naturalis historia* 8.31; Isidore *Etymologiae* 12.2.12; Solinus *Mirabilia* 53. Pliny's unicorns were more fearsome than the unicorns of the later medieval period – they were much larger and had the feet of elephants. Salvador-Bello badly misreads Aldhelm's description of this unicorn in order to fit this riddle into her assessment that the *Aenigmata* (and other literary riddles of the era) are rife with unconventional sexuality. She sees the unicorn and the virgin as a trope for bestiality, the baking bread of Riddle 70 as a trope for male arousal, Riddle 78 as a trope for a "female tavernkeeper and castanet-dancer, who exhibits her arts in her alehouse," and Riddle 80 as a trope for a prostitute; these readings say more about their author's politics than the *Aenigmata*. See Salvador-Bello, "The Sexual Riddle Type in Aldhelm's *Enigmata*, the *Exeter Book* and Early Medieval Latin," *Philological Quarterly* 90, no. 4 (2011) at 357–85. (Riddle 60 at 374–6, Riddle 70 at 369–70, Riddle 78 at 372–3, Riddle 80 at 374–6.)

l. 1 For the noun *discrimina* as "travails," see OLD 4, 5. The phrase *saevi discrimina Martis* ("a battle's fierce travails") probably echoes Lucan. See *Bellum civile* 3.336 (*discrimina Martis*); 4.770 (*discrimine Martis*), 5.723 (*discrimina Martis*); cf. Silius *Punica* 5.660 (*discrimina Martis*).

The phrase *collibus in celsis* ("In lofty hills") echoes Silius *Punica* 12.567 (*celsis adstans in collibus*).

l. 2 For *moloso* ("hound"), see n.10 *supra*. For the phrase *frustra latrante moloso* ("a foiled hound bays"), cf. Ovid *Tristia* 5.510 (*latrantem frustra*); cf. *Carmen de virginitate* 1956 (*Ut lacerare solent latrantes fauce molosi*).

l. 3 The phrase *contorquens spicula* ("With ... arrows ... falling") probably echoes Virgil *Aeneid* 7.165 (*spicula contorquent*).

l. 4 For *fretus viribus* ("spurred by might"), cf. Livy *Ab urbe condita* 7.14 (*viribus fretus*); Ammianus *Res gestae* (*viribus fretus*); Valerius Maximus *Mirabilia* 6.1.2 (*viribus fretus*), 9.11.101 (*viribus fretus*), 9.12.109 (*fretus viribus*).

l. 5 For *elefantes* ("elephants"), see n.96 *infra*.

I have not identified an earlier use of the idiom *vulnere sterno* ("I wound before my kill" – literally "I lay out by wound"). For later uses, cf. Bede *Homilae* 1.23.4 (*vulnere stravit*); Notkerus Balbulus *Sequentiae* 6.8 (*straverat vulnere*).

l. 8 My heavy alliteration with b's tries to mimic the extraordinary repetition of p's in the original text.

l. 9 The phrase *celsam ... ad urbem* ("to the city on the height") may seem to echo *Matthew* 5:14, particularly for those who recall John Winthrop's "city upon a hill" from his 1630 sermon "A Model of Christian Charity" or Ronald Reagan's "city on a hill" at the 1984 Republican National Convention. That conjecture is possible, but the *civitas ... supra montem posita* of the *Vulgate* is not that close to Aldhelm's Latin. The phrase may be a Virgilian echo. See *Aeneid* 3.293 (*celsam Buthroti ascendimus urbem*).

Riddle 61: l. 1 The phrase *De terrae gremiis* ("from Earth's breast") may echo Solinus *Mirabilia* 24.17 (*gremiis terrarum*).

l. 3 Lapidge and Rosier at 83 suggest that goats provide the horn for the handle despite the obvious difficulties of that suggestion.

l. 4 The phrase *clauduntur lumina* ("I close their eyes" – literally "through me their eyes are closed") probably echoes Virgil *Aeneid* 10.746 (*clauduntur lumina*).

l. 5 I have collapsed *nitor defendere* (literally "I try to defend") to "I ... protect."

Riddle 62: The term *famfaluca* ("bubble") was rare and not used in classical Rome; they used the term *bulla*. While it is not completely clear, *famfaluca* may be a corruption of *pompholyx*, a Greek word for bubble. The charming *fanfaluca* survives in Italian as "frothy gossip."

l. 2 For *flumina lapsu* ("where rivers flow"), see Claudian *In Rufinum* 1.1.159 (*flumina lapsu*).

l. 3 The phrase *udo gurgite nantem* ("while I'm swimming by" – literally "swimming in a wet stream") may echo Virgil *Georgica* 3.446 (*udisque aries in gurgite*).

Riddle 63 The raven feeds on carrion, and thus was a symbol of war sacred to Woden in pre-Christian Britain. This riddle probably precedes the next riddle on the dove so that Aldhelm can contrast the roles of the two birds following Noah's flood. Cf. Sedulius, *Elegiae*, 103–4 (*Sola columba redit, quae totum circuit orbem/Discedant corvi, sola columba redit*). It is unclear whether Aldhelm knew of works by Sedulius other than *Carmen Paschale*. See Lapidge and Rosier at 98.

ll. 1–2 The striking internal rhyme of *truculenta fluenta* ("bloody flooding") lightens the tone of this riddle. When one adds *aequora* ("seas") in line 2, one may hear a slight echo of *Hisperica Famina* A-Text 28–9 (*subterfugio aequeuum/Dum truculenta*). Cf. 29 (*truculenta*), 42 (*fluenta*), 98 (*truculentus*), 101 (*fluentum*), 184 (*truculentos*), 211 (*fluentum*), 260 (*fluentis*). The choice of *aequora* over about a dozen options increases the likelihood that Aldhelm was engaged in some etymological wordplay with words such as *aequum* ("equal" or "fair").

For *genus humanum* ("the human race"), see n.63.7 *infra*.

l. 4 I have not found a precedent for the phrase *foedera iuris* ("what law decreed" – literally "bonds of law"). Cf. Livy *Ab urbe condita* (*foedera alia aliis legibus*); Augustine *Sermones* 11.113.3 (*naturalis foederis legis*), *Sermones* 11.113.3 (*foederis lege*). See generally Gladhill 53–63.

l. 5 Aldhelm would have known the phrase *subdere colla* ("yielding" – literally "to submit the neck" with strong associations of slavery) from many texts. See e.g. Augustine *Enarrationes in Psalmos* 18.2.15 (*colla subdere*); Dracontius *Carmen de Deo* 3.453; Silius *Punica* 10.215 (*subdere colla*); Statius *Thebaid* 1.175 (*subdere colla*); Prudentius *Peristephanon* 11.90 (*subdere colla*); Avianus *Fabulae* 28.2, 37.11 (*subdere colla*).

l. 7 This quotation is from Sedulius *Carmen Paschale* 1.175. Patrick McBrine noted for me parallels between 1.73–4 of the *Carmen Paschale* and the first three lines of this riddle, particularly *genus humanum* in line 73.

l. 10 Aldhelm uses the medieval word for "raven" (*corbus*) rather than the classical *corvus*. Accordingly, when the letter "c" is dropped, the speaker becomes *orbus* ("without kin"). The same trick of dropping a letter for the punchline occurs at Symphosius *Aenigmata* 36.3.

Riddle 64: For a prose discussion by Aldhelm of the same subject, see Lapidge and Herren at 35. Aldhelm also discusses the significance of the dove in *Carmen de virginitate*, which perhaps for him contrasted with the image of the birds' "shrill music" in the prologue of Persius's *Saturae*. Cf. *supra* at n.Praef.10–14. Cf. Lapidge and Rosier at 112 ("This bird, therefore, is blessed by the Holy

Ghost, since it alone is lacking the bitterness of cruel poison with which the brawling crowd of other chafing birds is vexed: this radiant, prophetic bird bears a gentle heart").

l. 2 The phrase *scelerum contagia* ("sin's contamination") echoes Lucan *Bellum civile* 3.332 (*scelerum contagia*).

l. 3 The phrase that ends this line, *iussa parentis* ("The Father's proclamation"), was classical. See Virgil *Aeneid* 7.368; Ovid *Heroides* 14.43, 14.54, *Fasti* 2.708; Silius *Punica* 3.169. The noun *parentis* can refer to parents collectively or to a parent of either gender. A source for its Christian incarnation may be Juvencus *Evangelia* 3.697 (*jussa parentis*).

l. 4 With *portendens fructu* ("Marking with fruit") Aldhelm is referring to the proverbial olive branch. Cf. *Genesis* 8:11 ("And the dove came in to him in the evening; and, lo, in her mouth was an olive leaf plucked off: so Noah knew that the waters were abated from the Earth").

l. 5 I have shifted the verb *gesto* ("I will bear") from the present tense to the future to capture the continuous action signaled by *semper* (literally "always").

l. 6 The phrases *cum felle* ("with spleen") and *sine felle* ("without spleen") were popular with both classical and Christian authors. Few authors felt the need to describe spleen as black. But see Pliny *Naturalis historia* 11.195 (*in felle nigro*); Isidore *Etymologiae* 10.M.176 (*a nigro felle*); Seneca *Oedipus* (*felle nigro*); Sedulius *Carmen Paschale* 3.190 (*nigri qui felle veneni*). In the *Carmen de virginitate* Aldhelm speaks of God's ability to transform ravens into doves "without grey bile." Lapidge and Rosier at 113–14.

Riddle 65: The term *muriceps* is a combination of *mus* ("mouse") and *capio* ("hunt"), so for my translation of the answer/title I have used the colloquial American term for a barnyard cat who hunts mice as opposed to the standard label for the lazier family feline.

l. 1 The phrase *fida satis* ("somewhat faithful" – literally "faithful enough") is Virgilian. See Virgil *Aeneid* 2.377 (*fida satis*). Cf. Claudian *De raptu Proserpinae* 3.118 (*fida satis*); Festus Avienus *Ora maritima* 252 (*satis fides*). As in this riddle, Claudian uses *latebras* ("shadows") a few words after the phrase *fida satis*, another hint that *De raptu Proserpinae* was one of Aldhelm's guilty pleasures.

l. 2 The phrase *caecas ... latebras* ("the pitch-black night") parallels Lucretius *De rerum natura* 1.408 (*caecasque latebras*), but undoubtedly echoes Virgil *Aeneid* 3.424 (*caecis ... latebris*). Cf. Ambrose *De fide ad Gratianum Augustum* 1.6.47 (*caecis latebris*); Festus Avienus *Ora maritima* 661 (*caecae tenebrae*). For the unlikely possibility Aldhelm read Lucretius, see Orchard (1994) at 129–30.

l. 4 The phrase *farris acervos* ("the barley bin") is Virgilian. See *Aeneid* 4.402, *Georgica* 1.185 (*farris acervum*).

The noun *Furibus* ("For ... thieves") took on more ominous undertones in the Christian era because writers sometimes used it as a term for "devils."

l. 5 The phrase *mortis insidiis* ("fatal snares") parallels Cicero *Orationes pro Cluentio* 197 (*mortis insidiis*). Alcuin knew some of Cicero's rhetorical works, although he may have acquired that knowledge in France. See Scragg at 99. The extent of Aldhelm's knowledge of Cicero, Quintilian, and other rhetoricians merits more scholarly attention.

l. 6 The phrase *lustra ferarum* ("beasts' lairs") was common. See e.g. Virgil *Georgica* 2.471 (*lustra ferarum*); Silius *Punica* 3.438 (*lustra ferarum*), 16.552 (*lustra ... ferarum*); Macrobius *Saturnalia* 4.3.9 (*ferarum lustra*), 6.2.4 (*lustra ferarum*); Jerome *Commentarii in Osee* 2.7.36 (*ferarum lustra*); Juvencus *Evangelia* 1.400 (*lustra ferarum*); Festus Avienus *Ora maritima* 549.

l. 9 The closing words of this riddle, *nomen habendum* ("given name"), may echo the closing words of Symphosius 74.3 (*nomen habebo*).

The phrase *gens exosa* ("loathsome tribe") probably echoes Ovid *Metamorphoses* 14.92 (*exosus gentisque*). The adjective *exosa* ("loathsome") was sufficiently rare that a definition was included in Isidore *Differentiae* 1.E.182 (*Inter Exosum et odiosum, Exosus dicitur qui aliquem, odit, odiosus, qui oditur*). With Aldhelm's allegorical mindset, he may have been thinking of the Jews as another *gens exosa*; *gens* ("tribe") was often used for descriptions of the Jewish people. See Lapidge and Herren at 157 ("the cursed race of Jews"); see also Augustine *De civitate Dei* 16.11.8 (*Hebraea gens*), 16.11.10 (*gens Hebraea*), 16.21.5 (*gens Israelitica*), 16.29.4 (*gens Israel*), 18.45.1 (*gens iudaea*); Sedulius *Carmen Paschale* 5.12 (*gens Iudaea*); cf. Jerome *Vulgata Tobias* 1:18 (*filios Israhel exosos*). For an overview of Aldhelm's views on the Jewish people, see Herren, "Aldhelm the Theologian," in O'Keeffe and Orchard at 75–7.

Riddle 66: Mills were common in Anglo-Saxon life (5,624 mills in the *Domesday Book*) and often sophisticated, although we lack extensive knowledge of their operations because only a few have been excavated. See Rahtz and Bullough, "The Parts of an Anglo-Saxon Mill," *Anglo-Saxon England* 24 (1977) at 16.

l. 1 The phrase *aequales ... sorores* ("sisters, partners") echoes Symphosius *Aenigmata* 79.1 (*aequales ... sorores*).

l. 3 For *dispar fortuna duarum* ("both fortunes don't compare"), cf. Sedulius *Carmen Paschale* 5.206 (*par est poena trium sed dispar causa duorum*); Macrobius *Saturnalia* 6.1.58 (*Virtuti sis par, dispar fortunis patris*); Tacitus *Annales* 12.17 (*dispar fortuna*).

l. 5 The phrase *Nec ... stimulis agitamur* ("We're unmoved ... by ... spurs") may echo Arator *De actis Apostolorum* 2.100 (*stimulis agitata*). Given Arator's many debts to classical authors, it is hard to identify passages in Aldhelm that reflect Arator's influence. See Orchard (1994) at 166–70; cf. Lapidge and Rosier at 207, 214. The phrase *invidiae stimulis* ("envy's ... spurs") has several possible sources. See Claudian *In Rufinum* (*Invidiae quondam stimulis incanduit atrox*); Ambrose *De officiis ministrorum* 3.11.75 (*invidiae accensus stimulis*).

l. 6 The phrase *ore patenti* ("wide maw") is probably Isidorian. See *Etymologiae* 12.4.16 (*ore patenti*).

In using the past tense here I have followed the sense of the line.

l. 7 The phrase *sine fraude maligna* ("without cruel fraud") is puzzling because *maligna* seems close to redundant. After all, how often is fraud good-humoured? The adjective *maligna* might have been metrical filler or added some dimension I have been unable to discern, but it appealed to Aldhelm. See *Carmen de virginitate* 1639 (*fraude maligni*), 2247 (*sine fraude maligna*). Aldhelm's probable source is Juvencus *Evangelia* 2.113 (*sine fraude maligna*); see also *Evangelia* 4.2 (*cum fraude malignis*); cf. Avianus *Fabulae* 1.11 (*fraude maligna*).

Riddle 67: This riddle has received relatively little scholarly attention. The term *cribellus* does not appear in the classical era, and was a rare word in Late Antiquity. It appears to be a diminutive of *cribrum*, the classical term for a sieve.

Anglo-Saxons used sieves to make bread and beer.

l. 1 The adjective *pruinosam* ("frosty") is Ovidian. See *Amores* 1.6.65 (*pruinosus*), 1.13.2 (*pruinoso*), 2.19.22 (*pruinosa*), *Metamorphoses* 4.82 (*pruinosas*), 5.444 (*pruinosas*).

For *crebris ... fenestris* ("close-set windows"), cf. Horace *Carmina* 1.25.1–2 (*fenestras/iactibus crebris*). Aldhelm may have seen an entomological connection between *crebris* ("crowded") and *cribellis* ("sieve").

l. 5 I found no precedent for *funere leti* ("rites of death"). The noun *funere* often meant "death" or "corpse," but its primary meaning was "funeral rites," which would seem to make *leti* redundant. But see Paulinus Petricordia *De vita Martini* 6.376 (*funere mortis*).

l. 6 The verb *fatescit* ("fades away") is a variant of the classical *facessat*. See Hessels at 112.

l. 7 With the wordplay of *ditati* ("those with wealth") and *Ditis* ("Hell"), Aldhelm appears to be punctuating, albeit playfully, a serious theological point. There is no clear inspiration for the memorable phrase *limina Ditis* ("gates of Hell"). Cf. Servius *In Vergilii Aeneidos comentarii* 6.136.30 (*limina Ditis*); Seneca *Hercules Oetaeus* 9.165 (*in primo limine Ditis*); Pseudo-Columbanus *Ad Stethem* 55 (*limina Ditis*). Aldhelm's access to Seneca and Servius is possible but not proven; the authorship and dating of *Ad Stethem* is hotly disputed.

l. 9 The verb *indurescit* ("it does jell") is Ovidian. See *Metamorphoses* 4.745, 5.234, 9.219, 10.105, 10.241, 15.306; *Tristia* 5.85.

Riddle 68: The term *salpix* is a medieval variation of *salpinx*, a military trumpet of the ancient Greeks that was approximately a metre long and usually made of brass and iron with a bone reed. See Krentz, "The Salpinx in Greek Warfare," in Hanson at 110–20.

l. 1 Aldhelm is playing with the paradox of something without substance moving not just man's flesh, but his spirit; it suggests a trope for the divine.

l. 3 The use of both *reboans* ("echoed") in this line to discuss a military horn and *cava* ("hollow") in the first line strongly suggests inspiration from Prudentius *Apotheosis* 1.386 (*Quidquid in aere cavo reboans tuba curva remugit*). Cf. *Carmen de virginitate* 372 (*Tum tuba raucisonis reboat clangoribus alte*).

l. 4 For an intriguing possible source for *interius … vocem* ("a call within"), see Augustine *Confessiones* 12.22.15.1 (*interius vocem*). Aldhelm knew Augustine's *De civitate Dei* well; it is not clear whether he had read Augustine's *Confessiones*, although Bede knew at least parts of it. See Fitzgerald at 132.

l. 5 Aldhelm appears to be playing on the two senses of *spiritus* (in classical times the primary meaning was "breath," but the secondary sense of "soul" became stronger in the Christian era) in order to make a theological point.

l. 6 More than a thousand years after Aldhelm's death, his *garrula … cicada* ("chirpy cricket") became a species. See Walker and Gray at 118.

ll. 7–8 For more on the *luscinia/acalantida* ("nightingale"), see Riddle 22. For the "Christianization" of the image of the *luscinia*, see Williams at 34–74.

Riddle 69: The yew tree, which can live over a thousand years, is a coniferous tree with seeds and flaky bark that are toxic. For a description of the effects of ingestion of only fifteen grams of the bark, see Veltmann, Borgette, Schrimpf, and Wolpert, "Yew Causes Brugada ECG," *Circulation* 119 (2009) at 1836–7. Yew bark contains a chemical called taxane that has significant anti-cancer properties, and one species of yew almost became extinct in the 1990s because of demand for its bark in the preparation of a breast cancer drug called Taxol.

Like hellebore, see n.98 *infra,* yew was used in Aldhelm's era as a drug despite its risks. The yew tree was a significant product and symbol in both the Roman and Anglo-Saxon traditions. Romans saw the yew as a dreary tree that thrived in inhospitable soils and climates, and Ovid wrote that it lined the path to the underworld. See *Metamorphoses* 4.432; cf. Claudian *De raptu Proserpinae* 3.386 (*pestiferos … taxos*). Julius Caesar recorded that a Gallic chieftain committed suicide with yew rather than surrender. *De bello Gallico* 6.31. Its wood was used in shields and it was preferred for longbows; it also seems to have been important in Britain's pre-Christian rites. Aldhelm probably relied on Pliny or Isidore for his technical information on the yew. See Howe, "Aldhelm's *Enigmata* and Isidorian Etymology," *Anglo-Saxon England* 14 (1985) at 43–5. Aldhelm had a somewhat charitable view of the tree and remarked on its beauty. See Lapidge and Herren at 37 (" ... like a leafing yew tree or a sprouting plane tree was adorned with charming decoration ... ").

In the *Harry Potter* series the evil Voldemort (whose original name was Tom Marvolo *Riddle*) used a wand made of yew.

l. 1 For the phrase *semper habens* (literally "always having" but compressed into "always crowned in green"), cf. Sedulius *Carmen Paschale* 4.55 (*semper habens*); Claudius Marius Victor *Alethia* 1.13 (*semper habens*).

This line may echo Virgil *Aeneid* 5.129 (*Hic viridem Aeneas frondenti*).

l. 2 Both words of the phrase *tegmine spisso* ("woven screen") appear often in the *Hisperica Famina*. See *A Text* 318 (*tegminis*), 361 (*tegmine*), 456 (*tegmine*), *D-Text* 143 (*spisso*), *Rubisca* 32 (*spissis*).

ll. 3–4 Boreas, Caurus, and Circius were Greek gods of wind.

l. 4 The verb *deglobere* ("to strip ... clean") is a Late Antique version of the classical *deglubere*.

l. 5 The phrase *fata reorum* ("the fates of things") has no clear antecedent. Cf. Ovid *Tristia* 2.93 (*fortuna reorum*); Florus *Epitoma* 1.32.2 (*fata rerum*). The "o" in *reorum* has given commentators dyspepsia, and Lapidge and Rosier at 252 dismiss it as a metrical liberty. The best candidate for inspiration would be Paulinus Petricordia *De vita Martini* 2.190 (*fata reorum*).

l. 7 My "any body" is an attempt to capture the dark playfulness of Aldhelm's *plura cadavera*. In essence, the yew tree is describing people who threaten it by eating it as what we would call the "walking dead."

Riddle 70: Although the term *tortella* ("Loaf of Bread") evolved into the Spanish *tortilla*, here it refers to bread rounder and puffier than a modern tortilla. It is perhaps not accidental that the material of the Eucharist rises immediately after the previous riddle closes with a reference to *cadavera*.

One should reject the Salvador-Bello reading of the baking bread as a trope for male arousal. See n.60.8 *supra*.

l. 1 The sense of the verb *orior* ("I rise") is similar to *scando*. See n.5.4 *supra*.

l. 2 The term *nive* ("snow") is a reference to flour. Cf. Aldhelm *Aenigmata* 67. It is also provides a paradoxical contrast to Vulcan's heat that imbues the shield with a sense of wonder.

l. 3 The noun *duelli* ("that take a blow" – literally "of war") is a variant of *belli*.

My use of "plate" for *scuta* is an effort to imitate Aldhelm's etymological wordplay –*scuta* is derived from *scutra*, a shallow pan.

l. 6 For *artus* as "bodies," see OLD 4.

l. 7 The proper noun *Orco* ("Orcus") refers to a Roman god of the underworld.

The ancient phrase *validis ... viribus* ("with great force") was a favourite of Lucretius, but if there is a specific source, it is probably the *Aeneid*. See Lucretius

De rerum natura 1.287, 1.971, 3.494, 5.1098; Virgil *Aeneid* 2.50, 5.500; cf. Ennius *Annales* 9.298; Apuleius *Metamorphoses* 3.6.2; Ammianus *Res gestae* 24.2.5, 31.15.3; Prudentius *Cathemerinon* 5.62.

Riddle 71: Fish were a key part of a monk's diet because Benedict's Rule did not allow eating of four-legged animals. The definition of "fish" that monks used for their diet was broader than ours, and it included seals. Studies of monastic sites indicate that Anglo-Saxon monks ate more whale and dolphin than expected. See Lovelock, "Wealth, Whale and Conspicuous Consumption: Flixborough and Its Importance for Middle and Late Latin Saxon Rural Settlement Studies," in Hamerow and MacGregor at 44–6, 93–4.

   Bern Riddle 30 (*De pisce*) has the same answer.

   l. 1 The manifestly pedestrian phrase (pun intended) *pedibus manibusque* ("Of feet and hands" – in line 2 of the translation) occurs in many texts Aldhelm knew or may have known. See e.g. Pliny *Naturalis historia* 26.7, 28.86; Augustine *In Ioannis Evangelium* 124.36.4; Symphosius *Aenigmata* 39.1.

   ll. 1–2 For *Arbiter* ("Judge") see n.Praef.1 *supra*. For *almus/Arbiter*, cf. Aldhelm *Epistula ad Eahfridum* (*almus arbiter*) at Giles at 92.

   l. 4 The phrase *corpora flatu* ("flesh … with respiration") also appears at Prudentius *Contra Symmachum* 2.815. The combination of *spiritus* and *corpora* involves the same serious wordplay discussed at n.68.5 *supra*.

   Aldhelm's use of the verb *vegitat* ("stir") in this line has escaped scholarly attention. The Stork manuscript has the standard *vegetat*, but *vegitat* was an occasional variant arguably going back at least as far as Ausonius. See Hennig, "Verus de Mensibus," *Traditio* 11 (1955) at 68. It would be easy to write it off as a transcription error, but it seems to be part of a pattern, possibly Irish-influenced, of substituting the letter i for the letter e. See n.Praef.8 *supra*.

   l. 5 This line refers to the constellation Pisces. The phrase *convexa cacumina* ("vaulted canopy") may echo Ausonius *Mosella* 248 (*convexa cacumina*).

   l. 6 The primary meaning of the noun *ponti* is "bridge," but here Aldhelm is using a secondary definition of "flat expanse" in a manner reminiscent of Anglo-Saxon kennings for the sea. This phrase *marmora ponti* ("marble sea") was rare in Aldhelm's time, but became a stock phrase in later Anglo-Latin poetry. It is possible that Aldhelm picked up this phrase from Festus Avienus, who overused it. See *Descriptio orbis terrae* 171, 232, 247, 497, 715, 773, 782 (*marmora ponti*).

Riddle 72: The title refers to one of the Seven Wonders of the World, the Colossus of Rhodes. Aldhelm's most likely source is Pliny *Naturalis historia* 34.18. As in Riddle 11, Aldhelm argues that man's creations, despite superficial resemblances, are inherently inferior to God's.

l. 1 The verb *plasmavit* ("made") was common in the *Vulgate* as well as the writings of Prudentius and other Christian authors of Late Antiquity.

l. 2 The phrase *membrorum munia* ("my limbs' functions") probably echoes Juvencus *Evangelia* 1.744 (*membrorum munia*).

l. 3 Orchard (1994) at 214–15 shows that Aldhelm at *Carmen de virginitate* 2177 only slightly modified the first line of an anonymous four-line poem misattributed contemporaneously to Ovid or Virgil. This observation strengthens the likelihood that the phrase *cernere possum* (with *nec* as the negative rendered here as "I cannot ... see"), which appears in the same location in the third line of the anonymous poem, influenced this line of the *Aenigmata*.

l. 4 The phrase *patulae constent sub fronte fenestrae* ("below my brow there's ventilation," more literally "below my brow open windows would stay") probably combines Ovid *Metamorphoses* 14.752 (*patulis ... fenestris*) with Sedulius *Carmen Paschale* 4.38 (*sub fronte fenestras*).

l. 7 The adjective *inorme* ("giant") was rare. But see Sedulius *Carmen Paschale* 3.265 (*Pavit inorme virum*).

l. 8 The phrase *sensibus intus* ("sensation" – literally closer to "senses within") also appears at Prudentius, *Psychomachia*, 1.7. See Clarke, "Technological Innovation and Poetical Exegesis: The Glass Lamp in Prudentius," in Otten and Pollman at 113–14.

Riddle 73: l. 1 The adjective *cava* probably means "deep" here; the most common usage of translators is "empty," but that rendering just adds a superfluous modifier.

ll. 1–2 For a thoughtful comparison of the water flow in these lines with Symphosius *Aenigmata* 71, see Bitterli at 103.

l. 4 The term *laterculus* ("chart") was rare, though it appears in works of writers known to Aldhelm, such as Jerome and Isidore. It originally meant a brick or tile, but came to mean a list, a computus or a calendar. See Stevenson at 1. Its rarity increases the likelihood that it was taken from the *Laterculus Malalianus*, which Stevenson has attributed to Theodore of Tarsus, Aldhelm's teacher. See generally Stevenson; see also Siemens, "Preliminary Enquiries into the Place of the *Laterculus Malalianus* among the Chronicles of Late Antiquity," *Journal for Late Antique Religion and Culture* 4 (2010) at 68–80. The *Laterculus Malalianus* also opens with an image (*obstrusis cavernarum rivulis*) similar to the imagery of this riddle, although the point of the imagery is very different. See Stevenson at 120–1. The image was also a common one in the works of Augustine, perhaps inspired by his reading of the Neoplatonists; for instance, in *Confessiones* 7.8.12–13 he discusses the riddle of how we recall that we forgot something, and then goes on to compare memory to a cavern.

l. 6 For the phrase *rutilantis sidera* ("glowing stars"), cf. Jerome *Epistulae* 4.121a.10 (*astra rutilantia*), *Commentarium in Isaiam* 5.13.13 (*astraque rutilantia*).

l. 7 The term *fluctivagus* ("choppy") was a rare combination of *fluctus* ("wave") and *vagus* ("wandering"). But see Statius *Silvae* 2.1.94 (*fluctivagus volucrem*); Prudentius *Cathemerinon* 3.46 (*aequora fluctivagos*); Fortunatus *Carmina* 7.20.6 (*fluctivagi ... litora Rheni*). Cf. *Carmen de virginitate* 5 (*fluctivagi*), 423 (*fluctivagi*), 1102 (*fluctivagis*).

Riddle 74: For more detail on David and Goliath, see 1 *Samuel* 17.

l. 1 The phrase *aequore campi* ("flat ... fields") is Virgilian. See *Aeneid* 7.781, 12.710. See also Silius *Punica* 5.376; Statius *Thebaid* 10.736.

Translators have rendered the adjective *Glauca* ("light-blue") as "gleaming" and "bright," but I prefer a word that captures the colour of flax flowers. Classical and Christian writers often used *glauca* (from which our word "glaucoma" comes) to describe eyes. See e.g. Solinus *Mirabilia* 16.5 (*glauca oculis*), 53.37 (*glaucis oculis*); Isidore *Etymologiae* 9.2.65 (*glauca oculis*); Ambrose *Hexaemeron* 5.24.86 (*glaucis oculorum*); Pliny *Naturalis historia* 7.12 (*glauca oculorum*).

l. 2 Not that I am suggesting a direct connection, but Lucretius often used the rare *primordia* (collapsed into "my start" in line 1 – literally "my early destiny"); I suspect Aldhelm found the word in Juvencus. Cf. Juvencus *Evangelia* 2.203 (*primordia vitae*); *Carmen de virginitate* 176 (*primordiae vitae*).

The verb *tradebant* ("began") is problematic here. Cf. OLD 7.

l. 3 For *constant* (plus the dative *mihi*) as "make me," see OLD 8.

I retained Ehwald's *retinacula* ("bands") over Orchard's *nam bracchia* in the belief that *retinacula* makes better sense and *nam* is awkward.

l. 5 The term *falanges* ("brawlers") is derived from the Greek word *phalangos* for "fingers." Our term "phalanx" is derived from these words, which had a more technical meaning than it does today. In Aldhelm's time, *falanges* would have been close to a synonym for the Anglo-Saxon *sceld trume* ("shield wall"), which referred to a tightly-packed rectangular formation of soldiers who formed a human wall. The effectiveness of such phalanxes depended on troops holding their positions no matter how brutal the onslaught. Cf. *Carmen de virginitate* 1550 (*falanges*). The Lapidge and Rosier translation of this term at 86 as "Gentiles" is misguided.

l. 7 For the phrase *duris ... cuspite contis* ("hard-tipped ... spears"), cf. Virgil *Aeneid* 5.208 (*acuta cuspide contos*).

l. 8 The phrase *super ardua* ("to great height") may echo Symphosius *Aenigmata* 35.2 or Lucan *Bellum civile* 1.397, 4.739, 6.138. Cf. Ausonius *Mosella* 154;

Macrobius *Saturnalia* 6.2.25; Prudentius *Contra Symmachum* 1.1.148; Silius *Punica* 4.75, 11.243.

I have not translated *totum* ("all") due to metrical constraints, and would have liked to use "my whole body."

l. 9 The Stork manuscript has *extendor* for *et tendor* ("and … I soar"), which has some appeal, but the line does not work well without the conjunction.

Riddle 75: ll. 1–6 Aldhelm begins this riddle with the same end-rhyme in the first six lines, and then returns to that same end-rhyme in lines 10 and 12. This embrace of monorhyme (otherwise known as homoeoteleuton) almost surely reflects Irish influence.

l. 1 The verb *remigo* ("I thrash") meant "I row" in classical Latin, but eventually *remigo* would develop the sense in Italian of "I flap." While I will leave it to philologists to decide whether that sense had emerged in the Latin of Aldhelm's time, I thought it better to use "I thrash" instead of the "I row" of Orchard, the "I soar" of Lapidge and Rosier, the "I fly" of Stork, or the "I sail" of Pitman.

l. 2 The phrase *grossae … murmura vocis* ("low grumblings") probably echoes Ovid *Metamorphoses* 12.49 (*murmura vocis*). See also Dracontius *De laudibus Dei* 3.633 (*murmura voces*).

l. 3 Aldhelm also used the phrase *densis … turmis* ("thick swarms") in his *Carmen de virginitate* 2348. The most likely source is the *Appendix Virgiliana*. See *Culex* at 248 (*densas … turmas*). For a brief delightful attack on the legitimacy of this line from *Culex*, see Housman, "Remarks on the *Culex*," *Classical Review* 16, no. 7 (1902) at 343. Cf. Tibullus 3.7.196 (*densis … turmis*).

l. 5 Classical writers knew that some hornets produce honey. See Kelhoffer, "John the Baptist's 'Wild Honey' and 'Honey' in Antiquity," *Greek, Roman and Byzantine Studies* 45 (2005) at 64. Hornet honey is still generally considered inedible, although today there is a small market for honey from certain hornets.

l. 6 For *foedera pacis* ("bonds of peace"), see n.54.6 *supra*.

l. 12 For the verb *constant* ("carry") in the sense of "be comprised of," see OLD 3a.

Riddle 76: The answer to this riddle reflects Aldhelm's embrace of a legend that took root in Late Antiquity and continued to blossom until it culminated in the *Legenda aurea* (or *Legenda sanctorum*) of Jacobus de Voragine in 1260. The short version of the story is that the Cross on which Jesus was crucified was made from wood from the apple tree that produced the apple that caused Adam and Eve to sin. There is a huge amount of literature *after* Aldhelm that contains this version of the crucifixion, but very little *before* Aldhelm, which is why I am grateful to Maryann Corbett for bringing to my attention a possible source, the Fortunatus hymn *Pange lingua*.

l. 1 The phrase *nascentis origo* ("Our newborn race") echoes Corippus *Iohannis* 3.45 (*nascentis origo*). Aldhelm also uses it in *Carmen de virginitate* 744.

l. 2 The phrase *prostatus succumberet* ("made it cursed") is a bit problematic and a literal translation would probably closer to the "it was laid full low" of Orchard (forthcoming).

l. 4 Pitman at 77, albeit tentatively, notes the apple/evil pun in *mala*.

l. 5 The phrase *remeasse salutem* ("renewed salvation") echoes Juvencus *Evangelia* 1.748 and 2.343 (*remeasse salutem*). Cf. Paulinus Petricordia *De vita Martini* 5.611 (*remeasse salutem*).

l. 6 For *arbiter* ("the Judge"), see n.Praef.1 *supra*.

l. 7 The phrase *soboles veneranda Tonantis* ("Thunder's Holy Son") makes an identification of Jesus with Jupiter that was common in early Christian epics. See n.81.6 *infra*. This phrase most closely echoes Juvencus *Evangelia* 4.672 (*soboles veneranda tonantis*) and 4.786 (*proles veneranda tonantis*). Among others, Arator, Boethius, Cassiodorus, Dracontius, Fortunatus, Jerome, Prudentius, and Sedulius also used the name *Tonantis* to refer to the Christian God. See n.81.6 *infra*. The noun *soboles* ("son"), the medieval form of *suboles*, is a rare word whose primary meaning is "a young shoot of a mature plant," but it has a secondary meaning of "human offspring."

The phrase *poenas lueret* ("paid reparation") is a tricky one. Despite my respect for their work, I believe that Lapidge and Rosier at 86 mistranslated *poenas* by rendering it as "sins." *Poenas* generally means "pains" or "punishments," and "sins" stretches *poenas* beyond a defensible reading. Cf. *Carmen de virginitate* 1186 (*Traditur idcirco poenis torquendus acerbis*). Lapidge and Rosier then, in my opinion, compound this error by abandoning customary usages of *luere* and using an uncommon definition that means "cleanse." While those two decisions produce a defensible philological version of this line, my opinion is that their version misses Aldhelm's theological point.

This phrase predated the Christian era. See Tacitus *Annales* 13.21 (*poenas lueret*); Valerius Maximus *Mirabilia* 1.1.19 (*poenas lueret*); Livy *Ab urbe condita* 8.28 (*poenam lueret*). It was also popular with Christian writers known to Aldhelm. See e.g. Augustine *Sermones* 10.155.7 (*peccati poenam mortis lueret*), 20.214.8 (*poenas debitas lueret*); Dracontius *De laudibus Dei* 3.371 (*Dum lueret victor poenas*); Lactantius *Divinae instructiones* 4.11.2 (*poenas pro facinoribus suis lueret*); cf. Bede *Historia ecclesiastica* 1.7.3 (*poenam lueret*). The verb *luere* has meanings that make sense in narrow isolation, such as "avert," but in Christian writings *lueret poenas* consistently means something along the lines of "he paid the penalty." See e.g. Gregory of Tours *Historiae* 5.18.31 (*lueret poenas*); Bede *Historia ecclesiastica* 1.7.3 (*poenam lueret*). It has economic and legal connotations, and suggests that Christ suffered in order to extinguish a debt that mankind owed to God. The cleansing of sins may be a product of that act, but it is not the act itself.

Riddle 77: For references to fig trees, see e.g. *Genesis* 3:7; 1 *Kings* 4:25. Cf. *Matthew* 21:18–22; Sedulius *Carmen Paschale* 4.45–56; Solinus *Mirabilia* 33.34, 53.47. Aldhelm probably knew the special role that Ambrose assigned to fig trees in *Hexaemeron* 2.1.3 (*in hoc agro est ficus illa, sub qua sancti requiescunt spiritalis gratiae suavitate recreati*).

l. 1 The phrase *deprompsit tegmina vestis* ("covered us with clothes") probably echoes Juvencus *Evangelia* 4.561 (*tegmina vestis*). Cf. Quintilian *Institutio* 9.4.4 (*aut vestibus pellium tegmina*).

l. 2 This line echoes Sedulius *Carmen Paschale* 1.91 (*vinitor uvas*).

The adjective *egenum* ("broke") was rare in classical times, but popular among Christian writers. It often redundantly modified the noun *pauper*.

The rare adverb *elementer* ("kindly") perhaps came from Jerome *Commentarii in Isaiam* 15.54.51 (*et elementer quasi mixto cruore subrutilans*).

l. 3 For *irrita … verbis … frivola* ("a useless joke"), cf. 100.82. Jerome was almost the only writer prior to Aldhelm who used the phrase *irrita verbis*. See *Commentarii in Ezechielem* 8.26.15, 9.30.15, 9.30.33, 11.39; cf. Plautus *Amphitruo* 3.2.44.

ll. 4–5 These lines refer to Adam shielding his nakedness from Eve in *Genesis* 3:7.

ll. 4–6 Cf. *Altus Prosator* X.4

l. 6 My translation of *brumae … tempore* ("when winter blusters" – literally "in time of winter") is a bit more poetically intense than the language of the original text.

Riddle 78: l. 1 The term *Bacchi* literally refers to the god of wine, but his name was often used as a metonym for wine. For the phrase *pocula Bacchi* ("cups of wine"), see e.g. Virgil *Aeneid* 3.354 (*pocula Bacchi*); Ovid *Fasti* 3.301 (*pocula Bacchi*). Some poets who used this phrase used the ablative instead of the genitive *Bacchi*. See e.g. Priscian *Periegesis* 491 (*pocula Baccho*).

Salvador-Bello savages this line to read it as the beginning of a trope for describing a "female tavernkeeper and castanet dancer, who exhibits her arts in her alehouse." See n.60.8 *supra*.

l. 2 Aldhelm may have been putting a cheerier spin on a line from Sedulius. Cf. *Carmen Paschale* 1.75 (*sordidus inpressas calcabit vinitor uvas*).

l. 3 This line may echo Ovid *Metamorphoses* 13.395 (*purpureum viridi genuit de caespite florem*).

l. 10 This line may echo Virgil *Aeneid* 11.136 (*fraxinus evertunt actas ad sidera pinus*). Although there is no evidence that Aldhelm read Lucretius, *robora ferro* ("oaks by ... axe") parallels Lucretius *De rerum natura* 2.449 (*robora ferri*). In addition to *robur*, the Romans had *quercus*, *aesculus*, and other terms for oaks; it is not clear how they distinguished them.

Riddle 79: l. 1 The phrase *spurcissima proles* ("blighted son") also appears in Aldhelm *Carmen de virginitate* 1330.

l. 2 The likely source for *carmina vatum* ("bardic verse") is Persius *Saturae Praefatio* 7 (*vatum carmen adfero nostrum ad sacra*), the primary source for the *Aenigmata Praefatio*. Cf. Ovid *Epistulae ex Ponto* 3.4.65 (*vatum contra sua carmina*), 4.8.43 (*officio vatum per carmina facto*); Claudian *De Consulatu Honorii Augusti* 1.470 (*nunc mihi Tydiden attollant carmina vatum*); Festus Avienus *Descriptio orbis terrae* 1040 (*carmina vatis*); cf. *Carmen de virginitate* 1373 (*carmina vatum*), 1696 (*carmine vatis*), 1912 (*carmine vates*).

l. 3 The nouns *mater* and *creatrix* are nearly synonyms in a dense line, so I have collapsed them into "mother."

l. 4 For metrical reasons, I reluctantly collapsed *dicor* and *vocatur* into one "called."

l. 7 The phrase *communi lege* ("as we agreed" – literally "by mutual law") most likely echoes Jerome. See *Commentarii in Isaiam* 11.38.17, *Commentarii in Matthaeum* 1.5.6, *Epistulae* 3.79.7 (*communi lege*); see also Damasus *Epigrammata* 3.3 (*communi legi*); Ammianus *Res gestae* 14.7.9 (*lege communi*); Cicero *De re publica* 1.27 (*communi lege*); Cassiodorus *Exposito in Psalterium*, 2.96.2 (*lege communi*), *Variae*, 1.18.4 (*communi lege*).

I am grateful to Michael Herren for discussing *mundum ... quadratum* ("four-part world") and pointing me toward Isidore *Etymologiae* 3.12.1 ("De quattuor partibus caeli") as a possible source. He also indicated it is likely that Aldhelm was using *quadratum* interchangeably with the classical *quadrificus*. In subsequent research, I noted that the phrase appears in the possibly Irish tract *Commentarium in Marcum*. See Cahill, "Is the First Commentary on Mark an Irish Work?" *Peritia* 8 (1994) at 35–45. Cf. *Carmina de virginitate* 1632 (*per mundum soribuntur rite quadratum*); 1678 (*Sed Deus omnipotens quadrati conditor orbis*).

l. 9 The phrase *vaga saecula* ("passing time") has no clear antecedent and its meaning has divided translators. Pitman and Orchard have "wandering universe," Lapidge and Rosier have "unstable universe," and Stork has "wandering world." Given Aldhelm's interest in the dating issues of the Easter controversy and the fact that the previous line refers to the passage of time, I believe the better reading of *saecula* here is "time" instead of "world" or "universe." The adjectives "wandering" and "unstable" are inapt regardless of the translation of *saecula* because the line is describing the *status quo*, not the primordial chaos or the hypothetical chaos that *would* be created by an abdication of celestial objects. The adjective *vaga* must mean something closer to "changing."

l. 10 Pitman at 77 suggests that Aldhelm either confused *claudere* ("to close") with *claudere* ("to limp") or consciously accepted a metrical infelicity. The phrase *clauderet cuncta* is a cretic, which is an impermissible foot in dactylic hexameter. It is possible that *claudere* is a metrical joke – the metre limps at the point where the language hints at limping.

The phrase *chaos immensum* ("vast chaos") avoided the formulaic *chaos magnum*.

Riddle 80: Glass, both domestic and imported (mostly from Gaul and Rhineland), was common in Britain from around the beginning of Roman rule. Archaeologists have discovered many glass beads, cups and bowls in Anglo-Saxon graves. After the departure of the Romans, Britain produced little, if any, glass for several centuries until Christian conversion accelerated in the seventh century, although there is some evidence of glassmaking in Kent near Faversham. See Freestone, Hughes, and Stapleton, "The Composition and Production of Anglo-Saxon Glass in the British Museum," in Evison; Laing and Laing at 121; Blair at 283; Mitchell at 168–70; Lapidge and Rosier at 237.

l. 2 For *saxorum viscera* ("bowels of rocks"), cf. Cassiodorus *Variae* 12.15.4 (*montis saxorum visceribus excavatis*). Some of Cassiodorus's work might have been available to Aldhelm, particularly *De Anima* and *In Psalmos*, although it is unlikely that Aldhelm knew the *Variae*.

l. 5 Left-handedness was considered suspect ("sinister" comes from the Latin word for left), so most people in this period used their right hand. By holding the neck of a glass goblet, the crowds are "choking" the goblet. While there is a sexual undercurrent that begins in this line and continues through the end, Salvador-Bello's argument that this image is a trope for a prostitute is another example of her forced overreading. See n.60.8 *supra*.

l. 8 For *compressis* ("pressed thin") ... *buccis* ("kisses"), cf. Jerome *Epistulae* 4.96.2 (*labiisque compressis*).

l. 9 In order to make a tricky punchline work, I have taken liberties with *ruina* ("for nasty trips"). A literal translation would be closer to "for a disaster" or "with a fall," so I was trying to capture both the sense of disaster and the sense of falling in a way that tied in with feet.

Riddle 81: For classical authors, the name *Lucifer* (literally "light-bearer") meant simply "the planet Venus" or "the evening star." In the *Hexaemeron*, Basil describes it as part of God's plan and "the most beautiful of the stars ... thanks to the unalloyed and beautiful brightness which meets our eye." Schaff at 64. While Aldhelm also sees the star as *clarum* ("clear"), in lines 7–8, like early

Christian writers Tertullian and Origen, he makes the more modern connection of Lucifer with Satan's fall from grace. Cf. *Isaiah* 14: 3–20; *2 Peter* 1:19, *Revelation* 9:1; *Altus prosator* C.1-6.

l. 1 The phrase *lumine lumen* ("light with light") echoes the same phrase in Sedulius *Carmen Paschale* 1.313.

l. 2 The term *signifer* ("harbinger") literally means "sign-bearer."

l. 3 Aldhelm may have picked up the phrase *obliquo tramite* (collapsed into "angling" – literally "on an oblique path") from classical authors. See e.g. Seneca *Thyestes* 845 (*secat obliquo tramite zonas*); Ammianus *Res gestae* 16.2.10 (*tramite obliquo*). One cannot help suspecting that Aldhelm learned this phrase in his studies of astronomy and the Easter controversy. Orchard (1994) at 212–14 makes an intriguing case for influence of a poem by the Visigothic King Sisebut (ca. 565–ca. 621) that was often attributed to Isidore.

l. 4 Aldhelm may have found the phrase *Eoas partes* ("the East") in Ammianus. See *Res gestae* 16.10.1 (*Eoas partes*), 18.4.2 (*partes eoas*), 26.5.2 (*partes eoas*); see also Ovid *Fasti* 1.140 (*Eoas partes Hesperiasque*); Claudian *De Consulatu Stilichonis* 1.270 (*partes … Eoas*). Given this note and the previous note, one has to consider whether Aldhelm was reading *Res gestae* while composing this riddle. It is possible, though transmission of this text almost certainly relied on a single insular text copied prior to Aldhelm's time. See generally Clark.

l. 5 The phrase *Finis Indorum* ("India's lands") is probably Isidorean. See *Etymologiae* 9.2.45 (*Indorum fines*).

The phrase *lumina primi* ("early glow") may echo Virgil *Aeneid* 6.255 (*primi sub lumina*).

l. 6 Classical writers used the term *Tonantis* ("God's" – literally "the Thunder's" or "the Thunderer's") to describe Jove, but Christian writers of Late Antiquity often appropriated it to describe their God and to make it easier for pagans to relate to Christianity. *Tonantis* may have been a particularly useful appropriation for Aldhelm because many of his neighbors were still worshipping *Thunor*, the Anglo-Saxon god of thunder. See Dunn at 57–9. Similarly, *Phoebi* ("sun" here could be translated either as "sun" or as "Phoebus," another name for "Apollo"). Since the fall in line 7 clearly plays on "Lucifer" as both star and rebel angel, I have used the classical names as symbols.

It is possible that the phrase *lege Tonantis* ("to God's law") echoes an epigram of Pope Damasus. See Orchard (1994) at 207.

For the phrase *servata lege* ("service to … law"), cf. Ambrosiaster *In epistolas Beati Pauli* 1.2.51 (*Lex servata non fuerit*), 10.1.10 (*servata lege naturae*).

l. 7 The phrase *proterva mente* ("while feeling spiteful" – literally "with an impudent mind") probably echoes Gregory the Great *Dialogi* 1.4.25 (*proterva mente*).

l. 8 For *perculit hostem* ("undid a ... foe"), cf. Livy *Ab urbe condite* 30.35; Cassiodorus *Variae* 12.28.5; Claudian *De bello Gildonico* 16.

l. 9 The "six friends" are the other six planets of the seventh century (Venus is speaking and astronomers of this era counted seven planets, including the sun and moon).

For *gnarus* ("wise"), cf. 100.81.

Riddle 82: l. 1 The noun *quadripes* ("quadruped") probably came from Pliny. See *Naturalis historia* 8.89; 10.96; 22.17; 22.36; 25.83. Orchard (forthcoming) would emend this line to *Discolor in curvas deflecto membra cavernas*.

The phrase *in curvis ... antris* ("in burrows" – literally "in curved caves") is a curious one that I have found only in Claudian *Panegyricus Probino et Olybrio Consulibus* 209 (*curvis ... in antris*). Cf. Servius *In Vergilii Aeneidos libros* 3.674.1 (*curvis cavernis*).

l. 4 For the phrase *edidit alvus* (collapsed into "womb ... fertilize"), cf. Silius *Punica* 3.426 (*edidit alvo*).

l. 6 I have substituted *ore* ("mouth") for Ehwald's *aure* ("ear") based on the views of Isidore, the only writer known to Aldhelm with the bizarre opinion that weasels become impregnated through an unconventional orifice. Isidore *Etymologiae* 12.3.3. The phrase *praegnantur viscera fetu* ("My womb's impregnated" – literally closer to "My womb is planted with a fetus") may echo Juvencus *Evangelia* 1.140 (*viscera fetu*).

l. 7 The adverb *vero* ("though") is problematic here because its primary definitions suggest some connection between this line and the previous one, a connection which, if it exists, has escaped my interpretative abilities. Accordingly, I have uneasily relied on OLD 7b with its sense of "mild adversative force."

Riddle 83: I scoured this riddle looking for wordplay connecting the title and the Christian poet Juvencus, and found none. Despite his interest in Persius, Aldhelm restrained his satirical spirit and restricted his targets to animals, inanimate objects, and a few safely dead people from the pre-Christian era. Nicholas Howe, however, has argued for wordplay based on the verb *iuvare* ("to help"); in my opinion, this argument is one of the few in Howe's fine article that stretches too far. See Howe, "Aldhelm's *Enigmata* and Isidorian Etymology," *Anglo-Saxon England* 14 (1985) at 42. For a discussion of the influence of this riddle on Eusebius *Aenigmata* 37, *Collecteanea* 194, as well as *Exeter Book* 38, see Orchard, "Enigma Variations: The Anglo-Saxon Riddle Tradition" in O'Keeffe and Orchard at 297–300.

l. 1 The phrase *spumosis ... faucibus* ("with foamy lips") is a striking one without any clear literary antecedent. But see Claudian *De IV Consulatu Honorii Augusti* 549 (*spumosis morsibus*). While it may simply be the result of Aldhelm's observations of a creature common in his time, it may be drawn from martyrology, where both animals and their victims frequently foam at the mouth. Cf. n.83.6 *infra*.

l. 2 The phrase *bis binis ... fontibus* ("twice two fountains") describes a cow's udder. See Meritt at 81 (*stricelum*); n.90.2 *infra*. Anglo-Saxon cattle were small by today's standards, no larger than Iron Age cattle. See Wilson at 379–80. The heavy alliteration and assonance of *bis binis bibulus* introduced a comic effect.

l. 3 The phrase *cum stirpibus imis* ("with roots down deep" in line 4 of the translation) echoes Virgil *Georgica* 2.209 (*cum stirpibus imis*).

l. 5 The adjective *algida* was rare, which increases the chances that *algida membra* ("limbs gone cold") echoes Orientius *Commonitorium* 1.124 (*algida membra*). There has been regrettably little scholarship on the influence of Orientius on poets of Late Antiquity, but this parallel is one of several that suggests Aldhelm was familiar with Orientius.

l. 6 Aldhelm's basis for calling leather thongs *nexibus horrendis* ("horrible constraints") becomes clearer when one reads Aldhelm's descriptions of how leather thongs were used in the torture of the martyr Chrysanthus. Lapidge and Rosier at 129; Lapidge and Herren at 98.

Riddle 84: l. 2 For *bis duodenis* ("twice six"), see n.90.2 *infra*.

l. 5 The word *sinzigias* ("feet") was spelled erratically in Aldhelm's time; unpredictably, the initial "i" would become a "y," the "n" would become an "m," the "z" would become an "s," or the second "i" would become a "u." Section 142 of Aldhelm's *De pedum regulis* lays out a more detailed description of the concept. See Lapidge and Rosier at 218–19. Wordplay between metrical feet and human feet was almost a thousand years during Aldhelm's time, but the comparison to pigs' feet is a fresh twist that suggests that Aldhelm did not allow his poetry to feed his ego.

l. 6 For a discussion of the yew, see n.69 *supra*. This line echoes Virgil *Georgica* 2.13 (*populus et glauca canentia fronde salicta*).

l. 8 The phrase *florenti vertice* ("with flowered crowns") appears in the anonymous *Carmen ad flavium felicem* 20. Orchard (1994) at 200–2. Aldhelm was taken with it; he also used it at *Carmina Ecclesiastica* 2.20 and *Carmen de virginitate* 1698. Orchard (1994) at 202 notes a number of parallels between *Carmen ad flavium felicem* and Aldhelm's other poetry.

Riddle 85: There are many possible literary and religious sources for this riddle, but Aldhelm almost certainly had *John* 9:13–41 in mind, and in particular verse 39 ("For judgment I have come into this world so that the blind will see and those who see will become blind").

l. 5 The phrase *munere claro* ("a gift that's bright") may echo Statius *Silvae*

1.2.209 (*munere claro*). While *munere* may be a bit ambiguous, I think it is clearly closer here to OLD 5 than the "bounty" of Lapidge and Rosier at 89; Orchard (forthcoming) independently came to the same conclusion.

Riddle 86: Aries is a sign of the Zodiac named after the golden ram that rescued Phrixus but dropped his twin sister Helle in a strait later named for her called the Hellespont. Phrixus was stunningly ungrateful to his rescuer; he sacrificed the ram to Poseidon and gave the fleece to King Aeëtes. This fleece was later sought by Jason and the Argonauts in a myth retold in the *Argonautica* of Apollonius of Rhodes.

Orchard (1994) at 208 argues that an anonymous riddle, *De pariete et ariete*, which exists in fragmentary form in a ninth century French manuscript, may have influenced this riddle.

l. 1 For *rugosis* ("wrinkled"), see n.40.1–2 *supra*; for *rugosis … horrens* see also Ammianus *Res gestae* 19.2.3 (*rugosa horrenda*).

l. 3 The adjective *astrifero* ("starry" – literally "star-bearing") was rare, and I found it in the ablative singular among major classical and Christian writers only at Martial 8.28.8 and 9.20.6. Intriguingly, it appears twice in the ablative singular in the *Hisperica Famina*. See *A Text* 233, 387 (*astrifero*); cf. *B-Text* 177 (*astriferos*). In addition, at *A Text*, 233 it is preceded by the very rare word *ageas*, a word sonically similar to the *agmine* ("swarms") of this line.

l. 4 I have tried to mimic Aldhelm's heavy alliteration, albeit with a different consonant.

ll. 5–6 A battering ram was often used in military assaults.

l. 6 For *arcibis* ("fortress") *altis* ("tall") and perhaps a hint of a mock-heroic tone, cf. Virgil *Aeneid* 2.56 (*arx alta*).

l. 8 The punchline is only accessible in Latin. If you remove the *p* from *paries* ("wall"), you have *aries* ("ram").

Riddle 87: For more information about Anglo-Saxon shields, see generally Stephenson.

l. 4 Orcus was a god of the underworld who became a personification of death.

Riddle 88: l. 1 If you know your *Vulgate*, the first line of this riddle gives away the answer. Cf. *Genesis* 3:1 (*Sed et serpens erat callidior cunctis animantibus terrae quae fecerat Dominis Deus*).

l. 2 I have taken a slight poetic liberty with *late in mundum* ("through every field"), which literally is "widely in the world."

The striking phrase *semina mortis* ("seeds of death") echoes Corippus *Iohannid* 2.39 (*semina mortis*). Cf. Ovid *Remedia amoris* 81 (*semina morbi*).

l. 4 The epithet *scortator* ("The Old Goat") is derived from the verb *scortari*, which means "to be a whoremonger" or "to go whoring."

The phrase *metit ... falce* ("sickle reaps") echoes Corippus *Iohannid* 8.537 (*falce metit*).

ll. 5–6 The phrase *cornigeri ... cervi* ("antlered bucks") was probably inspired by Ovid *Metamorphoses* 7.701 (*cornigeris ... cervis*). Cf. Lucretius *De rerum natura* 3.752 (*cornigeri ... cervi*). For more on stags and snakes, see Pliny *Naturalis historia* 8.20, 22.37. The stag was a symbol of Christ and its struggle with a snake was often seen as a struggle between good and evil. See Bitterli at 155–7.

l. 6 The phrase *pelle vetustus* ("my ancient hide") raises interesting questions. I have identified it only in Ovid *Ars amatoria* 3.77 (*cum pelle vetustus*), a text Aldhelm would have considered scandalous, but one should not assume that Aldhelm read the text; he may have come across it in a quotation in some other text, or the linguistic parallel may be a coincidence. It is also possible that Ovid's racier works were guilty pleasures.

Riddle 89: The phrase *arca libraria* appears for the first time as the answer to this riddle; it probably refers to a wooden chest for books instead of what we would call a bookcase. See Lapidge (2006) at 61–2. This definition is reinforced by glosses referring to Old English equivalents such as *bocciste* and *boccest* that were written several centuries after Aldhelm wrote this riddle. For a fascinating article on maintenance of books in Late Antiquity and the early medieval period, see Humphreys, "The Early Medieval Library," in *Münchener Beiträge Zur Mediävistik und Renaissance-Forschung 32 Palaographie 1981* (1982); see also Ó'Néill, "Celtic Britain and Ireland in the early Middle Ages," in Leedham-Green and Webber at 69–90.

l. 1 Orchard (1994) at 154–5 notes a possible echo of Claudian *Carmina* 23.9 (*compleri viscera*) as well as a possible intertextual pun. See also Thornbury at 55.

l. 2 Lapidge and Rosier at 89 translate the noun *praecordia* ("my heart") as "entrails" – in other words as synonymous with *viscera* (translated as "inwards") in the previous line. In classical times *praecordia* was a vague term for the area of the chest. See Orians at 38–43. In the Christian era the definition narrowed to the tissue immediately surrounding the heart. See e.g. Prudentius *Psychomachia* 10 (*furiis inter praecordia mixtis*). For Isidore of Seville's thinking on this topic, which probably influenced Aldhelm, see Lockett at 211–12.

l. 3 The phrase *nequeo cognoscere quicquam* ("I'm not much edified") may echo Juvencus *Evangelia* 4.221 (*cognoscere quisquam*).

l. 5 For *tollunt* as "steal" instead of the customary "darken," see OLD 11–15, particularly 11. Orchard (forthcoming) at 18 independently came to the same conclusion with his "deprive."

For *parcae* ("Fates"), see n.45.6 *supra*.

Riddle 90: This riddle echoes Symphosius *Aenigmata* 92 on the same subject.

l. 1 The phrase *auribus hausi* ("to hear" – literally "to drain with ears") was common. See e.g. Virgil *Aeneid* 4.359; Ovid *Metamorphoses* 13.787, 14.309; cf. *Carmen de virginitate* 1132 (*Auribus hausisset*).

l. 2 The phrase *in corpora gesto* ("on my frame were borne" – active voice in the original) may echo Prudentius *Contra Symmachum* 2.301 (*corpore gestent*).

Heikkinen at 54 cites *decies senos* ("sixty" – literally "ten sixes") as an example of use of a phrase involving multiplication when the more straightforward expression will not fit a metrical scheme.

l. 4 For *quinquies … quaternos* ("twenty" – literally "four times five"), see n.90.2 *supra*.

Riddle 91: *Bern Riddle* 15 (*De palma*) is on the same subject.

l. 1 This line may echo Claudius Marius Victorius *Alethia* 2.42 (*omnipotens auctor mundi rerumque creator*), although Orchard (1994) at 217–18 rejects Manitius's arguments that Aldhelm knew *Alethia*.

l. 2 The Stork manuscript has *cui* for *mi*.

ll. 2–4 Based primarily on *John* 12:13, early Christians embraced the palm as a symbol for celebrations of the victories of the faithful, especially martyrs, over enemies of the Church, hence the reference to *victrix* ("victor") in line 2 and *martiribus* ("martyrs") in line 4, although it is likely that Palm Sunday celebrations did not begin in Britain until after Aldhelm's time. See Bedingfield at 90.

The phrase *nomen habendum* ("has named") in line 2 echoes Symphosius *Aenigmata* 74.3 (*nomen habebo*).

l. 4 The phrase *proelia mundi* ("worldly strife" - literally "battles of the world") also appears at *Carmen de virginitate* 2022. See Orchard (1994) at 16. Cf. Silius *Punica* 12.336 (*proelia mundo*). Corippus *Iohannis* 4.347 (*proelia mundi*).

l. 5 The phrase *caelestis … praemia vitae* ("their reward … of lofty life") probably echoes Sedulius *Carmen Paschale* 1.341 (*perpetuae … praemia vitae*) or Orientius *Commonitorium* 1.1 (*praemia vitae*). Cf. Claudius Marius Victor *Alethia* 3.621 (*praemia vitae*).The phrase *praemia vitae* had an Epicurean sense before it was appropriated by Christian poets. See e.g., Lucretius *De rerum natura* 3.900, 5.1151 (*praemia vitae*); cf. *Carmen de virginitate* 1226, 2019, 2275 (*praemia vitae*).

l. 7 For a helpful discussion of *victor* ("the … victor"), see Howe, "Aldhelm's *Enigmata* and Isidorian Etymology," *Anglo-Saxon England* 14 (1985) at 44–5. Cf. *Altus prosator* O.5.

l. 9 By rendering *frondigeris* as "from bowers" I took some liberties from the more literal "leaf-bearing."

ll. 10–11 Although the anonymous Greek author of *The Periplus of the Eryth-raean Sea* probably tells us (there is disagreement about the Greek term often translated as "coconut") that the lost coastal town of Rhapta (probably in to-day's Tanzania) had an active coconut trade as early as around 60 AD, I have found no literary or archaeological reference to coconuts in Britain – or most of the Continent – during Aldhelm's era. See generally Schuiling and Harries, "The Coconut Palm in East Africa," *Principes* 38, no. 1 (1994) at 4–11.

It is virtually certain that Aldhelm's palm is the date palm of Northern Africa and the Near East (with its delightfully Aldhelmian technical name *phoenix dactylifera*), and his likely primary source is Pliny's *Naturalis historia* 13.9.45, which describes three particularly juicy types of dates. Aldhelm refers to palm branches twice in his *Carmen de virginitate* and mentions Saint Paul being nourished by dates. Lapidge and Rosier at 106, 118, 120; Lapidge and Herren at 105–6. Dates from date palms were the source of still-popular wine; wine was also made from the sap of the tree itself. The *nectare* ("nectar") of the date is also a metaphor for the Holy Word in much the same way that the bees' honey is in Riddle 20.

I am grateful to W.F. Lantry for bringing the *Periplus of the Erythraean Sea* to my attention.

l. 11 Stork and Pitman have *ciborum* at the end of this line – almost surely it is a gloss mistakenly copied into the text.

Riddle 92: In his *Laudibus de virginitate* Aldhelm, blissfully unaware of Freud-ian psychology, compares a tall lighthouse to "the sublimity of praiseworthy virginity." Lapidge and Herren at 66. Lapidge and Rosier express some doubt about whether Aldhelm knew about lighthouses other than through Isidore *Et-ymologiae* 15.2.37, but I think that view underestimates marine activity during this period. Cf. Isidore *Etymologiae* 20.10.10. If one accepts the persuasive cir-cumstantial evidence that Aldhelm travelled once to Rome, he may have seen lighthouses in France, Italy, or elsewhere. His well-travelled tutors, Theodore of Tarsus and Hadrian, also undoubtedly saw lighthouses in their travels.

There is a persistent, but unconfirmed, legend that the Chapel at St. Aldhelm's Head in Dorset is the site of a lighthouse from Aldhelm's time. See Barker and LePard, "St. Aldhelm and the Chapel at Worth Matravers: Sea-mark, Lighthouse or Bell Tower?" *Proceedings of the Dorset Natural History and Archaeological Society* 126 (2005) at 148–56. One can see remains of two Roman lighthouses at Dover. See Blair, "Whitby in the Seventh Century," in Lapidge and Gneuss at 10.

l. 1 The phrase *rupibus ... cautes* ("the craggy cliffs" – literally "the cliffs with crags") appears at Festus Avienus *Ora maritima* 215.

l. 3 My translation of the catch-all noun *machina* ("scaffold") reflects intuition more than information. But see OLD 2. Lapidge and Rosier tried "construction-work," Stork and Pitman "mechanic art," and Orchard "construction."

l. 6 The exact meaning of the phrase *tramite flexo* ("as they lurch" – literally "on a curved path") is open to some interpretation. It may echo Claudian *De raptu Proserpinae* 2.1.99 (*tramite flexo*).

l. 7 The phrase *immensis fluctibus ... actos* ("pushed by huge waves") probably conflates phrases from several sources. See Virgil *Aeneid* 1.333 (*fluctibus acti*), 7.213 (*fluctibus actos*); Ovid *Metamorphoses* 11.721 (*fluctibus actum*). Cf. Dracontius *Carmen de Deo* 148 (*fluctibus immensis*), 150 (*fluctibus actum*).

l. 9 The phrase *in turribus altis* ("In lofty towers") is Virgilian. See *Aeneid* 4.187 (*turribus aut altis*), 9.70 (*turribus altis*), 10.121 (*turribus altis*). See also *Appendix Virgiliana Ciris* 192 (*in turribus altis*); cf. Ovid *Heroides* 16.181 (*turribus altis*); Silius *Punica* 13.102 (*turribus altis*); Statius *Thebaid* 11.219 (*turribus altis*).

For *flammiger ... torres* ("inflagrations" – literally "flame-bearing heat"), cf. *Carmen de virginitate* 1350 (*flammigeris*), *Carmen rhythmicum* 65 (*flammiger*). See Howe, "Aldhelm's *Enigmata* and Isidorian Etymology," *Anglo-Saxon England* 14 (1985) at 40–1.

l. 10 The phrase *ignea ... sidera* ("bright constellations") probably echoes Juvencus *Evangelia Praefatio* 3 (*ignea sidera*). It may also echo Lucan *Bellum civile* and its much-debated, possibly corrupt, 1.75 (*sidera ... ignea*).

The phrase *brumales ... nimbi* ("clouds of winter") seems as if it should be a common one, but I found it only in Festus Avienus *Descriptio orbis terrae* 1276 (*nam cum brumali ceciderunt sidere nimbi*).

Riddle 93: *Bern Riddle* 23 (*De ignis scintilla*) has the same answer.

l. 1 The phrase *robore tanto* ("with such great might") may echo Lucan *Bellum civile* 4.633 (*robore tanto*). Cf. Valerius Maximus *Facta et dicta memorabilia* 3.3.ext 1.5 (*tanto robore*). Aldhelm's wordplay here resists effective translation. The noun *robore* can mean either toughness or an oak; Aldhelm is implicitly comparing the spark to the matter it consumes.

l. 2 The words *viribus* ("force") and *audax* (collapsed into "terrify" with *fungi*) may echo Virgil *Aeneid* 5.67 (*viribus audax*), although *audax* may function here as an adverb modifying *nitatur* or *fungi*.

l. 3 The likely sources for the phrase *exordia vitae* ("life's beginnings") are Prudentius *Apotheosis* 1.169 (*exordia vitae*) or Juvencus *Evangelia* 2.190 (*exordia vitae*). Given the echoes of Juvencus in the next lines, it appears that Aldhelm wrote this riddle while rereading Juvencus.

l. 4 The phrase *prosternere leto* ("to slay" – literally "lay low with death") echoes Juvencus *Evangelia* 4.406 (*prosternere leto*).

l. 5 The phrase *penetralia ventris* ("internal organs") echoes Juvencus *Evan-*

gelia 3.394 (*penetralia ventris*). Cf. Cassianus *Collationes* 2.16.18.6 (*penetralia ventris*).

l. 6 Later poets picked up the phrase *nemorum … frutecta* ("bushes" – literally "shrubs of the forest") from Aldhelm, but it does not seem to have been used in poetry prior to the *Aenigmata*. This phrase does appear, however, in the Prologue to Book I of Fulgentius *Mitologiorum* (*Tandem inter sentosa nemorum frutecta*). Helm at 6. It is unclear whether Fulgentius's popular text travelled to Britain before Aldhelm's death, but it would be a mistake to rule out the possibility that the *Mitologiorum* was a source of Aldhelm's mythological references – as well as his attitude toward those myths.

l. 7 The Stork text has *collibus altis* for the Ehwald *molibus* ("mass") *altos* ("high").

l. 8 This line begins with a remarkable litany of rhymes and off-rhymes.

l. 10 As in Riddle 11 on bellows and Riddle 72 on the Colossus, Aldhelm's wonder at man's creations always falls short of his wonder at God's creations. The spark's *dura … alvo* ("stony womb") punctuates his point. The adjective *dura* flags that the *genetrix* ("mother") here is a flint. Flint mining in Britain started in approximately 3000 BC at the remarkable Graves Grimes flint mines. Shafts descended forty feet in order to remove tons of flint from these mines. See Longworth & Varndell.

I gingerly disagree with previous translators about the admittedly obscure *gentis*. Pitman just left it out of his version. Lapidge and Rosier at 90, as well as Stork at 218, use "of her race," but I think *gentis* refers to *primitus*, not to *frigida genetrix* ("My cold mother"). Literally *primitus … gentis* ("first in class") would be along the lines of "first of breed." Orchard (forthcoming) renders this line as "producing from the first the offspring of her kin out of her womb." Remember the significance of being first-born in Anglo-Saxon society; one can read this line as saying that the enablement of fire was more important than flint's other uses.

Riddle 94: The dwarf elder, *Sambucus ebulus,* is also known as "danewort."

l. 1 There is wordplay in the first and final lines. Both *putris … fronde* and *olidas fibras* mean "stinking leaves," although *fibras* might also refer to parts of an internal organ – in this case perhaps the bowel. I rendered *olidas … fibras* in the singular in order to introduce some similar wordplay with "relieves."

The Stork manuscript has the unlikely *botris* for *putris*. It also has the plausible *rubescit* for *virescit* ("grows").

l. 2 With *surculus* ("shrub"), Aldhelm has dropped a hint that the answer is the dwarf form of the *sambucus* ("elder").

The verb *glesco* ("I spread") is the Late Antique version of the classical *glisco*.

l. 3 The noun *corimbos* ("clusters") is the Late Antique version of the classical *corymbos*.

l. 6 Leprosy was spreading in Europe during Aldhelm's time; it is probable that leprosy reached Britain during his life. See Richards at 4–5; see generally Rawcliffe. It is also possible that Aldhelm confused leprosy with smallpox, severe psoriasis, syphilis, or other diseases. The *Canterbury Biblical Commentaries* and the *Iudicium de penitentia Theodori* (both probably notes of Theodore's students) have sections on leprosy. See Stevenson at 52–3.

Riddle 95: In *Carmen de virginitate* Aldhelm cites Christ as the pilot who can navigate the righteous through perils of the flesh comparable to the perils of Scylla and Charybdis. Lapidge and Herren at 67. Scylla was a gorgeous sea nymph who attracted the amorous attentions of a fisherman named Glaucus. A jealous witch named Circe, the daughter of Titan, transformed Scylla into a grotesque monster who inhabited one side of the Strait of Messina in Sicily while another monster, Charybdis, prowled the other side; her enormous mouth created massive whirlpools. In Ovid *Metamorphoses* 14.248–308, Aldhelm's most likely source, Ovid, described Scylla as having a female upper body and barking dogs below. Odysseus made it through the strait by passing closer to Scylla, but she ate a number of his sailors. Jason and the Argonauts made it through unharmed.

For a discussion of the relation between this riddle (and to a lesser extent Riddles 15, 28, 39, 72, and 96) and the anonymous *Liber monstrorum* (sometimes, but almost surely wrongly, attributed to Aldhelm), see Orchard (1995) at 86–102.

l. 1 For more information on Scylla's *molosorum nomen* ("canine name"), see Tsitsiou-Chelidoni, "Nomen Omen: Scylla's Eloquent Name and Ovid's Reply (Met. 86–151)," *Materiali e discussion per l'analisi dei testi classici* 50 (2003) at 195–203.

l. 2 The phrase *Argolicae lingua loquelis* ("Greek vocabularies") probably echoes Sedulius or Prudentius. See Sedulius *Carmen Paschale* 4.63 (*lingua loquellas*); Prudentius *Peristephanon* 10.928 (*"Christum loquenti lingua numquam defuit"*), 10.945 (*linguam loquellae*). Though practice varied, by Aldhelm's time *loquelis* was more common than the classical *loquellis*. The adjective *Argolicae* was a fancy way of saying "Greek," perhaps comparable to "Hellenic."

l. 3 The *dirae ... carminae Circae* ("spells of dreaded Circe") were evil because Circe summoned the powers of Hecate, the goddess of necromancy. Cf. Ovid *Metamorphoses* 14.44 (*et tritis hecateia carmina miscet*), 14.405 (*convocat et longis hecatem ululatibus orat*).

l. 4 The phrase *fontis liquidi* ("clear flow" in line 3 of the translation) is Virgilian. See e.g. *Georgica* 2.200 (*liquidi ... fontes*), 4.18 (*liquidi fontes*).

l. 5–6 The Stork manuscript has the unlikely *polite* for *poplite* ("knees").

This line may echo the *fumorum crurumque pedumque* of Ovid *Metamorphoses* 14.64, which describes the replacement of the lower half of Scylla's body with a whirlwind of loud canines. Primarily for this reason I have rejected Ehwald's *Cruraque cum coxis* for the *Femora cum cruribus* ("thighs with calves") of Orchard (forthcoming).

l. 7 The gerund *ululantia* ("wailing") was common in the *Vulgate*.

l. 8 The striking phrase *caerula findunt* ("cleave blue seas"—literally "cleave blue") may echo Fortunatus *Vita Sancti Martini* 4.275 (*caerula findens*).

l. 11 The phrase *latrant inguina* ("my loins … my ... bay") echoes Ovid *Metamorphoses* 14.60 (*latrantibus inguina*). Cf. *Altus prosator* K.6.

l. 13 The phrase *salsis fluctibus* ("on salt waves") probably came from Jerome. See *Commentarii in Amos* 3.8.28, *Commentarii in Danielem* 7.5, *Commentarii in Ezechielem* 8.25.32, 8.26.20, *Commentarii in Isaiam* 7.18.5, *Commentarii in Matthaeum* 2.14.23, *Commentarii in Zachariam* 3.14.11; cf. Cicero *Tusculanae Disputationes* 2.19; Augustine *Enarrationes in Psalmos* 64.11; Gregory the Great *Moralia in Iob* 28.19.2.

Riddle 96: War elephants were a regular part of the Roman army until the time of Julius Caesar. See generally Glover, "The Elephant in Ancient War," *Classical Journal* 39, no. 5 (1944) at 257–65; Cross, "The Elephant to Alfred, Aelfric, Aldhelm and Others," *Studia Neophilologica* 37, no. 2 (1965) at 367–73. Basil discusses the use of elephants in phalanxes in Homily VIII of his *Hexaemeron*. Cf. Solinus *Mirabilia* 26, 31, 53.

l. 1 This riddle's opening words, *Ferratas acies* ("As armoured troops"), probably echo Prudentius *Cathemerinon* 5.48 (*ferratasque acies*). See also Dracontius *Romulea* 5.28 (*ferratas acies*).

l. 2 For *vana cupido* ("with vain lust"), cf. Virgil *Aeneid* 9.769 (*furor ardentem caedisque insana cupido*).

l. 3 The phrase *foedera regni* ("civil loyalties") echoes Lucan *Bellum civile* 1.4, 1.86 (*foedera regni*).

l. 4 The *salpix* ("A trumpet") is the medieval version of the Roman *salpinx*. See *supra* at n.68.

The phrase *ventosis flatibus* ("with bursts of breeze") echoes Juvencus *Evangelia* 7.345 (*ventosis flatibus*).

l. 9 The phrase *gloria formae* ("pulchritude" – literally "the glory of my beauty") may echo *Appendix Virgiliana Culex* 408 (*gloria formae*). Cf. n.6.3 *supra*.

l. 10 I have not identified an antecedent for the phrase *letifer … finis* ("Doom" – literally the quintessentially Aldhelmian "The death-bearing end").

ll. 12–13 These lines refer to the ivory that remains after the elephant's death. The scholarly consensus had long been that ivory rings found in Anglo-Saxon graves of both men and women were made not from elephant bone, but from whale or walrus bone. See e.g. Lapidge and Herren at 254. However, DNA tests prove that elephant ivory, as well as Cowrie shells and amethyst bands of indisputably African origin, were buried in Anglo-Saxon graves. See Hills, "From Isidore to Isotopes: Ivory Rings in Early Medieval Graves," in Hamerow and Macgregor at 132–5. Cf. Symphosius *Aenigmata* 49.

ll. 15–16 Elephants are notoriously light sleepers.

Riddle 97: l. 1 The phrase *corpore tellus* ("with flesh of Earth") echoes Virgil *Aeneid* 12.900 (*corpora tellus*).

l. 2 The second "e" in *stereli* ("sterile") instead of the standard *sterili* may reflect Irish linguistic influence. See n.Praef.8 *supra*. The Stork manuscript, though, has *sterili*.

l. 3 *Eumenidum* ("The Eumenides") were Greek gods of vengeance. The fact that Aldhelm used Servius's description of these gods rather than Virgil's, a fact noted by Herren, suggests that Aldhelm knew Servius's commentary on the *Aeneid*. See Herren, "The Transmission and Reception of Graeco-Roman Mythology in Anglo-Saxon England 670–800" *Anglo-Saxon England* 27 (1998) at 96.

l. 4 *Tartaream* ("Tartarus' ") describes the lowest part of the underworld, the closest equivalent in classical mythology to the Christian Hell.

l. 6 For *quadratum mundi* ("the four-cornered world"), see n.79.7 *supra*.

For *caerula* as "gloom," cf. *caeruleum* OLD 9.

l. 7 The phrase *Est inimica mihi* ("incurs my enmity") probably echoes Virgil *Aeneid* 1.67 (*inimica mihi*).

l. 8 For *lampas Titania* ("torch of Titan" in line 7 of the translation), cf. Priscian *Peregesis* 45 (*lumine Titan*).

l. 9 Herren sees wordplay on *diri* in this line. See Herren, "The Transmission and Reception of Graeco-Roman Mythology in Anglo-Saxon England 670–800," *Anglo-Saxon England* 27 (1998) at 96.

l. 10 In the Stork manuscript this riddle ends on this line; the remaining lines become a separate riddle with the title *De fama*. See Stork at 224–6. Given Aldhelm's fascination with numbers, it is unlikely that the *Aenigmata* has 101 riddles instead of the 100 that would pay tribute to Symphosius's 100. After Aldhelm's death, Eusebius continued Tatwine's *Aenigmata* (which is highly derivative of Aldhelm) until there were exactly 100 riddles.

l. 12 This line quotes Virgil *Aeneid* 4.177 and 10.767, which are identical.

ll. 13–16 These lines quote Virgil *Aeneid* 4.181–4.

Riddle 98: Hellebore is a flowering plant mentioned by Horace and other classical writers that was used as a treatment for mental illness and other diseases despite its nasty side effects. To illustrate the general point that everything

God makes has a purpose, Basil's *Hexaemeron* states " … many times hellebore has taken away longstanding disease." Schaff at 77–8. See generally Brennesel, Drout, and Gravel, "A Reassessment of the Efficacy of Anglo-Saxon Medicine," *Anglo-Saxon England* 34 (2005) at 183–95; M. Cameron, "Anglo-Saxon Medicine and Magic," *Anglo-Saxon England* 17 (1988) at 191–215. Alaric Hall has made a persuasive case that Aldhelm confused what we call woody nightshade with what was called hellebore by classical authors. See Hall, "Madness, Medication – and Self-Induced Hallucinogen? *Elleborus* (and Woody Nightshade) in Anglo-Saxon England, 700–900," *Leeds Studies in English* 44 (2013) at 43–69. Aldhelm's tutor, Theodore of Tarsus, had an extensive knowledge of classical (primarily Greek) and Byzantine medicine. See Stevenson at 47–55.

l. 1 The term *ostrum* ("purple") was derived from the Greek *ostreon*, but the term *ostriger* ("decked with purple" – literally "purple-bearing") does not seem to appear before Aldhelm. See Lapidge, "The Career of Aldhelm," *Anglo-Saxon England* 36 (2008) at 42; Pheifer at 107. The term appears in an eighth-century glossary. See Hessels (1890) at 87. The suffix *iger* is derived from the verb *gerere* ("to bear"). The *iger* suffix survives in French in words such as *voltigeur* ("acrobat"). The adjective refers to the plant's flowers, not the stem or berries.

l. 2 The phrase *cocci … rubro* ("red-stained" in line 3 of the translation) echoes Sedulius *Carmen Paschale* 5.165 (*rubri … cocci*).

l. 3 In this line Aldhelm creates an image similar to his description of the death of Saint Paul in the *Carmina Ecclesiastica*. Cf. Lapidge and Rosier at 51.

The Stork manuscript has *vertice* for *palmite* ("branch").

l. 5 Severe neurological effects were among the side effects of hellebore.

l. 6 There has been little scholarly attention to the fascinating phrase *dementia cordis* ("heart flutter"), which may have been coined by Aldhelm and was not embraced by later writers. The wordplay of a heart being out of its mind must have almost surely amused him. Lapidge and Rosier read *dementia cordis* at 92 as "a certain touch of insanity." Stork at 228 is closer to the mark with her "madness of the heart," as is Orchard (forthcoming) with his "a madness of spirit." Hellebore does cause heart palpitations.

Riddle 99: Pitman points out that Aldhelm may be mimicking Symphosius here by building a poem around dubious wordplay on the name of a Roman historical figure. Symphosius Riddle 25 on the mouse (*mus*) puns on the name of Publius Decius Mus, and Riddle 32 on the bull (*taurus*) puns on the name of Statilius Taurus. Here Aldhelm is punning on the name of Camillus, the consul who captured Veii. Lapidge and Rosier at 254–5 are probably right that Aldhelm learned of Camillus through Lucan rather than Livy. Stork at 229 notes Isidore *Etymologiae* 12.1.35 and Gregory the Great *Moralia in Iob* 1.28.39 as possible sources of information on camels. Another possible source of information about camels for Aldhelm was Solinus *Mirabilia* 50. Cf. *Carmen de virginitate* 1496–7 (*Idcirco gelida constrictum morte camellum/Perdebat gippum*).

l. 1 The phrase *miles equester* ("knight") was not standard and might reflect beliefs of Anglo-Saxon culture rather than a detailed understanding of the hierarchy of Roman nobility. Cf. Sidonius Apollonaris *Epistulae* 9.13.34 (*miles ordo equester*).

l. 3 The term *gippi* ("hump's") is the Late Antiquity version of *gibbi*.

The Stork manuscript has *convectant* for *reportant* ("supports").

l. 5 The phrase *agmen equorum* ("herds of ... steeds") probably echoes Fortunatus *Vita Sancti Martini* 3.328 (*agmen equorum*). Cf. Caesar *Bellum civile* 2.42.5.3 (*agmen equorum*).

l. 6 The noun *quadripedante* (literally "four-footed") is a variant of the classical *quadrupedante*. Combined with *meatu* (literally "movement"), I have rendered the phrase as "gallop."

l. 7 The phrase *corporis ... artus* ("frame's ... limbs") probably echoes Corippus *In laudem Iustini* 2.193 (*corporis artus*).

Riddle 100: l. 2 Steen at 102 notes that *rector regnorum* ("Lord of lands") echoes the *regum regnorum* ("King of kingdoms") of the *Vulgate* and perhaps its Old English equivalent, *rice reccend* ("powerful ruler").

l. 3 For a helpful discussion of Aldhelm's use of the stock phrase *culmina caeli* ("spacious skies"), see Lapidge, "Aldhelm's Latin Poetry and Old English Verse," *Comparative Literature* 31, no. 3 (1979) at 226–8.

l. 5 The Stork manuscript has *valebo* instead of *iuvabit* ("it ... helped").

The phrase *pervigil excubiis* ("I stay on watch") may echo Arator *De actis apostolorum* 1.752 (*pervigil excubiis*). This line is the first part of a paradox, a recurring feature of this riddle perhaps inspired by *Carmen Eucheriae*. Cf. n.56.5.

l. 6 The phrase *lumina somno* ("I sleep as eyes") is Virgilian. See *Aeneid* 4.185, *Georgica* 4.414.

l. 8 Orchard (1994) notes that this line may echo Claudian *In Rufinum* 2.274 (*sub cardine caeli*).

l. 9 The term *larbula* ("ghosts") is the medieval form of *larvula*. This line is another that concludes with a paradox. See n.100.5 *supra*.

l. 11 The phrase *vexilla triumphi* ("trophy" – literally "flag of victory") echoes Statius *Thebaid* 8.238 (*vexilla triumphi*). Cf. *Carmen de virginitate* 1104 (*vexilla tropei*).

l. 13 The Stork manuscript has *fraglantior* instead of *fragrantior* ("more fragrant").

l. 15 This line's first two words *lilia* ("lilies") *purpureis* ("scarlet") probably echo the first two words of Sedulius *Carmen Paschale* 1.262 (*lilia purpurei*). Cf. Dracontius *De laudibus Dei* 2.442 (*purpurea lilia*).

l. 17 This line may echo Sedulius *Carmen Paschale* 3.82 (*sordibus … olida*).

l. 19 The epithet *arcitenens* ("the Archer" – in line 18 of the translation) was rare, but Aldhelm would have seen it at Ovid *Metamorphoses* 1.441, 6.265. Perhaps more importantly, it was an old Latin name for one of the constellations, so Aldhelm would surely have known it from his work on the Easter controversy. Cf. Bede *De temporum ratione* 16.1.

l. 22 The adjective *tetra* ("foul") is the Late Antique version of the classical *taetra*.

l. 26 The phrase *vilior algis* ("more vile than low-tide litter") probably echoes Virgil *Eclogae* 7.42 (*vilior alga*). Cf. Horace *Sermones* 2.5.8 (*vilior alga*). This line may also echo Prudentius *Peristephanon* 10.245 (*in algis vilibus*), a reference to plants in a pond.

l. 29 For *candente pruina* ("gleaming frost"), cf. Avianus *Fabulae* 34.7 (*candentes pruinas*).

ll. 30–2 For a longer discussion of this subject in *Laudibus de virginitate*, see Lapidge and Herren at 69. Vulcan was the blacksmith of the gods.

l. 33 *Ciclopum* ("Cyclopes") were an ancient and primitive race of one-eyed giants. In Book III of Virgil's *Aeneid*, Aeneas and his men landed on an island inhabited by Cyclopes.

l. 37 For the scansion of *testudo* ("turtles"), see n.Praef.18 *supra*.

The beetle here is probably the Anglo-Saxon *tordwifel* ("dung beetle" or more literally "turd weevil").

l. 40 The Stork manuscript has *sic* instead of *sum* ("I'm").

l. 41 For *tippula* ("pond-spiders"), see the notes on Riddle 38.

l. 42 The Stork manuscript has *fundit* rather than *fudit* ("shed"). The phrase *viscera flammas* ("flames … from bowels") may echo Virgil *Aeneid* 6.253 (*viscera flammis*).

l. 43 The phrase *tostis … extis* ("kidney stew") is on its face vague – we know only that it refers to internal organs cooked in some fashion. Since the dish is an example of something soft, it seemed appropriate to pick something stewed or braised. It could, however, just as easily be rendered as "grilled liver" or other menu items I find unappealing.

ll. 46–9 Hairstyle was a symbol of identity for Aldhelm and his contemporaries that distinguished monks and priests from the laity. See Cullen at 31, n.73; James, "Bede and the Tonsure Question," *Peritia* 3 (1984) at 85–98. Failure to adopt the proper tonsure was a point of contention in Aldhelm's letter to King Geraint. See Lapidge and Herren at 156–7.

l. 48 The noun *axungia* in the phrase *multo … axungia* ("greasy" – literally "with much lard") was rare, and it derived from the most common use for lard, which was greasing axels. The noun *axun* meant "axel" and the verb *ungere* means "to grease." See Harris, "Lubrication in Antiquity," *Greece and Rome* (Second Series) 21, no. 1 (1974) at 32–6.

l. 49 Lapidge and Rosier at 255 argue that Aldhelm substituted *referunt* ("they fill") for *referciunt* for the sake of metre.

l. 52 The phrase *dapibus … opimis* ("meals of luxury") occurs in the same location in the line as Virgil *Aeneid* 3.224 (*dapibusque epulamor opimis*). See also Juvencus *Evangelia* 3.87 (*dapibus … opimis*).

l. 54 The verb *ningit* ("shed" – literally "snow") was rare in literature, but this form of the verb must have been common colloquially for a long time before Aldhelm in order for it to be dismissed as improper by the second century grammarian Flavius Caper in *De verbis dubiis*, 7.110.16. (*Ninguit sic effer non ningit*). Cf. Virgil *Georgica* 3.367 (*ninguit*). I have extended the metaphor of the fleece with "have shed" because with *nivibus* ("snow") I did not want to repeat a word in the translated line when there was not a repeated word in the original text.

The phrase *candidior nivibus* ("brighter than the snow") may echo the same phrase in Ovid *Amores* 3.5.11. Most scholars think that Aldhelm did not have access to the *Amores*, so this parallel could be a coincidence, it could be a phrase quoted in a grammar or some other text, or it could have resulted from copies of the *Amores* circulating surreptitiously due to the subject matter. This phrase was common with "snow" in the singular. See e.g. Martial 4.42.5 (*nive candidior*); Cassiodorus *Exposito in Psalterium* 0.17.3 (*nive candidior*); Prudentius *Peristephanon* 3.162 (*nive candidior*).

The phrase *vellera nimbus* ("fleece … clouds") echoes Fortunatus *Vita Sancti Martini* 2.26 (*vellera nimbi*). Cf. *Carmen de virginitate* 54 (*vellera nimbus*); *Miracula Nynie Episcopi* 36 (*vellera celo*).

l. 57 The phrase *teres atque rotunda* ("round, smooth") may echo Horace *Sermones* 2.7.86 (*teres et rotundus*), although scholars have some doubt as to Aldhelm's access to the works of Horace. Orchard (1994) at 145 also notes Ausonius *Carmina* 7.3.5 (*teres atque rotundus*).

l. 58 For the scansion of *cristalli* ("crystal"), see n.Praef.18 *supra*; Orchard (1994) at 76. Excavations of Anglo-Saxon graves found crystal beads and a smaller number of crystal balls. See Huggett, "Imported Grave Goods and the Early Anglo-Saxon Economy," *Medieval Archaeology* 32 (1980) at 70–2. There is some evidence that these balls were worn on chains around the neck. See Owen-Crocker at 94–5. Although these balls probably had magical or religious significance in pre-Christian Britain, at some point their successors made the Christ/crystal connection. One of Aldhelm's favourite authors, Gregory the Great, described crystal as symbolic of Christ in *Homilarium in Ezechielem* 1.7.

See Karkov at 27–30. Like Alcuin and Bede, Aldhelm probably believed that crystals were petrified ice. See Garrett at 15–16.

l. 59 For the term *Serica* ("Chinese silk" in line 60 of the translation), see n.12 *supra*.

l. 61 The source for Aldhelm's "six zones" is unclear. Isidore believed the world had five climatic zones. See Woodward, "Reality, Symbolism, Time and Space in Medieval World Maps," *Annals of the Association of American Geographers* 75, no. 4 (1985) at 511. Ovid believed that the heavens had five zones. See Ovid *Metamorphoses* 1.46 (*zonae quinta*). Others argued for four zones. See e.g. Jerome *Isaias* 11.12 (*quattuor plagis terrae*); Gregory of Tours *Historiae* 3.19.2 (*quattuor plagis mundi*). If you assume that Aldhelm intended that the term *orbis* "the world" refer to the area around the Earth instead of to the Earth itself, one would expect to see *seven* "zones" – one for each of the seven "planets" Aldhelm believed revolved around the Earth (the sun, the moon, Mercury, Venus, Mars, Jupiter, and Saturn).While I cannot solve this riddle within a riddle, I suspect that the answer relates to early Christian numerology. Augustine in *De civitate Dei* 11.30 explains the perfection of the number six – it is the first number that is the sum of its parts; i.e., one multiplied by two multiplied by three. For the dubious, remember this warning from Augustine: "Hence the theory of number is not to be lightly regarded, since it is made quite clear, in many passages of the Holy Scriptures, how highly it is to be valued." Bettenson at 465. He then quotes *Wisdom* 12:21 as authority for this proposition.

In the *Laterculus Malalianus* Theodore of Tarsus repeatedly stresses the significance of the number six in the life of Christ (emphasis added throughout): the Archangel Gabriel witnesses the betrothal of Mary in the *sixth* month of Octavian's forty-first year (Stevenson at 121, 123); most gospels say that Christ was crucified in the *sixth* hour (*id.* at 125, 127, 135); Christ was crucified on the *sixth* ferial day (*id.* at 135); Christ remained in Mary's womb for nine months plus *six* days (*id.* at 137, 139); semen retains the appearance of milk for *six* days before turning into blood (*id.* at 139). Theodore explains this calculation in this way: "So *six* and nine, twelve and eighteen together make forty-five, add one, and make forty-*six*, and from there you extend through the parts, that is, to *six* forties, 240. And the same again through the *six*; *six sixes*, thirty-*six*, a three and a *six* … For forty and *six* signified the *sixth* age … God, therefore, for the fortieth and *sixth* number, the *doubled threes*, coagulated the whole lump of humankind into a single faith with scattered leaven." (*id.* at 139). Later Theodore talks of the *six* "grades of office," although, oddly, he lists seven (*id.* at 147).

l. 64 Juvencus was probably the source of the phrase *rerum genitor* ("God" – literally "the producer of things"). See e.g. *Evangelia* Praef. 4 (*genitor rerum*).

l. 67 The most likely source for the unusual word *atomo* ("motes"), from which our word "atom" is derived, is Isidore *Etymologiae* 13.2–4.

l. 72 For the importance of syllables to Aldhelm, see Ruff, "The Place of Metrics in Anglo-Saxon Latin Education: Aldhelm and Bede," *Journal of English and German Philology* 104, no. 2 (2005) at 156.

l. 78 The phrase *machina mundi* ("the … world's configuration") was originally Lucretian. See *De rerum natura* 5.96 (*machina mundi*); cf. *Carmen de virginitate* 158, 1679 (*machina mundi*); *Carmen rhythmicum* 17 (*machina mundi*). This line may be echoing *Altus prosator* E.1 (*mundi machinam*). Cf. Eugene of Toledo *Carmina* 1.1 (*machina mundi*). For the scansion of this phrase, see Orchard (1994) at 27.

l. 83 This closing line has more of the feel of a closing line of Symphosius than Aldhelm's other closing lines because it poses a question, albeit in the form of a request.

Sources

Texts, Commentaries, and Translations

Ehwald, R. *Aldhelmi Opera Omnia*. Berlin: Monumenta Germaniae Historica. Auctores Antiquissimi XV, 1919.

Giles, J. *Sancti Aldhelmi Opera*. Oxford: Parker, 1844.

Glorie, F., and K. Minst. *Collectiones Aenigmatum Merovingicae Aetatis, Corpus Christianorum, I*. Turnhout: Brepols, 1968.

Lapidge, M., and M. Herren. *Aldhelm: The Prose Works*. Cambridge: D.S. Brewer, 1979 (includes English translation).

Lapidge, M., and J. Rosier. *Aldhelm: The Poetic Works*. Cambridge: D.S. Brewer, 1985 (includes English translation).

Manitius, M. *Zu Aldhelm und Beda*. Vienna: In Commission Bei Carl Gerold's Sohn, Kaiserlichen Akademie der Wissenschaften, 1886.

Orchard, A. *The Anglo-Saxon Riddle Tradition*. Cambridge: Harvard University Press, forthcoming (includes English translation).

Pitman, J. *The Riddles of Aldhelm*. New Haven: Yale University Press, 1925 (includes English translation).

Stork, N. *Through a Gloss Darkly: Aldhelm's Riddles in the British Library MS Royal 12 C.xxiii*. Toronto: Pontifical Institute of Mediaeval Studies, 1990 (includes English translation).

Other Sources

Anderson, G. *King Arthur in Antiquity*. London: Routledge, 2004.

Augustine. *City of God*. Translated by H. Bettenson. London: Penguin, 1984.

Basil. *Basil: Letters and Select Works*. Translated by P. Schaff. Edinburgh: T & T Clark, 1895.

Bedingfield, M. *The Dramatic Liturgy of Anglo-Saxon England*. Woodbridge: Boydell Press, 2002.

Bischoff, B. *Latin Palaeography: Antiquity and the Middle Ages*. Cambridge: Cambridge University Press, 1990.

Bischoff, B., and M. Lapidge, eds. *Commentaries from the Canterbury School of Theodore and Hadrian*. Cambridge: Cambridge University Press, 1994.

Bitterli, D. *Say What I Am Called: The Old English Riddles of the Exeter Book and the Anglo-Latin Riddle Tradition*. Toronto: University of Toronto Press, 2009.

Blair, P. *An Introduction to Anglo-Saxon England*. Cambridge: Cambridge University Press, 2003.

Bracken, D., and E. Graf. *The Schaffhausen Adomnán, Volume 2, Commentary, Irish Manuscript in Facsimile*. Cork: Cork University Press, 2014.

Bremmer, R., K. Dekker, and D. Johnson, eds. *Rome and the North: The Early Reception of Gregory the Great in Germanic Europe*. Louvain: Peeters Publishing, 2001.

Bright, D. *The Miniature Epic in Vandal Africa*. Norman: University of Oklahoma Press, 1987.

Bruce, S. *Silence and Sign Language in Medieval Monasticism: The Cluniac Tradition ca. 900–1200*. Cambridge: Cambridge University Press, 2007.

Bynum, C. *Wonderful Blood: Theology and Practice in Late Medieval Northern Germany and Beyond*. Philadelphia: University of Pennsylvania Press, 2007.

Cameron, M. *Anglo-Saxon Medicine*. Cambridge: Cambridge University Press, 1993.

Carey, J. *King of Mysteries: Early Irish Writings*. Dublin: Four Courts Press, 1998.

Chance, J. *Medieval Mythography: From Roman North Africa to the School of Chartres AD 433–1177*. Gainesville: University Press of Florida, 1994.

Clark, C. "The Text Tradition of Ammianus Marcellinus." PhD thesis, Yale University, 1904.

Colafrancesco, P., and F. Bücheler. *Carmina Latina Epigraphica*. Bari: Edipuglia, 1986.

Colgrave, B., and R. Mynors. *Bede's Ecclesiastical History of the English People*. Oxford: Clarendon Press, 1969.

Cook, E. *Engimas and Riddles in Literature*. Cambridge: Cambridge University Press, 2006.

Corona, G., ed. *Aelfric's Life of Saint Basil the Great*. Cambridge: D.S. Brewer, 2006.

Cramp, R. *Corpus of Anglo-Saxon Stone Sculpture: Volume VII: South-west England*. Oxford: Oxford University Press, 2006.

Cullen, O. "A Question of Time or a Question of Theology: A Study in the Easter Controversy in the Insular Church." PhD thesis, Pontifical University, St. Patrick's College, Maynooth, 2007. Available at: eprints.nuim.ie/1331/.

Curley, M. *Physiologus: A Medieval Book of Nature Lore*. Chicago: University of Chicago Press, 1979.

Dunn, M. *The Christianization of the Anglo-Saxons c.597–c.700: Discourses of Life, Death and Afterlife*. London: Continuum, 2009.

Dyck, A. *A Commentary on Cicero, De Legibus*. Ann Arbor: University of Michigan Press 2004.

Evans, J. *The Age of Justinian: The Circumstances of Imperial Power*. London: Routledge, 1996.

Evison, V. *Catalogue of Anglo-Saxon Glass in the British Museum*. Oxford: Oxbow Books, 2008.

Fitzgerald, A., ed. *Augustine through the Ages: An Encyclopedia*. Grand Rapids: Eerdmans Publishing, 1999.

Frakes, J. *The Fate of Fortune in the Early Middle Ages: The Boethian Tradition*. Leiden: E.J. Brill, 1988.

Frantzen, A. *The Key of Heaven: Penance, Penitentials and the Literature of Early Medieval England*. Charlottesville: University of Virginia Press, 1976.

Frantzen, A. *The Literature of Penance in Anglo-Saxon England*. New Brunswick, Rutgers University Press, 1983.

Fulgentius. *Fabii Planciadis Fulgentii V.C. Opera*. Edited by R. Helm. Leipzig: Teubner, 1898.

Garrett, R. "Precious Stones in Old English Literature." PhD thesis, Kgl. Ludwig Maximilians-Universität München, 1909.

Garrod, H. *The Profession of Poetry and Other Lectures*. Oxford: Clarendon Press, 1929.

Gladhill, C. "Foedera: A Study in Roman Poetics and Society." PhD thesis, Stanford University, 2008.

Halsall, G. *Humour, History and Politics in Late Antiquity and the Early Middle Ages*. Cambridge: Cambridge University Press, 2002.

Hamerow, H., and A. Macgregor, eds. *Image and Power in the Archaeology of Early Medieval Britain: Essays in Honour of Rosemary Cramp*. Oxford: Oxbow Books, 2001.

Hanson, V. *Hoplites: The Greek Battle Experience*. London: Routledge, 1993.

Heikkinen, S. "The Christianisation of Latin Metre: A Study of Bede's *De arte metrica*." PhD thesis, University of Helsinki, 2012.

Herren, M. *The Hisperica Famina*. Cambridge: Cambridge University Press, 1974.

Herren, M. *The Hisperica Famina: Related Poems*. Toronto: Pontifical Institute of Mediaeval Studies, 1987.

Herren, M. *Latin Letters in Early Christian Ireland*. Aldershot: Variorum, 1996.

Herren, M., and S. Brown. *Christ in Celtic Christianity: Britain and Ireland from the Fifth to the Tenth Century*. Woodbridge: Boydell Press, 2002.

Hessels, J., ed. *An Eighth Century Latin-Anglo Glossary Preserved in the Library of Corpus Christi, Cambridge, MS. No.144*. Cambridge: Cambridge University Press, 1890.

Hessels, J., ed. *A Late Eighth Century Latin-Anglo-Saxon Glossary Preserved in the Library of Leiden University*. Cambridge: Cambridge University Press, 1906.

Howe, N. *Migration and Mythmaking in Anglo-Saxon England*. New Haven: Yale University Press, 1989.

Hofmann, P. "Infernal Imagery in Anglo-Saxon Charters." PhD thesis, University of St. Andrews, 2008. Available at http://hdl.handle.net/10023/49.

Isidore. *The Etymologies of Isidore of Seville*. Translated by S. Barney, B. Lewis, J. Beach, and O. Berghof. Cambridge: Cambridge University Press, 2006.

Karkov, C. *The Ruler Portraits of Anglo-Saxon England*. Woodbridge: Boydell Press, 2004.

Karkov, C., S. Keefer, and K. Jolly, eds. *The Place of the Cross in Anglo-Saxon England*. Woodbridge: Boydell Press, 2006.

Kendall, C., and P. Wells, eds. *Voyage to the Other World: The Legacy of Sutton Hoo*. Minneapolis: University of Minnesota Press, 1992.

King, M., and W. Stevens, eds. *Saints, Scholars and Heroes: Studies in Medieval Culture in Honor of Charles W. Jones*. Minnesota: Hill Monastic Library, 1979.

Laing, L., and J. Laing. *Britain before the Quest: Anglo-Saxon England*. London: Routledge & Kegan, 1979.

Lapidge, M. *Anglo-Latin Literature 600–899*. London: Hambledon Press, 1996.

Lapidge, M. *The Anglo-Saxon Library*. Oxford: Oxford University Press, 2006.

Lapidge, M., and H. Gneuss, eds. *Learning and Literature in Anglo-Saxon England*. Cambridge: Cambridge University Press, 1985.

Leedham-Green, E., and T. Webber, eds. *The Cambridge History of Libraries in Britain and Ireland, Volume 1*. Cambridge: Cambridge University Press, 2006.

Lees, C., and G. Overing, eds. *Double Agents: Women and Clerical Culture in Anglo-Saxon England*. Philadelphia: University of Pennsylvania Press, 2001.

Lewis, C., and C. Short. *A Latin Dictionary*. Oxford: Clarendon Press, 1879.

Lindsay, W. *Studies in Early Medieval Latin*. Brussels: Union Académique Internationale, 1924.

Lockett, L. *Anglo-Saxon Psychologies in the Vernacular and Latin Traditions*. Toronto: University of Toronto Press, 2011.

Longworth, J., and G.Varndell, eds. *Excavations at Grimes Graves, Norfolk 1972–1976: Fascicule 5: Mining in the Deeper Mines*. London: British Museum Press, 1996.

Marcellus, Nonius. *De compendiosa doctrina Volume I*. Edited by W. Lindsay. Leipzig: Teubner, 1903.

Marsden, R. *The Text of the Old Testament in Anglo-Saxon England*. Cambridge: Cambridge University Press, 1995.

Marshall, C. "Late Medieval Liturgical Offices in Acrostic Form: A Catalogue and Study." PhD thesis, University of Toronto, 2006.

Masters, J. *Poetry and Civil War in Lucan's "Bellum Civile."* Cambridge: Cambridge University Press, 1992.

McBrine, P. "The English Inheritance of Biblical Verse." PhD thesis, University of Toronto, 2008.

McCluskey, S. *Astronomies and Cultures in Early Medieval Europe*. Cambridge, Cambridge University Press, 1998.

Meritt, H. *Fact and Lore about Old English Words*. Stanford: Stanford University Press, 1954.

Mitchell, B. *An Invitation to Old English & Anglo-Saxon England*. Oxford: Blackwell Publishing, 1995.

Mousourakis, G. *A Legal History of Rome* Abingdon: Routledge, 2007.

Neville, J. *Representations of the Natural World in Old English Poetry*. Cambridge: Cambridge University Press, 1999.

Norberg, D. *An Introduction to the Study of Medieval Latin Versification*. Translated by G. Roti and J. de la Chapelle Skubly. With an introduction by J. Ziolkowski. Washington: Catholic University of America Press, 2004.

O'Keeffe, K. *Visible Song: Transitional Literacy in Old English Verse*. Cambridge: Cambridge University Press, 1990.

Orchard, A. *The Poetic Art of Aldhelm*. Cambridge: Cambridge University Press, 1994.

Orchard, A. *Pride and Prodigies: Studies in the Monsters of the Beowulf-Manuscript*. Toronto: University of Toronto Press, 1995.

Orchard, A., and K. O'Keeffe, eds. *Latin Learning and English Lore: Studies in Anglo-Saxon Literature for Michael Lapidge*. Toronto: University of Toronto Press, 2005.

Orchard, A., and S. Zacher, eds. *New Readings in the "Vercelli Book."* Toronto: University of Toronto Press, 2009.

Orians, R. *The Origins of European Thought about the Body, the Mind, the Soul, the World, Time and Fate*. Cambridge: Cambridge University Press, 1951.

O'Sullivan, S. *Early Medieval Glosses in Prudentius' Psychmachia: The Weitz Tradition*. Leiden: Brill, 2004.

Otten, W., and K. Pollman, eds. *Poetry and Exegesis in Premodern Latin Christianity: The Encounter between Classical and Christian Strategies of Interpretation*. Leiden: Brill, 2007.

Owen-Crocker, G. *Dress in Anglo-Saxon England*. Woodbridge: Boydell Press, 2004.

Patterson, K. "A Christian Virgil: The Function of Virgilian References in the Writings of Aldhelm." PhD thesis, Brown University, 2007.

Pheifer, J. *Old English Glosses in the Épinal-Efrurt Glossary*. Oxford: Clarendon Press, 1974.

Pitman, J., and A. Cook, trans. *The Old English Physiologus*. New Haven: Yale University Press, 1921.

Rajak, T. *Translation and Survival: The Greek Bible of the Ancient Jewish Diaspora*. Oxford: Oxford University Press, 2009.

Rawcliffe, C. *Leprosy in Medieval England*. Woodbridge: Boydell Press, 2006.

Retsch, M. *The Intellectual Foundations of the English Benedictine Reform*. Cambridge: Cambridge University Press, 2004.

Richards, M. *Anglo-Saxon Manuscripts: Basic Readings*. London: Routledge, 2001.

Richards, P. *The Medieval Leper*. Cambridge: D.S. Brewer, 1977.

Rock, D. *The Church of Our Fathers as Seen in St. Osmund's Rite for the Cathedral of Salisbury*. London: John Murray, 1905.

Schmidt, G. *The Iconography of the Mouth of Hell: Eighth Century Britain to the Fifteenth Century*. Selingrove: Susquhenna University Press, 1995.

Schmitt, R. *Dichtung und Dichtersprache in indogermanischer Zeit*. Weisbaden: Harrassowitz, 1967.

Schoff, W. (trans.). *The Periplus of the Erythrean Sea*. London: Longmans, Green & Co., 1912.

Scholfield, A. (trans.). *On Animals Books VI–XI*. Cambridge: Harvard University Press, 1959.

Scragg, D. *Textual and Material Culture in Anglo-Saxon England: Thomas Northcote Toller and the Toller Memorial Lectures*. Cambridge: D.S. Brewer, 2003.

Sobiecki, S. *The Sea and Medieval British Literature*. Cambridge: D.S. Brewer, 2008.

Steen, J. *Verse and Virtuosity: The Adaptation of Latin Rhetoric in Old English Rhetoric in Old English Poetry*. Toronto: University of Toronto Press, 2008.

Stenton, F., and Dolley, M., eds. *Anglo-Saxon Coins*. Norwich: Jarrold & Sons, 1961.

Stephenson, I. *The Anglo-Saxon Shield*. Stroud: Tempus Publishing, 2002.

Stevenson, J. *The "Laterculus Malalianus" and the School of Archbishop Theodore*. Cambridge: Cambridge University Press, 1995.

Stokes, M. *Six Months in the Apennines*. London: George Bell & Sons, 1892.

Stokes, W., and J. Strahan. *Thesaurus Palaeohibernicus Volume I*. Cambridge: Cambridge University Press, 1901.

Stone, J. *Human Law and Human Justice*. Palo Alto: Stanford University Press, 1965.

Straus, R. *Carriages & Coaches: Their History & Their Evolution*. Plymouth: William Brendon & Son, 1912.

Symphosius. *The Hundred Riddles of Symphosius*. Translated by E. Dubois. Whitefish: Kessinger Publishing, 2009.

Thornbury, E. *Becoming a Poet in Anglo-Saxon England*. Cambridge: Cambridge University Press, 2014.

Walker, F., and J. Gray. *List of the Species of Homopterous Insects in the Collection of the British Museum*. London: Edward Newman, 1850.

Williams, J. *Interpreting Nightingales: Gender, Class and Histories*. Sheffield: Sheffield Academic Press, 1997.

Wilson, D. *The Archaeology of Anglo-Saxon England*. London: Methuen & Co., 1976.

Ziolkowski, J. *Talking Animals: Medieval Latin Beast Poetry, 750–1150*. Philadelphia: University of Pennsylvania Press, 1993.

Index

.

Lightning Source UK Ltd.
Milton Keynes UK
UKHW041550191222
414163UK00020B/218

9 781442 628922